DRIVE

TIM FALCONER

DRIVE

A ROAD TRIP THROUGH OUR COMPLICATED
AFFAIR WITH THE AUTOMOBILE

VIKING
CANADA

VIKING CANADA

Published by the Penguin Group

Penguin Group (Canada), 90 Eglinton Avenue East, Suite 700,
Toronto, Ontario, Canada M4P 2Y3 (a division of Pearson Canada Inc.)

Penguin Group (USA) Inc., 375 Hudson Street, New York, New York 10014, U.S.A.
Penguin Books Ltd, 80 Strand, London WC2R 0RL, England
Penguin Ireland, 25 St Stephen's Green, Dublin 2, Ireland
(a division of Penguin Books Ltd)
Penguin Group (Australia), 250 Camberwell Road, Camberwell, Victoria 3124, Australia
(a division of Pearson Australia Group Pty Ltd)
Penguin Books India Pvt Ltd, 11 Community Centre, Panchsheel Park,
New Delhi – 110 017, India
Penguin Group (NZ), 67 Apollo Drive, Rosedale, North Shore 0632, New Zealand
(a division of Pearson New Zealand Ltd)
Penguin Books (South Africa) (Pty) Ltd, 24 Sturdee Avenue, Rosebank,
Johannesburg 2196, South Africa

Penguin Books Ltd, Registered Offices: 80 Strand, London WC2R 0RL, England

First published 2008

1 2 3 4 5 6 7 8 9 10 (RRD)

Copyright © Tim Falconer, 2008

Manufactured in the U.S.A.

LIBRARY AND ARCHIVES CANADA CATALOGUING IN PUBLICATION

Falconer, Tim, 1958–
Drive : a road trip through our complicated affair with the automobile / Tim
Falconer.

Includes index.
ISBN 978-0-670-06569-1

1. Automobiles—Social aspects. 2. Automobiles. I. Title.

HE5611.F35 2008   303.48'32   C2008-901399-9

ISBN-13: 978-0-670-06569-1
ISBN-10: 0-670-06569-2

Visit the Penguin Group (Canada) website at **www.penguin.ca**

Special and corporate bulk purchase rates available; please see
www.penguin.ca/corporatesales or call 1-800-810-3104, ext. 477 or 474

FOR CARMEN

"The evil genius of our time is the car," Barry Byrne, an elderly architect, observed several years ago. "We must conquer the automobile or become enslaved by it." … Less than a year after our conversation, Mr. Byrne, on his way to Sunday mass, was run down by a car and killed.

— From the introduction to *Working*, by Studs Terkel (1972)

Contents

DRIVE

1 Toronto Cars. Can't Live with 'Em, Can't Live without 'Em

EVEN THOUGH I LEFT EARLY to avoid the worst of the Friday afternoon snarl, the city roads are thick with cars and I don't reach the highway as quickly as I'd hoped. Once I do, three lanes of high-speed congestion surround my car. I'm heading north to a cottage for the weekend, but suburban sprawl mars the landscape for most of the next hour; the subdivisions seem to creep a little farther every time I drive up here and I feel old remembering how all this land was nothing but fields when I was a kid. As soon as the traffic eases and I hit open road, and the dispiriting tract housing gives way to lush farms and dense forest, I sit back, crank the tunes a little louder and step on the gas. Within an hour, I will be lakeside, far from the smog, a cold beer in my hand—though it's not just my destination that makes me happy. My car is not a convertible, but as I rejoice in the speed, the power and the freedom it offers, I imagine the sun on my face and the wind in my thinning hair. I press the pedal a little harder. I feel exhilarated.

That doesn't mean I don't feel guilty. I do. After all, I'm contributing to the traffic I curse, I'm spewing greenhouse gases and other harmful emissions and I'm part of the reason we build cities for cars instead of people (not that we're doing even that well). Most North Americans, and increasingly those in other countries, have convinced themselves that a car is a necessity. I'm not that addicted, but my relationship to the automobile—a complicated mix of desire and disgust—is still a powerful one. While car lovers can make a passionate case for the object of their affection and car haters can marshal the facts against it, most of us are conflicted: the more we've allowed ourselves to be sucked into the car's considerable charms, the more brutal and complete our subjugation to it has become. If intelligent life forms on a distant planet ever bothered to study our civilization, they would surely conclude that the vehicles were the dominant creatures while the humans, who build roads, provide warm, dry spots to park and do the cleaning and fixing, were the servants.

The closer the aliens looked, the more baffled they would become. Even as road engineering and automobile safety have improved dramatically, the death toll remains ludicrously high: 1.2 million people die on the world's roads each year. The thirst for oil has led to many conflicts around the world, including two wars in the Persian Gulf and civil unrest in Nigeria, and it threatens environmentally sensitive habitats. All the while, the humans fret about their tailpipe toxins, lament the lost hours spent stuck in traffic and cluck at the urban sprawl that makes no economic, environmental or aesthetic sense.

BEYOND ITS PIVOTAL ROLE in our day-to-day lives, the automobile has worked its way into our psyches. From the sunny California of the Beach Boys to the darker New Jersey of Bruce Springsteen, the car is a central image in American music. And from the chicken run in *Rebel Without a Cause* to the main-street cruising in *American Graffiti* to every road trip movie ever made, the car plays an essential role in film. It's not just that the automobile is a handy device for storytelling. Through music, movies, television and literature—and advertising—vehicles have become metaphors for freedom and symbols of status and success.

Though it started developing earlier, the iconography of the car generated by movies and music really took hold in the 1950s and 1960s, when the automobile posed no pressing problems. With the building of the interstate highway system in the 1950s, the American economy boomed. People moved around easily and trucking quickly became the preferred shipping method. But it didn't take long for the true cost of these freeways to surface:

bypassed towns slowly withered and died while inner-city neighbourhoods succumbed to a similar fate quickly because of expressway construction. That led to a flight to the suburbs, exacerbating the urban sprawl the highways had already spurred. Today, it's no stretch to live without a car in a few cities—and in Manhattan, it's actually advisable—but I wouldn't want to try it in Atlanta or Houston.

And yet, for some people, a car is still an *objet d'art* to be collected and fawned over, though perhaps seldom driven. Talk show host Jay Leno has more than 150 cars, trucks and motorcycles, and a full-time staff to keep them running. No doubt buying and maintaining a fleet of collectible cars puts little strain on Leno's fortune, but for most regular folk, a vehicle is the second-most expensive purchase they'll ever make. And between loan payments, insurance, gas, maintenance, parking and other costs, some people spend more each month to keep their car going than they do on their rent or their mortgage. That's even more likely for those with more than one set of wheels: so many families insist on owning several—they should be thankful they don't live in Bermuda, where automobile ownership is limited to one per household—that the United States now has more vehicles than drivers. Americans, who represent just 5 percent of the global population, own 200 million of the more than 520 million cars in the world.

This proliferation has shaped where and how we live. Many businesses, from drive-in cinemas to drive-thru banks, cater to those behind the wheel (and often exclude those on foot). No wonder people say we either love cars or we need them. Even some activists dedicated to protesting against the auto and oil industries and to promoting environmental awareness find they have no choice but to own what they hate—or at least take a lot of taxis.

CITY DWELLERS COME IN three categories: drivers (and passengers), cyclists and pedestrians. Each one can't stand the other two.

Drivers have nothing but contempt for pedestrians who jaywalk or, even when crossing the street legally, take too long, and they detest cyclists who sneer at the rules of the road. Cyclists despise drivers because too many of them refuse to admit bike riders have a right to be on the road and they hate pedestrians the way a bully hates the smallest kid in the playground. Pedestrians fear and loathe aggressive and distracted drivers, especially the ones who prefer yakking on a cell phone to paying attention, and they dread and abhor cyclists who won't obey stop signs and seem to take joy in running down people on sidewalks.

I am a pedestrian.

My first choice has long been to walk whenever possible, but I always intended to get my licence. Someday. Owning a set of wheels isn't essential where I live, so I was able to avoid getting a driver's licence until I was in my late thirties. Finally, a friend who was a magazine editor asked me if I wanted to rent an RV for two weeks and write about it. Turning down such a fun assignment was so painful—and felt so pathetic—that I decided it was finally time to grow up. Driving *seemed* like the adult thing to do. And so I joined the ranks of the drivers, and then, a few years later, the owners.

When I finally did, I regretted having waited so long. True, my 1991 Nissan Maxima, my first—and so far, only—automobile, is no aficionado's idea of a sweet ride. Light blue (or Silver Blue, according to the manufacturer), the body is still in good shape, but it's old, and even when it was new, it wasn't the most stylish car on the road. The horsepower isn't impressive, and I don't spend any time tinkering with it, let alone tricking it out. I don't even use it that much. In the summer, I love to escape the city without cadging a ride from friends, but in the winter, it just sits on the street for days until I throw two sticks and a big equipment bag into the back seat and drive to a hockey arena. Since 1999, I've added just sixty thousand kilometres to the hundred thousand that were already on the odometer. I certainly could live without a car, and I know I should, but I don't want to give it up.

THE STREET WHERE I park my car is a short, leafy cul-de-sac in midtown Toronto. In most American cities, my street, which is just a block from a six-lane north–south arterial road, would be no place for single-family homes. Fortunately, my city never suffered an exodus to the suburbs. The evacuation that killed the central core of too many cities didn't happen here because a group of citizens killed a highway.

The Spadina Expressway—which would take suburbanites from the northwest corner of the city into downtown in the morning, and then out again in the evening—was all part of a master plan that featured five expressways. Plenty of putative experts thought the scheme was an excellent one; after all, the great American cities were doing it. And in the 1960s, Toronto was anything but a great city: it was puritanical, placid and parochial. A good time was hard to find. My parents, like a lot of people who lived here back then, drove to Buffalo or Detroit to shop and enjoy some nightlife. Today, that seems laughable because those places are decaying cities with dead downtowns, while Toronto is now a vibrant place. It will never have the energy of Manhattan, the joie de vivre of Montreal or the architecture of Chicago (a town Toronto looks up to the way a kid reveres his big brother), but to most objective observers, the city is largely a success. True, the place is still a bit uptight, developers seem to take pride in throwing up unremarkable buildings and the wasted opportunity of the waterfront is a disgrace, but it is also dynamic, tolerant, wealthy, safe and among the most livable cities in the world.

Some good decisions and a huge dollop of luck helped make this possible, but stopping the Spadina Expressway was crucial. In 1971, the road was already under construction. Suburbanites were all for it; downtowners, not so much. They knew the highway would mean the end for central neighbourhoods. Some of the most vocal opponents were from the Annex, which was right on the path of the planned construction. Annex resident Jane Jacobs led the activists who stopped Spadina. Born in Scranton,

Pennsylvania, she moved to New York City, where she took on Robert Moses, the autocratic master builder who was, for more than four decades, one of the most powerful people in New York. Though he never learned to drive, he favoured highways over public transit, suburbs over cities and grand projects over neighbourhoods. His plan for the Lower Manhattan Expressway would have destroyed Greenwich Village and SoHo. Jacobs and her first book, *The Death and Life of Great American Cities*, galvanized opposition to the proposed road. After that defeat, Moses lost much of his influence in New York, but by then his ideas had infected other cities across the continent.

A few years after helping to save it, Jacobs left the West Village. Appalled that their taxes were being used to fight the Vietnam War—and with two sons eligible for the draft—she and her architect husband moved to Toronto and settled in the Annex. She stayed until she died in April 2006, just a few days shy of her ninetieth birthday. In the rest of the world, she'll be best remembered for *The Death and Life of Great American Cities*, but in many ways her legacy is modern Toronto. Along with leading the crusade against Spadina, she was prominent in many other fights (for public housing, for intensification) and was a mentor to some of our better municipal politicians. The central plan that shaped Toronto from 1975 to 2000 incorporated many of her ideas.

The Annex became one of the most desirable parts of the city. John Barber, the city columnist for *The Globe and Mail*, lives there—on a street where his great-grandparents bought their first house in 1880. Though he and his wife ride their bikes to work, he loves American V8s and is the proud owner of a 1998 Mercury Grand Marquis LS, which he calls the Grand Monkey. I had lunch with him two weeks before Jacobs died, and when, inevitably, the subject of the Spadina Expressway came up, he pointed out that many people who complain about the traffic in the city still argue that the big mistake was not building Spadina. I stated the obvious: "You wouldn't live where you live if it had gone through."

"I'd be living on an off-ramp," he agreed.

Other residential areas—including mine—would likely have been collateral damage. Some of the highway's opponents may have been motivated more by NIMBYism than anything else, but when the provincial government finally agreed to kill the project—along with three of the other proposed inner-city expressways—it not only saved the Annex but also changed the way the city thought about its neighbourhoods. (The fifth highway, the Don Valley Parkway, had already been built in a bosky river valley. Environmentalists would never let that happen these days, but it did mean that fewer homes were destroyed. And though it usually seems closer to a parking lot than a parkway, it does offer a lovely, winding and tree-lined drive into Toronto and an impressive view of downtown.) With the scrapping of the planned inner-city highways, Toronto became a city of neighbour-hoods—and, more important, a city that valued them. Aside from meaning fewer people fled to the suburbs, that mindset was also an ideal fit with the waves of immigration that would, over the next couple of decades, transform Toronto from a sleepy regional town full of dull, white Protestants to the most multicultural place on the planet.

While much of downtown Detroit remains a no-go zone, the American cities having the most success revitalizing their downtowns—San Francisco, Portland and Washington, D.C., for example—boast extensive, if often aging, transit systems. So Toronto is fortunate it didn't tear up all of its streetcar tracks and for a while built subways, but the transit system is now under-funded, overcrowded and struggling to keep riders happy. For downtowners at least, it offers an alternative to driving, though apparently I'm not alone in thinking that walking is an even better option. After a study found that 45 percent of people who live close to the waterfront walk to work, Rod McPhail, the city's director of transportation planning, told the *Toronto Star* in October 2004, "What we found, it blew me away."

Inner-city success couldn't stop the surrounding suburbs from sprawling, but the vigour of the downtown made the region a magnet for newcomers from across Canada and around the world. The city now has a population of almost 2.5 million and a healthy density greater than 10,000 people per square mile, but the Greater Toronto Area has more than 5 million residents, most mired in car dependency and poorly served by public transit. Many of those people commute to Toronto for work, but only 20 percent take public transit. Solo drivers account for 67 percent of the trips into the city each morning, and since the road infrastructure hasn't kept pace with the growth, travel times continue to rise.

I'VE ALWAYS THOUGHT Hogtown, as we call it, was akin to older East Coast American cities that have grown in a radial pattern around a downtown core, and I was surprised to hear that many American urban planners see Toronto as closer to the polycentric cities of the American West. Perhaps it has a chance to combine the best of both. Or it could become everything it fears. Eric Miller, a professor at the University of Toronto's Department of Civil Engineering Joint Program in Transportation, worries the city has been dining out on some good choices, such as killing Spadina, that are now decades old. "I don't think we've made any smart decisions since," he told me, citing the failure to continue building subways and the sprawling suburbs as examples. "We lost control over the situation and we lost our will to make decisions and to see the vision through. We still talk about it but we don't really do it and we haven't done it for a long time and now we have a lot of catching up to do. We're resting on our laurels."

Unfortunately, now is the worst time to be coasting. The city's population is growing rapidly, and already 49 percent of the people who live in Toronto were born in another country and 43 percent of the population are part of a visible minority. This is our great experiment, and so far the results have been encouraging. If it is a success, that diversity will be our greatest strength and could turn Toronto into a model of multicultural urban living for the rest of the world. But pulling it off won't mean a thing if we don't solve the problem of the car.

My hometown isn't the only place facing this challenge: as a society, we can't live with the car and we can't live without it. Although the suburbs promise more space and relief from inner-city woes, they are too often dismal, wasteful and unhealthy communities filled with soulless shopping malls, drive-thru fast-food joints and clogged roads. And we've now sprawled so much that commutes of over an hour—once unthinkable—are now commonplace. And that's on a day without lane-closing crashes. All that time in the car is not good for us. Traffic tie-ups are costly in terms of wasted fuel and productivity—and human health and sanity. Many suburbanites suffer from frazzled nerves and neck and back problems brought on by long commutes, and because they must get in a car just to pick up a litre of milk, they are less fit and more likely to be overweight or obese than their inner-city counterparts. Even if governments could afford to build as many highways as they wanted, they'd never get ahead of demand: more roads beget more cars. And although most politicians prefer subsidizing roads to public transit, many highways are in dis-repair. So no one's happy.

More worrisome is the prospect of people in other countries joining in. So far, the obsession with the automobile has been most acute in North America. Europeans love their cars, but their societies don't revolve so completely around the automobile: the vehicles are smaller, the gas more expensive, the transit systems better, the urban densities greater and the distances people travel shorter. Nevertheless, traffic in London was so bad that the city introduced a congestion charge for cars entering the central core. Worse, as emerging economic powerhouses such as China and India—where automobile ownership is 10 percent but growing rapidly—fall in love with the car the way we have, we're headed for deeper trouble. Mexico City gives us a hint of what could happen:

the streets are so overwhelmed with cars that it takes several hours to drive across town, while the pollution is so bad that many visitors cannot even wear their contact lenses. And all those cars don't necessarily mean a vibrant economy: the most car-dependent cities are the least efficient.

As always, though, there is some hope. Many companies, trumpeting a variety of technologies, work feverishly to find the alternative fuel that will be clean enough, efficient enough and cheap enough to make future generations wonder what the hell a gas-guzzler was. And despite the disappointing results of experiments such as New Urbanism, planners can take comfort in the knowledge that many North Americans actually want to live downtown again.

The glory days of the automobile, extended beyond all good sense by twenty-five years of cheap gasoline, are finally over. Despite what the auto industry and the oil industry and the politicians in their pockets would have us believe, we won't survive our current addiction—yet the Utopians calling for a ban on all cars are equally deluded. A carless future won't happen anytime soon because we couldn't go cold turkey even if we wanted to. Before I could consider solutions in between those two extremes, I knew I had to develop a better understanding of our peculiar love–hate relationship with our wheels. And the best way to do that, I figured, was to take a road trip to the heart of car culture: Los Angeles, California.

2 The Border
Leaving Minivan Nation

JUST AFTER EIGHT O'CLOCK on Monday morning, I loaded my last bit of luggage into my Nissan Maxima and hopped into the driver's seat. After turning the ignition key, I flicked on the wipers to get rid of the heavy dew on the windshield and hit the rear defrost button. I plugged in my iPod and drove away in search of some insight into why we love our cars so much and what we can do about it.

I'd gassed up the night before so I wouldn't have to stop until I hit the border, almost four hours away. The drive out of the city was relatively painless—better than a lot of the trips to Sunday lunch at my in-laws' I've taken along the same route—but traffic in the other direction on the Gardiner Expressway and the Queen Elizabeth Way was downright ugly as countless commuters put up with a soul-crushing amount of congestion just to get to the office. The morning was crisp and clear, though the blue skies eventually gave way to cloud cover around the time I hooked up with Highway 401 near Woodstock on my way to the border between Sarnia, Ontario, and Port Huron, Michigan.

I knew I was about to cross into a country that had, in many ways, a similar relationship to the car as the one I was leaving. But there are significant distinctions, too, as I learned when I met David MacDonald, vice-president (automotive) with Toronto-based Environics Research Group. A tall, easygoing man with a moustache, MacDonald has always been a car guy, the kind whose wife says he'd let his dinner go stone cold while talking about his favourite subject. When I visited him in his midtown office on a

Friday afternoon, we spent two and a half hours chatting—and I got the impression he'd have happily kept at it all weekend.

After getting his licence at the age of seventeen in 1986, he drove a 1969 Valiant that had been his grandmother's—"a piece of crap," it was true, but he absolutely loved it. A man always remembers his first love and his first car. Today, his wife drives a 1999 Honda CR-V because it's sporty and nimble, while he's just as happy to take the family's 1998 Honda Odyssey because it's big; he is, after all, six foot five. But his dream car is an old Dodge Charger. His new office had nothing on the walls yet, but he had found the time to place a model of a green 1969 Charger and a framed ad for a 1969 Dodge Charger Daytona from an old *Playboy* magazine on the credenza. He also showed me a May 1981 issue of *Cartoons*, the first auto magazine he ever bought, which he keeps in his office because his wife, a high-school teacher, threatened to throw it out. She's also not that keen on the Charger. "You want a forty-year-old car that gets zero miles per gallon, drives like a drunken pig and pollutes left, right and centre. And now it costs forty thousand dollars," she told him. "Give your head a shake!" Still, when they got married, they made a pact that once they could afford it, she would get a cottage and he would get his Charger. They have the cottage, but with the recent arrival of a third child, his prize isn't exactly imminent.

In the meantime, MacDonald compensates by doing what he's done for more than a decade: making his living researching and talking about cars. In 2004, his company did a survey comparing Canadian and American attitudes on a variety of topics, including whether people agreed with the statement "A car says a lot about a person—it must reflect my personal style and image" or instead thought, "A car is just an appliance, something to get me from point A to B." Turns out, 54 percent of Americans preferred "style and image," while only 34 percent of Canadians did. On the other hand, 62 percent of Canadians and just 40 percent of Americans saw their cars as appliances. (This may explain the popularity of the practical, but rarely stylish, hatchback north of the border.) "If Americans have a passionate love affair with the automobile," concluded MacDonald, "Canadians have a mild crush."

That the two peoples view cars slightly differently should come as no surprise to anyone who understands the fundamentally different cultural values of the two nations. Michael Adams, the president of Environics and the author of books such as *Fire and Ice: The United States, Canada, and the Myth of Converging Values*, believes that cars play an even greater symbolic role in America. In 2005, he wrote a piece for *Marketing*, a trade publication, arguing that for Americans, the car has always represented not only socio-economic status but also mobility, independence and freedom. "Cars were to middle class suburbanites what horses were to cowboys: keys to movement and productivity and, if everything else went sour, tickets to a fresh start in another town," he wrote. "When it comes to how we imagine ourselves, Canadians seem happier to admit that their cars really are just appliances that mostly travel in circles: away from home and back again. Americans are more attached to the ideal of the car as an extension of themselves: an expression of their individualism, and a means of heading off toward a new frontier should they so desire."

THE INTENSITY OF THEIR PASSION for their rides may differ, but both nations experienced the bulk of their population growth after the turn of the last century, so most North American urban centres are designed for cars, though that's proven to be not such a good thing. In addition, both have economies built on cars and trucks. In my home province of Ontario, one in six jobs is related to automobile manufacturing. And almost all of our jobs are dependent in one way or another on the ability for people and goods to move along roads.

Roads such as Highway 401. More than 815 kilometres long, it runs from just shy of the Detroit River all the way to the Quebec border—and always seems to be clogged. The section through

Toronto can be particularly infuriating: it's the busiest in North America, busier even than California's famed Santa Monica Freeway. Originally completed in 1956 as a northern bypass, the 401 wasn't a way to avoid the city for long. Since Toronto sits on the northern shore of Lake Ontario, southward expansion was impossible, and the expressway accelerated the northward spread of people and businesses. Decades of sprawling growth mean the 401 now takes commuters, truckers and other drivers right through the continent's fifth-largest city and fourth-largest conurbation.

On weekdays, this part of the highway regularly carries more than 420,000 cars—and half a million people. Compounding the congestion is the design of the road, which doesn't offer much in the way of what traffic engineers call lane continuity. Two lanes in each direction—with a capacity of 35,000 cars a day—seemed like more than enough when construction started, but by 1959, as many as 85,000 cars jammed the 401 daily. In 1963, the provincial government finally announced plans for the first expansion of the highway. Today, at its widest point, the road has eighteen lanes. Since drivers must contend with lanes that appear and disappear, transfers between the express and collector lanes, and frequent exit ramps, the congestion is exacerbated by a lot of merging and lane changing. "There's no doubt that the 401 violates one of the basic principles of simple is better," observed Les Kelman, director of transportation systems for Toronto. "We're trying to squeeze capacity so much that it has introduced a degree of unpredictability, which is not necessarily good in a driving environment. Even for an experienced driver, it's a nightmare."

That nightmare gets worse for the people involved in the average of twenty-five collisions a day on this thirty-six kilometres of highway. Most of these incidents are minor, but the ones that aren't can create real havoc. One of the worst in recent years occurred just after three o'clock in the morning on September 29, 2004. The fiery crash involving two tractor-trailers closed most of the highway's lanes until well past the time the morning rush would normally have morphed into just heavy traffic. Nearly twelve hours later, police and clean-up crews had finally finished clearing the mess, meaning the crash wasn't just a huge inconvenience for commuters, but also a big hit to the economy. Although the 407, an electronic-toll highway that opened a little to the north in 1997, offers an alternative for those willing to pay the ever-increasing charges to the private consortium that now owns it, the 401 remains the economic spine of the region, and more than $1.4 billion worth of goods move through Toronto on the old highway each day.

Fortunately, because I'd left the city from the south, I didn't join the 401 until west of Toronto. And then, just after London, I exited onto Highway 402 to Sarnia, which meant I also missed Carnage Alley. The London to Windsor stretch of the 401 has been the site of several gruesome crashes over the years, including an eighty-seven-car pile-up in thick fog on Labour Day in 1999. Eight people died and another forty-five suffered injuries.

The carnage on our roads and the economic significance of our freeways are far from the only elements of car culture that Canada and the United States share. Both are geographically big, with vast, wide-open spaces and gorgeous landscapes that lure people into their cars and out onto the roads. And both countries are home to car lovers. In a couple of weeks, I would meet several members of the Guthrie Flashbacks at an auto show in Depew, Oklahoma. One of them—retired attorney Dennis Doughty—told me about an internet forum called ChevyTalk, where enthusiasts from both countries hang out. "We don't always get along on politics," he said dryly, "but on the old Chevys we seem to have common ground."

And yet that ground may not be quite as common as Doughty thinks because car culture does change north of the forty-ninth parallel. While some Canadians may like to spread their car knowledge, lefty politics and other charms on the ChevyTalk site, their fellow Canucks are less likely than their American cousins to be members of car clubs, to spend time fixing, restoring or other-wise tinkering with their vehicles, or to accessorize them. Rather than a hobby, in Canada a car is probably just a means of trans-portation or even a "necessary evil," according to industry analyst and automotive consultant Dennis DesRosiers, whose research also suggests, "Canadians tend to buy vehicles to fill fundamental needs rather than desires, whereas Americans are more aspira-tional with their vehicle purchases."

OBLIVIOUS CAR LOVERS ASIDE, many North Americans watch the automobile with increasing alarm, a predicament that's eerily reminiscent of the one people faced when they travelled on four hoofs instead of four wheels. The horse wasn't convenient or efficient: most people had to go to a livery stable to arrange trans-portation, and even for the few who had their own, spontaneous trips weren't practical, so no one said, "Let's go down to the five-and-dime. I'll bring the horse and buggy around!" But traffic was still a growing problem in cities, and the congestion was exacer-bated by the absence of rules of the road. Horses also created health problems: they relieved themselves frequently, and rotting carcasses often stayed on streets for days before someone bothered to clean up the mess. People needed an alternative. The bicycle spurred social change—including acting as a catalyst in the women's movement because it provided previously undreamed-of mobility and even encouraged less-restrictive clothing—as well as creating the need for better roads, but bikes weren't practical for everybody or for long distances.

Automobiles first appeared in Germany in the 1880s, but the development soon moved to France, where more people could afford to buy them. Initially a luxury, or even a toy, for the wealthy, the car quickly became a necessity in the United States. By the early 1900s, even before the automobile was really practical, Americans embraced it with an optimism that seems laughable today. Instead of urine, manure and dead horses attracting flies and spreading disease, American streets would be clean, quiet and uncluttered. The car never delivered on that promise, of course, but it changed just about everything. Society-altering inventions—including air travel, antibiotics and the birth control pill—seemed common in the twentieth century, but the automobile may have been the most profound of all.

The auto and oil sectors were soon giant engines of the U.S. economy, while many other industries, including restaurants and hotels, changed and grew. Aside from making shopping easier, cars fostered consumerism because automakers introduced the concept of credit. Since the banks wouldn't lend money to people to buy cars, the manufacturers offered financing, and by 1925, three-quarters of the cars sold in the United States had been purchased on instalment plans. Although Henry Ford hated the idea of people buying anything they couldn't afford to pay for with cash, his competitors left him with no choice and he caved in 1928.

Ford may have lost that battle, but he won on another front. He refused to contribute to projects such as the Lincoln Highway, the first link between New York and San Francisco, because he believed that if the private sector built roads, the people never would. So the government stepped in. Today, the widespread adoption of just-in-time delivery means private-sector manufacturers have essentially turned public highways into warehouses, increasing congestion, harming the environment and damaging the infrastructure, which taxpayers then have to pay to fix. And once politicians started building roads, the welfare state wasn't far behind.

Automobiles also helped to attract immigrants. Many Europeans loved their cramped cities, but most of the people who came to America wanted land, and the car helped to gratify that thirst for green, open spaces. Women also benefited. Almost from the beginning of the era, carmakers created advertising aimed at them, and several technological advancements, including power steering and automatic transmissions, were overtly promoted as enablers for female drivers. And once she was armed with an automobile, a woman was less likely to accept staying barefoot and pregnant in the kitchen. Homes were also changing. In the 1800s, garages were unnecessary. By the 1920s, more and more houses had detached garages tucked away in the back, usually on a lane. In the 1950s, the typical suburban home featured a big driveway leading to an attached garage at the front. And by 2001, 18 percent of American houses had a three-car garage, up from 11 percent in 1992. Viewed from the street, many appear to devote more space to cars than to humans. More dramatically, the automobile dictated the form of the modern city by drawing us from dense downtowns to the sprawling suburbs, trading efficiency for a feeling of space, safety and freedom.

How we spent our leisure time also changed with our increased mobility. There's an old joke that asks why we drive on a parkway and park on a driveway, but parkways were originally scenic routes designed for recreational trips to the country (though, ironically, they soon helped to stimulate the suburban development that destroyed much of the countryside). And though the concept may now seem bizarre, for generations the Sunday drive was a popular pastime: people simply climbed into a car and went for a slow, leisurely trip-to-nowhere drive. My father took me on a few, but the practice fell out of favour when oppressive traffic took all the relaxation out of it. (The Sunday driver—someone who is pokey, distracted or even incompetent behind the wheel—is still out there, though.) National Park visits rose dramatically after the sites opened to automobile traffic in 1908 and the driving holiday and the road trip became common activities, especially after the Second World War. And as cruising the main drag became increasingly popular, so did teenage rebellion.

Tailgate parties—gatherings outside sporting events to barbecue some food, enjoy a few drinks and socialize with other fans—proved cars could be fun even when parked. Of course, that wasn't news to teenagers. Indeed, the car loosened our morals as courting practices changed because the back seat promised to be much more fun than sitting on the front porch under the watchful eye of parents. For people past that stage in their relationship, meeting for trysts became much easier, which led to an increase in adultery and divorce. In the 1950s, drive-in movie theatres were known as passion pits—for self-evident reasons. And just about everyone has a sex-in-a-car story. (Even as a non-driving teenager, I always made sure I invited a girl with a car to the high-school dance.) As MacDonald put it, "Cars shape our lives from conception in the back seat to being hauled out in the hearse."

THE AMERICAN LOVE AFFAIR with the automobile really became serious in the 1920s. Early cars were expensive and, like bug-plagued early personal computers, not that user-friendly. Before Charles Kettering invented the electric self-starter that first appeared on the 1912 Cadillac, the only way to get a car going was with a hand crank, which was not just hard work but also dangerous as more than a few drivers broke thumbs, wrists and even arms trying to start their automobiles. The new starters were great for Caddy owners, but it took at least a decade before the technology trickled down to lowlier models. And for all its popularity, Henry Ford's Model T was open to the elements, and that meant it wasn't practical except in temperate weather. In 1920, about 90 percent of cars were open, but several manufacturers began producing affordable alternatives, and by 1930, about 90 percent of cars were closed. The growth in auto sales was striking: the United States had 8.1 million registered cars in 1920 and 24 million by October 1929, when the stock market crashed.

As usual, American literature reflected the social change that followed this boom. In *Babbit*, Sinclair Lewis's classic 1922 satire of conformity and social climbing, the striving protagonist buys an automobile: "To George F. Babbitt, as to most prosperous citizens of Zenith, his motor car was poetry and tragedy, love and heroism. The office was his pirate ship but the car his perilous excursion ashore." Lewis goes on to describe the daily challenge of starting the thing and later writes: "It took but little more time to start his car and edge it into traffic than it would have taken to walk the three and a half blocks to the club." But of course, Babbitt—who desires all the latest technology—feels powerful and important in his shiny ride.

Cars play a central role in what is arguably the greatest American novel ever written, *The Great Gatsby*. The setting of F. Scott Fitzgerald's 1925 masterpiece is the Long Island suburbs of West Egg and East Egg, and Jay Gatsby's Rolls-Royce is a symbol of his nouveau riche wealth. "At nine o'clock, one morning in July, Gatsby's gorgeous car lurched up the rocky drive to my door and gave out a burst of melody from its three-noted horn," recounts narrator Nick Carraway. At a time when most cars were black, Gatsby drove one that was "a rich cream color, bright with nickel, swollen here and there in its monstrous length with triumphant hat-boxes and supper-boxes and tool-boxes, and terraced with a labyrinth of wind-shields that mirrored a dozen suns. Sitting down behind many layers of glass in a sort of green leather conservatory, we started to town." Bad driving is rampant in the book. After Carraway tells Jordan Baker, the dishonest golfer, "You're a rotten driver," she claims it doesn't matter because other people are careful. "'They'll keep out of my way,' she insisted. 'It takes two to make an accident.'" (Both Jordan and Baker Electric were early automakers, and in 1923 the Jordan Motor Car Company ran ads that featured an independent, convention-breaking woman.)

The roadside billboard for oculist Doctor T. J. Eckleburg, complete with giant blue eyes behind massive yellow glasses, watches over the gas station about halfway between West Egg and Manhattan. That's where Daisy Buchanan, driving Gatsby's car back from the city, runs down Myrtle Wilson, the wife of the gas station owner (and her husband's mistress). At the end of the book, Carraway decides, "They were careless people, Tom and Daisy—they smashed up things and creatures and then retreated back into their money or their vast carelessness, or whatever it was that kept them together, and let other people clean up the mess they had made ..."

The nation's great novelists may have seen cars as symbols of the dangers of conformity, materialism and industrial society, but the general public sure didn't. Even as the Roaring Twenties ended and the Great Depression began, Americans didn't give up their wheels. New-car sales did plummet, but gasoline consumption dipped only slightly. And many real people did exactly what the fictional Joad family did in John Steinbeck's *The Grapes of Wrath*: drove to California in search of a better life. The Soviets, hoping to discredit American free enterprise and make the peasants feel better about life, showed newsreels about those fleeing the dust bowl. The plan backfired; when the Russians saw the films, their reaction was, "'They have cars!'"

After the Second World War, military men returned home looking for a job, a wife and a car—not necessarily in that order. At the same time, older people had more money because of the upswing in the economy, women who'd worked while the men had fought were feeling increasingly independent and even teenagers with part-time jobs could afford used models. Freed to once again produce cars instead of military vehicles, the automakers were initially unable to meet the demand.

Advances in technology and the economic benefits of war soon catapulted America into the future predicted by the 1939 World's Fair with its "The World of Tomorrow" theme. The promotion of science and technology as the path to prosperity and personal happiness was as naive as it was optimistic, but influential nonetheless. One of the fair's highlights was Futurama. Designed by Norman Bel Geddes and sponsored by General Motors, the exhibit took people on a ride through what the world would be like in 1960—a future dominated by cars and highways. Cities would separate their residential, commercial and industrial areas for the sake of efficiency and the suburbs would sprawl. (Alas, this all came to pass.) Futurama's "express motorways," engineered to improve safety while increasing speed, helped to sell Americans on the idea of superhighways, though the interstate system the government started building twenty years later did not include the automated radio control system to keep cars a safe distance from each other.

By the mid-1950s, American culture and car culture were becoming almost synonymous. And the automobile was taking on greater meaning, according to cultural anthropologist Grant McCracken. In "When Cars Could Fly: Raymond Loewy, John Kenneth Galbraith, and the 1954 Buick," an essay collected in *Culture and Consumption II: Markets, Meaning and Brand Management*, McCracken focuses on the style known as the "Forward Look," the distinctive appearance of mid-century cars. "The Forward Look was not very streamlined, forsaking the 'least possible resistance' for the greatest possible show," writes McCracken, who describes it as imposing, dramatic and heavy with chrome. "Consumers might be embracing modernist simplicity in their homes, offices, clothing, and appliance designs. But when it came to cars, they wanted something else."

Many experts—including industrial designer Loewy and economist Galbraith—hated the style, deriding it as vulgar and gaudy and a triumph of marketing over engineering and common sense. But everybody else loved the tail fins, the grinning grilles, the oversized bodies, the wraparound windshields, the hood ornaments, all that chrome—even the obvious references to air and space travel in the names. To the buyers, according to McCracken, these cars represented the future: "The 1954 Buick was science and technology 'come down to earth,' proof of what the cascade of progress could do for the consumer."

The Forward Look may have lasted for only a few short, but wildly successful, years, but it helped change the relationship people had with their cars. "To take the wheel in 1954 was to control three and a half tons of metal and glass and gain dramati-

cally in the speed, grace, and power with which one moved,"
argues McCracken. "Unable (or unwilling) to see exactly where
driver leaves off and car begins, drivers were inclined to take credit
for properties that belonged to the car. They were now large,
gleaming, and formidable. The speed, grace, and power of the car
now belonged to them."

More than that, in the 1950s, people talked about "getting
ahead," "travelling in the fast lane" and "heading straight for the
top." And there was no better way to show off social status than
with a car. As the post-war baby boom peaked, parents wanted a
house in the sprawling suburbs, a television (ideally a colour one)
and maybe a mahogany dining room set. And they wanted to be
able to trade in their automobile every couple of years. There was
so much homogeneity in society—practically everyone watched
The Ed Sullivan Show on Sunday night—that a great new set of
wheels was one of the few ways to stand out in the crowd. A car,
right down to its age and even the trim level, defined social status,
and people were jealous of what their neighbours drove. "The
automobile was a consumer good that didn't merely claim or
show or seek to prove mobility," McCracken contends in his essay,
"it was mobility."

MCCRACKEN REMEMBERS seeing the way young men identified with their
cars in 1962. As an eleven-year-old boy in suburban Vancouver, he
and his buddies liked to stand on a street corner in the Saturday
evening dusk and wait for big Chevys and Fords to stop. Once the
boys caught the eye of the driver, one of them would hork on the
hood. And then, as soon as the enraged owner had stepped out of
his beloved machine—often leaving it unattended on the street—
the little imps would run like hell. Since they called the drivers
greasers, the boys dubbed their game "calling grease." It was just a
mischievous bit of fun, but it taught McCracken something about
the relationship between people and their cars (even if it took him
years to really understand it). After one getaway, the boys smoked

their victory cigarettes and pondered the reaction of the drivers. That's when the sagest of the spitters explained to his co-conspirators, "They don't see any difference between themselves and the car. You spit on their car, you spit on them."

Eight years after those carefree days of "calling grease," McCracken got a job as actress Julie Christie's chauffeur while she filmed Robert Altman's *McCabe and Mrs. Miller* in Vancouver, though he drove her around in a Volkswagen instead of a limo. Later, he became a contemporary cultural anthropologist who studied the value of objects in our consumer society and now works around the world as a consultant to companies such as Coca-Cola, Microsoft and Kraft. His services, which he describes as ethnographic and anthropological research, help these clients understand the "head and heart of the consumer." He now lives in Connecticut, where "the signature car is a tiny, stick-thin blonde in a gigantic black SUV." McCracken still believes there is a lot of meaning to be found in our cars, though there's much more diversity today, both in what we drive and how other people react to it.

One reason the car is such a powerful communicator is that it sends out its intended and unintended messages even when we aren't using it. "The weird thing about cars is—and that's why every brand has to say something—people put them in their driveway," said Dave Kelso. Now a consultant, he was a creative director with MacLaren McCann, a Toronto ad agency, where he spent a decade working on the GM account. A carpenter before he was a creative director, he has been driving Chevy trucks for twenty-five years. Currently, he has a Silverado that he still uses to haul lumber and tools. He pointed out that people never put, say, a box of soap on display in the same way they do a car. "What you put in your driveway says something about you. Now it may say that you've got a deal, it may say that you're cheap, it may say that you make more than everybody thinks or that you think you make more than anybody thinks." Even cars that don't appear to make a statement often say something about the driver: the rich man who drives a battered old jalopy may want to appear frugal or he may simply not care about cars, preferring to spend his dough on his watch or his sailboat.

The car we own can express who we are—or, at least, who we think we are—but the image we think we're projecting may not be the same as the one other people are getting when they look at us. When I was a teenager, my friends and I all thought the Dodge Dart was a car for senior citizens, but surely the people who bought them didn't want to advertise their advanced age. The same goes for those who traditionally bought Buicks, which many people consider the current equivalent of the Dart. One friend of mine, while stuck behind a slow-moving Buick, vehemently insisted, "Every Buick driver is a ninety-year-old man who hasn't checked his mirror in decades and has a wife who has never been behind the wheel of a car."

Such snap judgments are, of course, often wrong. Buick's image is changing, for example. And while the minivan driver could be a soccer mom, minivans are also popular with seniors because they're easy to get in and out of. And the same vehicle can mean two completely different things to two different people. Luxury cars are no longer universally admired the way they once were. For decades, the Cadillac was the symbol of success; then, in the 1980s, a German sedan meant power and wealth; and lately, celebrity athletes and actors have made the Escalade, Cadillac's SUV, the ride to be seen in. Regardless of the most-desired make and model of the moment, some cynics will dismiss them as symbols of crass consumerism and their drivers as people with more money than brains or taste.

Environmental awareness also affects the way we see vehicles and their drivers. To some people (including the owners, presumably) an SUV is stylish, powerful and practical, but others think anyone who drives one is a selfish jerk who doesn't care about the planet. At the same time, drivers of hybrids such as the Toyota Prius can be perceived as either virtuous or obnoxiously smug.

"Hummers are now deeply antagonizing and will remain so," McCracken argued, "even as the Prius can seem a little pious."

Even a car's colour may have meaning. According to Leatrice Eiseman, a colour consultant and author of several books on the subject, a black car suggests the owner is not easily manipulated, loves elegance and appreciates classics; white conveys fastidiousness; dark blue indicates credibility, confidence and dependability while light blue denotes someone who is calm, faithful and quiet; orange implies the driver is fun-loving and talkative, but also fickle and trendy. According to Dupont Automotive, silver (which projects an image of cool elegance) remains the most popular colour for car buyers, and urban legend has long held that drivers of red cars—who are sexy, high-energy and like speed—get more than their fair share of speeding tickets.

The way we drive says even more about us than the cars we own. Aside from the relentless speeders, some aggressive drivers go too fast while recklessly switching lanes in an attempt to shave a few seconds off their travel time, while others tailgate in the hope the vehicle in front will get out of the way. Good luck to them when they get behind those drivers who pick a lane, travel at or just above the speed limit and go on autopilot as if expecting everyone else on the road to drive the way they do.

Some people keep their vehicles immaculately clean and meticulously maintained while others let the junk-food wrappers, newspapers and other debris pile up as they run their cars into the ground. Some people spend hours a day in their car while for others it is simply a utilitarian device to make doing errands easier.

All this diversity makes deciphering what the car means to our society harder than it was in the 1950s, so McCracken is reluctant to draw definitive conclusions. "The modernist message captured by the cars of the 1950s is long gone, and it's not clear what the message now is," he suggested. "Perhaps it will reveal itself to an anthropologist fifty years into the future."

JON TURK HAS PERHAPS a more extreme relationship with his pickup truck than most people, but it has nothing to do with style or image. An adventure-travel writer and textbook author, he has homes on both sides of the border—in Darby, Montana, and in Fernie, British Columbia—and says that on one level his 1995 Ford Ranger is a toy that takes him to fun, but it also represents womb-like comfort.

He spends a lot of time in the backcountry, skiing, climbing and hiking; it's cold in the winter and tiring in the summer. "The truck is the first interface of civilization," he explained, "and it's always a whole huge amount more comfortable than where I've been."

When Chris, his wife of twenty-five years, died in an avalanche, he tried to cope with the loss by driving around the continent and visiting friends. "Chris said that for some people, travelling is a place. I would stay somewhere for weeks, or a few months, and then move on." His truck was the only constant. Whenever he grabbed the steering wheel, he felt safe—even though he knew there was danger on the highway—and comfortable. "I always knew that as soon as I got in the truck I was out of there. That was my escape and that was my home. That was what was reliable to me."

At one point in his journey, a friend asked him, "How're ya doing, Jon? I haven't seen you around."

"Oh, I'm not doing very well. I'm living out of my pickup and spinning."

His friend looked at him and said, "What's wrong with living out of your pickup and spinning?"

Not many people want to make a home out of their vehicle, even temporarily, but plenty have deep attachments with their rides. Tuners, for example, spend all their time and money customizing and accessorizing cars such as Honda Civics. But tuners make up only a tiny percentage of the population. We live in a society with so much choice that we can spend our money and our leisure time in many ways. Some people define themselves by the sports they play, some by their cottages, some by other hobbies or possessions. In the 1950s, people had fewer ways to define themselves or seek ego gratification. So while car owners are still unlikely to take kindly to local kids "calling grease" on their cars, fewer people now identify with their vehicles as strongly as they did in the past.

As ever, an unhealthy attraction to cars is most apparent among the young, but that doesn't mean that as we get older, we all turn into appliance people. "You'd be surprised: there are elders who agree very strongly that it's about style," said MacDonald. "And there are young males—we have some working here—who wouldn't know a dipstick from a key slot." In fact, many car clubs are struggling to attract younger members. Nostalgia is part of it: a car can be a powerful symbol of lost youth.

Whether a person lives in a city, a suburb or a rural area, on the other hand, does play a role in how he or she views cars. Four out of five Canadians live in urban centres and 39 percent live in Toronto, Montreal or Vancouver. The country's three largest metropolises all have reasonable population densities and good public transit—a mode of transportation Canadians are happier than Americans to take—meaning that more families can get by with one car or even none at all. By contrast, only 17 percent of Americans live in New York City, Los Angeles or Chicago; and few people want to live in LA without a car.

Money is an even bigger factor. Canadians make less money, suffer higher taxes and pay more at the gas pump than Americans, and that certainly shapes their ownership, usage and purchasing patterns. They tend to buy smaller, cheaper vehicles—more Toyota Corollas than Toyota Camrys is the standard example— and keep them longer: 8.2 years versus 5.

Canadians are also more sensitive to hikes in gas prices. Between January and April 2007, when Vancouverites watched the cost of gas climb above $1.25 a litre, they didn't just grumble and pay—instead, they took Translink, the city's light rail system, more often, leading to an 11 percent jump in ridership. All that may help explain why when I ask Torontonians if they are car buffs, I'm likely to hear: "I would be if I could afford it."

South of the border, some people have started buying more fuel-efficient cars, including Priuses, Corollas and Honda Civics, without giving up their SUVs or pickups; the small cars are just another addition to the family fleet. Americans buy more niche vehicles, including sports cars, luxury cars and convertibles, so while there is one car for every two out of three licensed drivers in Canada, vehicles outnumber drivers in the United States. Bigger stables of cars mean more less-practical, single-purpose rides and fewer one-size-fits-all machines. "Americans are getting some on the side," suggested MacDonald, continuing the love affair metaphor, "whereas Canadians are monogamous, or even celibate."

For many families, this reliance on a single vehicle means driving a minivan. In fact, minivans are twice as popular north of the border because they are cheaper and better on gas than SUVs and are more understated, just like the people who own them. American values, it turns out, are close to those of typical SUV drivers, while the values of Canadians and minivan drivers are similar. "We are," confessed MacDonald, "the quintessential minivan nation."

TO SERIOUS CAR LOVERS, the thought of their beloved machine being dismissed as something akin to what they'd find in a kitchen is more than a little unsettling. For his part, auto journalist David Booth doesn't even believe the numbers. The publisher and editor of *Autovision* magazine and columnist with the *National Post* is a wound-up, fast-talking guy who swears with abandon, doesn't mind indulging in hyperbole and calls environmentalists enviro-weenies. Balding, he keeps his hair closely cropped, has a goatee and wore a black T-shirt the day I met him at his suburban

Toronto office. He said he had only ten minutes as we sat down in a lunchroom, and after fifteen minutes asked me to walk with him to the Acura CSX he was reviewing. Even as he drove away, leaving me standing in the middle of the street, he was still talking excitedly. He was skeptical of the Environics research because he's convinced people don't want to publicly admit, "I bought this car with my heart." So they make up an excuse. He pointed out that the Ford 500 and the Chrysler 300 came out at about the same time. "One appeals to the brain—the Ford 500—and the other appeals to the heart—the Chrysler 300," he said, noting that while the powerful and impressive-looking 300 has been a huge success, "Ford comes up with this bland thing and they can't fucking give them away."

Less aggressively, Wayne Cherry, retired vice-president of design at General Motors, suggested that style and image are more important than many people realize. "I hate to talk about people who think about cars as appliances, but I know there are some out there," he admitted before laughing ruefully. "But given that, some appliances are better looking than other appliances." Indeed, even those new car buyers who just want something to get from A to B may compare several similarly priced practical models and end up buying the most attractive one. That's why he couldn't completely shake his skepticism about people who say design would never influence their buying decisions. "And here they've got the very latest suit cut, the right lapels, the tie, the shoes," he pointed out. "A lot of it is subconscious. Something looks right. Some people say they wouldn't buy something for the looks, but subconsciously they do."

I wasn't surprised that an auto journalist and a car designer would make such arguments, but I also ran the results of the survey by a few other people, including a couple of car dealers, the people in the auto industry closest to the consumer. Mike Shanahan is a guy I played hockey with for many years, though I hadn't seen him for a while when I drove up to Shanahan Ford

Lincoln Sales in Newmarket, Ontario. A strapping guy with a bushy moustache and huge hands that dwarfed mine—his handshake stopped a little short of crushing—he is the fourth generation of his family in the vehicle business: his great-grandfather started making buggies and sleighs in 1880, his grandfather manufactured bumpers and motor bodies and his father opened a Ford dealership in 1965. In 1974, as a sixteen-year-old high-school student, Shanahan spent the summer working for his father as an apprentice mechanic. He's been with the company ever since and now owns it.

He sat behind his big wooden desk in an office decorated with a model ship, nautical paintings and an old musket. Behind him, eight scale model cars—including an Edsel, a Cadillac and a Fairlane—sat on a credenza. "Interestingly enough, once I got into the car business I fell out of love with cars," said Shanahan, who grew up a big fan of auto and drag racing. He last owned his own vehicle, a five-year-old Pinto, in 1979. Since then he's driven an ever-changing array of company cars, usually the dealership's flagship or hottest-selling product. "To me, those aren't automobiles and trucks out there on the lot. That's $6.1 million in new cars and $710,000 in used cars. And if you ever take your eye off that ball, that's when you get in trouble in this business. Then you become the bar owner who loves booze."

Despite his own mercenary relationship with the car, he strongly dismissed the idea that his customers see their automobiles as appliances. For downtowners, a car might be a necessary evil, but not for most of the people living forty-five kilometres north in Newmarket. "People are very interested in what their vehicle looks like in their driveway. It's amazing listening to people argue about what side of the driveway they get—it's like what side of the bed!" said Shanahan. "A real estate agent who shows houses around here will tell you, 'Look at the cars in the neighbourhood. Don't just look at the houses; the cars will tell you the personality of the people who live there.'"

Although this fast-growing suburb of more than seventy-seven thousand is no longer a farming community, the residents still love their trucks. In fact, roughly 65 percent of Shanahan's sales are pickups and SUVs. Of course, today's pickups are a long way from the bare-bones vehicles with sheet-metal dashboards and bench seats that I remember from my summer jobs in the 1970s and 1980s. But beyond the newfound comfort and the addition of luxurious features, Shanahan thinks the popularity of the pickup has a lot to do with the "psyche of room" that attracts city dwellers to a place like Newmarket. "People say, 'I'm going to move out of the city and I'm going to own a truck.' On Saturday, they want to be able to drive to the Home Depot and maybe they'll buy a box of nails, but they won't put it in the cab, they're going to put it in the box of the truck." The pickup, in other words, is a functional vehicle that many people buy for the sake of image.

Next, I went to visit Ken Shaw, Jr., who co-owns Ken Shaw Lexus Toyota, a dealership in Toronto, with his brother. Like Shanahan, he started out working for his dad; unlike Shanahan, he prefers to stick to one car, a Lexus RX. "When you're in the car business, people think it's glamorous to have a new car every two weeks, but I just like having my own," he said. "I know where my sunglasses are and where my CDs are and I guess after all the years I've been in the business there are not too many cars that make me wild. If someone said, 'What would you drive if money was no object?' Maybe some of the exotics—a Ferrari or something—but it's not practical and I would never spend my money on it."

Toyota is a brand that built its reputation on value, and while he wouldn't want to put it quite as coldly as comparing a car to an appliance, he admitted there's a difference between an intellectual purchase and an emotional one. "The Toyota buyer typically buys with his brain not his heart. He's not riding that roller coaster of adrenalin," Shaw said. "When people buy a Camry, they're using their head: they know the reliability, the quality issues, they know the resale values. Somebody who buys a Mustang would be on a much higher high than somebody who buys a Camry."

Or maybe the buying decision is akin to finding the right settings on a stereo equalizer. "You've got all these bars that equalize the sound," said Dave Kelso. "So this one over here might be financial. This is what your grandfather said. This is what your neighbour said. And these are your practical needs. So how do you like your stereo to sound? That's what car you're going to buy."

Even if a growing number of people see their cars as closer to an appliance than a status symbol or personal statement, that doesn't mean they're willing to give up their wheels. Not even our aging demographics will change that. David MacDonald was at a conference where some people were suggesting that when the baby boom generation retires, the car market will suffer because retired couples will need only one car. He and his colleagues thought that was "a crock," and to prove it they said to everyone in the room, "Okay, stand up if you and your spouse both own cars now." Then they said, "Okay, sit down if you will be the one to give up your car." No one sat down. MacDonald's conclusion: "That speaks to the love affair. It's not just the physical car, it's also the idea of mobility and freedom."

Before I left his office, he assured me, "Even though Canadians are more rational in our love affair with cars, we do love cars and we can't imagine life without them."

"Do you agree it's a love–hate relationship?" I asked.

"I'd say it's mostly love. It's not the first year of lust, it's like a marriage: there are spats along the way, but it's not hate," he said. "Definitely not hate."

IF THAT WAS TRUE IN CANADA, then I was excited to find out what it was like on the other side of the border. When I finally rolled to the head of the line, the guards were in the midst of a midday shift change. A tall, thin older man was just finishing up, and a younger woman with dark hair was taking over. The man started the questions, and when I explained that I was driving to Los Angeles to research car culture, the woman asked why I needed to do it in the United States.

"When it comes to cars," I responded, "America's the place, isn't it?"

"No," said the man, as he walked away from the booth. "It's Japan."

Now, it's no secret that the Big Three automakers—General Motors, Ford and Chrysler—are facing some hard times even as several of their foreign rivals go from strength to strength, but I didn't expect to hear something so treasonous, so soon, from someone who works so close to Motor City. And yet it didn't take long before I began to wonder if he wasn't on to something. I knew I would see cars from around the world in big cities, especially LA, but I expected there'd be little but American cars in Michigan and the heartland. As I drove through the suburban sprawl around Detroit, it became clear my expectation of a steely allegiance to American cars in Michigan was positively naive. I saw a lot more Cadillacs than I see in Toronto, but I also saw many Toyotas, Hondas, BMWs and other non-American cars—rides that not too long ago many people considered un-American. That was my first surprise.

3 Detroit
Motor City Sadness

SHORTLY AFTER 5 P.M. on the first day of my road trip, I drove from Sterling Heights to Novi, Michigan, along roads and highways that were in surprisingly bad shape. Back home, I would do just about anything to avoid being in my car—especially on a highway—at the peak of rush hour. So I was thrilled to be able to bomb along at or above the speed limit, which much to my delight was seventy miles per hour—a speed I'm not legally allowed to travel anywhere in Ontario, where the top speed limit is one hundred kilometres per hour (about sixty-two miles per hour). But while the light traffic may be a pleasure for drivers, it says a lot about the health of the Detroit area. As director of transportation systems for Toronto, Les Kelman has a tough job, but he's glad he does: "Never wish congestion away," he warned me, "because if you want to see a city without congestion, you'll find a city with high unemployment rates, high vacancy rates and an incredibly depressed economy. Congestion is a sign of success."

Detroit was once one of the most successful cities in the United States. In 1950, when cars were American and no one thought that would ever change, close to 1.85 million people lived there. Even in 1970, after the population had slipped to just over 1.5 million, Motown was the fifth-largest city in the country and an essential engine of the national economy. When I was in Detroit in 2000, on a road trip to Tiger Stadium before it closed, a cab driver pointed to an abandoned train station and said that when he first arrived in the city as a ten-year-old, the place was so crowded that his mother made him hold her hand. But the downtown diaspora started long before foreign automakers became a serious threat to the Big Three. As in many other American cities, new suburban freeways made nearby communities more attractive while the construction of inner-city freeways made the core less appealing. Worse, although the city boasted the highest rate of home owner-ship among blacks in the country, many of the communities destroyed to make room for the expressways and so-called urban renewal projects were African-American ones. The historic Black Bottom neighbourhood, just east of downtown, for example, gave way to Interstate 75 (also known as the Chrysler Freeway) and Lafayette Park, a seventy-eight-acre project featuring apartment buildings designed by renowned architect Mies van der Rohe. This development exacerbated simmering racial tensions that eventu-ally exploded into violence during the infamous Twelfth Street Riot in 1967. (Though Gordon Lightfoot wrote the song "Black Day in July" about it, the riot actually lasted several days.)

White flight from the city accelerated in the following years and, during the 1970s, it accounted for much of the more than 20 percent decline in the population. Today, Detroit is a rust-belt donut city with a population of just over 886,000 at the centre of a metropolitan area that's home to almost 4.5 million people. Unemployment is high in the suburbs, and higher in the city. And racial politics—invariably fraught at the best of times—compli-cate the relations between the city and its suburbs because more than 80 percent of Detroit is black while the surrounding munici-palities are mostly white. On our 2000 trip, my friends and I looked out the car window in amazement as we drove through poverty and urban decay we had never imagined could exist in North America and then crossed into predominantly white Grosse Pointe, where we saw imposing mansions and massive manicured lawns that made the ritzy sections of Toronto seem modest.

That sequestered wealth is a lavish reminder of what Motor City once was. But while Detroit may no longer be a great metropo-lis, it was the obvious first stop on my journey for both geographic reasons—it's just four hours from Toronto—and historical ones. If I wanted to understand our relationship with the automobile, I needed to learn about the lucrative past, rocky present and uncertain future of the industry that built the American dream machine.

THE PAST ACTUALLY BEGINS in Germany, where Karl Benz built a "motor carriage" with a gas-powered internal combustion engine and three wheels in 1885. Within six years, he started selling a four-wheel version. Brothers Charles and Frank Duryea may not actually have been the first automakers in the United States, but the bicycle builders from Springfield, Massachusetts, usually get the credit because they generated so much media attention when they tested a gas-powered car—with a one-cylinder, four-horsepower engine—in 1893. They'd sold thirteen of their "motor wagons" by 1896 when they formed the Duryea Motor Wagon Company to market their inexpensive limousines commercially. A year later, Ransom Olds started the Olds Motor Vehicle Company in Lansing, Michigan, but sold it in 1899, staying on as an executive with the business, which moved to Detroit and became the Olds Motor Works. By 1904, when the founder left, it was selling five thousand curved-dash Oldsmobiles a year. Even then, four years before Henry Ford introduced the Model T, almost half of the cars made in the country came from the Detroit area. In *A Nation on Wheels: The Automobile Culture in America Since 1945*, Mark S. Foster argues that was no accident. First, the region had resources: "Excellent hardwood forests had made the upper Midwest a natural location for production of wagons and carriages," he writes, "and the same materials were used, initially, in automobile bodies." Second, the area was home to a great number of ambitious entrepreneurs. Third, the presence of many manufacturers—including those of bicycles and carts—meant an abundance of skilled workers. In addition, the roads in the Midwest were even worse than those in the East and "gas-powered vehicles were far superior to electrics and steamers in less-than-ideal conditions."

The Model T ensured that Detroit would be Motor City. Henry Ford, who test-drove his first automobile prototype in 1896, saw the potential for an inexpensive car that millions of people, rather than a few thousand, could afford; he wasn't the only businessman with that idea, he was just the most successful at reaching his goal. He created the Ford Motor Company in 1903, introduced the Model T in 1908 and started building the cars on a moving assembly line in 1913. Tin Lizzies weren't stylish, but they were functional, rugged and reasonably reliable—and their height meant they could handle almost any bad road at a time when almost all roads were bad. Most of all, they were affordable, initially selling for $850 in 1908 when most others cars went for more than $2,000. As he increased production, Ford's costs fell, and by the mid-1920s he was able to lower the price to as little as $300 (less than $3,600 in today's dollars). Meanwhile, Ford's decision to double the wages he paid to $5 a day, while cutting the workday by two hours, helped to create a middle class with enough money and leisure time that a car seemed like a necessity. More than fifteen million Model Ts rolled off the line before a decline in sales forced the company to stop production in 1927. While Ford stuck with his car longer than he should have, the success of the Model T led to an industry shakeout. From the early days of the industry, more than 1,500 companies had made cars, but by 1929, when the stock market crashed, only 15 remained in business.

For all his innovation in manufacturing, Ford didn't have much interest in advancing the technology that went into his automobiles; instead, he was almost monomaniacal about creating a car for everyone and pushing the price down. So the design of the Model T stayed basically the same for nineteen years, and by the early 1920s, people joked that the Tin Lizzie was like a bathtub: everybody had one but nobody wanted to be seen in one. That's why Ford needed his competitors as much as they needed him.

One of those competitors was General Motors. William Durant, who already controlled Buick, wanted to create an automobile-manufacturing conglomerate. In 1908, he formed General Motors in Flint, Michigan, and later that year bought the Olds Motor Works. The next year, GM purchased Cadillac and the Oakland Motor Car Company, which later became known as Pontiac. In 1911, after leaving GM, Durant helped to start Chevrolet, which became part of the conglomerate in 1917. Even as the Model T kept selling well, GM was quickly becoming a serious rival to Ford. It formed the General Motors Acceptance Corporation in 1919, to offer financing, and by the mid-1920s was coming up with new marketing ideas. "Top-level executives determined that many buyers wanted something more than basic, reliable transportation," according to Foster. "Perhaps they could be sold on comfort, styling, and aesthetically pleasing choices of colors for both exteriors and interior fabrics." The company also started making regular design changes to emphasize that last year's model was, well, last year's model. But GM wasn't a technological innovator either: in fact, the company only wanted to lead in technology when that was the best way to make money for its shareholders.

Chrysler, the youngest of the Big Three, had a different approach. Essentially an engineering company, it played Apple to GM's Microsoft—at least when it came to launching new technology. In 1925, a year after introducing a well-received eponymous car, Walter Chrysler, who had worked in the railroad industry, formed the automaker out of the wreckage of the Maxwell Motor Company. In 1928, he bought the Dodge Brothers Motor Vehicle Company and launched Plymouth as an inexpensive brand and DeSoto as a mid-market brand. Chrysler was convinced that the way to success was to build more advanced automobiles at a competitive price, and the company developed cars, notably the Plymouth, that were practical, comfortable and affordable.

In the 1940s, following the Depression and the Second World War, the economy boomed and Americans started lining up to buy cars. Even with expanded production capacity after switching from making automobiles to manufacturing for the war effort, the carmakers had trouble meeting the demand. But once they did, they needed to find a way to keep people buying cars. The result was a horsepower race: between 1940 and 1955, the horsepower of the average American automobile doubled and V8 engines grew from 40 percent of the market in 1950 to 80 percent in 1957. In addition, companies began to segment the market and got serious about making their previous models obsolete by introducing regular styling changes. That boosted demand—and the investment needed to keep up with the competition. Packard, which had built its first car in 1899 and had a rock-solid reputation for great luxury automobiles, merged with Studebaker in 1954. That same year, Nash, which had been one of the most consistently profitable of the small makers, merged with Hudson, which had been the country's largest carmaker in 1929, to create American Motors. By the mid-1960s, the U.S. auto industry included just the Big Three plus American Motors and Kaiser Jeep. But then American Motors bought Kaiser Jeep in 1970 and Chrysler bought AMC in 1987.

Only three are left, and they're struggling. The healthiest of the trio is probably GM, but that's not saying much, and over the years its market share has withered from about 50 percent to 25 percent. The people who work there eagerly point out that most companies would drool over a quarter of the market in such a huge industry. That's true if GM stays at that level; it's not true if the company is like the guy going past the sixth floor after jumping out of a twelfth-floor window.

EACH OF THE BIG THREE automakers now has a museum of one kind or another in suburban Detroit. The oldest is the Henry Ford in Dearborn. Established in 1929 by the man himself, it features a broad range of exhibits, from technology to architecture to decorative arts, and is part of a complex that includes an IMAX theatre and a factory tour and bills itself as "America's greatest history attraction." The impressive car collection includes several presidential vehicles, including the 1902 horse-drawn Brougham carriage that Theodore Roosevelt rode in, the Lincoln "Bubble Top" that transported Dwight D. Eisenhower and the Lincoln Continental that John F. Kennedy was riding in when he was shot. The last in this line of limos is the one that served three Republicans and one Democrat: Richard Nixon, Gerald Ford, Jimmy Carter and Ronald Reagan. All subsequent presidential cars have been or will be destroyed in Secret Service experiments. I also saw the bus Rosa Parks was on in Montgomery, Alabama, when she refused to give up her seat to a white man; a yellow 1923 Stutz Bearcat, usually considered America's first sports car; and the Oscar Mayer Wienermobile. In addition, the museum has several exhibits that look at the social and cultural history of the car, including automobile advertising, food stands and drive-ins and the role of the car in movies. And I got a kick out of seeing a 1934 hand-written letter from outlaw Clyde Barrow (of Bonnie and Clyde fame) to Henry Ford that read: "While I still have got breath in my lungs I will tell you what a dandy car you make. I have drove Fords exclusively when I could get away with one. For sustained speed and freedom from trouble the Ford has got ever other car skinned and even if my business hasen't been strickly legal it don't hurt enything to tell you what a fine car you got in the V8." A few months later, police gunned down the notorious pair in an ambush that left their stolen 1934 V8 Ford riddled with bullets.

Unlike the Henry Ford Museum, which displays cars from many manufacturers and is a popular, if expensive, tourist spot, the GM Heritage Center, in Sterling Heights, is dedicated to GM products and isn't open to the public, though private events such as business meetings, training sessions and fundraising dinners take place there almost daily. More than 150 vehicles—including concept, rare and historic cars—were on display in the eighty-thousand-square-foot exhibit hall when I visited. Open since 2004, the centre boasts a collection of more than 800 automobiles, but only about 275 regularly go on display; the staff rotates about 25 in and out every week. Although everything was in immaculate shape, many of the exhibits hadn't been saved off the line—I saw a 1940 Buick sedan that had more than eighty thousand miles on the odometer—because only relatively recently did the company realize that the first and last cars off the line would be more valuable saved than sold.

Finally, the smallest of the lot is the Walter P. Chrysler Museum in Auburn Hills. It opened in 1999 and stakes out middle ground between the other two, attracting about sixty thousand visitors a year. All polished red granite and black glass, the building sits behind a large sculpture called *Motus Historia* at the end of an impressive avenue-style driveway on a ten-acre site at the edge of the Chrysler campus. Green lawns surround the huge parking lots. After completion of the fifty-five-thousand-square-foot building, the company had a long "laundry list" of what it wanted to exhibit, but with no experience in the field, it lured Barry Dressel from his job at the national museum in the Turks and Caicos Islands. He was a good fit as manager: the son of a man who'd opened a driving school in Washington, D.C., in 1921, he started restoring a Model A Ford when he was fifteen, so he knew cars, and in the 1980s, he was the head of the Detroit Historical Museums, so he knew the area.

Dressel wore a brownish tweed jacket, brown pants, an olive shirt and a gold tie. A few months shy of his sixtieth birthday, he was a bit aloof and professorial, with a slightly patrician air about him. After we chatted in his small office for a while, he took me on a tour of the museum. We ended up in the basement, where the muscle cars are, and Dressel, who drives a Chrysler Pacifica and a Dodge Stratus, admitted that he wasn't really a fan of these classics. In fact, I got the impression that he considered this part of his job slumming. But he enjoys giving lectures on the social impact of the car to groups of schoolchildren and other visitors to his museum. In an effort to make the place less of an "automobile ghetto" and attract a broader audience, he has plans to create several digital audiovisual tours using an iPod-like device that would allow visitors to select the information that most interests them, whether it be technical specifications or social history or car sounds or vintage ads or even—for those not particularly interested in automobiles—details about fashion and design in the 1930s. "Here in the Big Hubcap, some people call themselves car guys, but what they really are is hardware guys," he said. "We discovered that the only way we can surprise people who know more about the cars than we do is to talk about the social context."

The museum displays about sixty-five automobiles out of its collection of more than three hundred. Unlike the GM Heritage Center, which arranges most of its cars in rows in one large room, the Chrysler Museum creates a sense of movement with exhibits arranged at different angles and on a rotating tower with space for three vehicles in the atrium. We started at a display about Walter Chrysler and then moved on to his first prototype and came to a cream-coloured 1934 Airflow CU Sedan. "They kind of stumbled into it, but what they ended up doing was coming up with a new paradigm for how automobiles are built," he explained. "The real significance was the fact that the cabin was moved forward and the engine was moved forward on the axles. It gave you a more roomy cabin and a closed, integrated trunk, an even weight distribution and a better ride. And that really makes it the prototype of a modern automobile."

By the time we got to models from the 1980s, Dressel admitted, "Everybody walks by one of the most significant cars on the floor." We were standing in front of the first Plymouth Voyager minivan—light brown with wood panelling—to roll off the line, in 1984. "Unquestionably a revolution," my tour guide assured me. Beside it was a 1981 Plymouth Reliant, the first K-car off the line. The Reliant and the Dodge Aries featured front-wheel drive, and while they weren't much to look at, they were inexpensive and economical—and, best of all, from the beleaguered company's point of view, they sold well. "You can't get anybody to look at the K-car, and yet K-cars dominated Chrysler in the 1980s, and as all the executives used to say, 'We wouldn't be standing here if it wasn't for that car.'"

THE MINIVAN and the K-car were much-needed hits after the U.S. government bailed out the company with a $1.5 billion loan in 1979. During the 1990s, Chrysler built some successful cars— including the Jeep line—but it remained ripe for takeover when a wave of international consolidation crashed over the industry. During a decade or so of corporate coupling, Ford bought Aston Martin (which it later sold), Jaguar, Land Rover, Volvo and a controlling share of Mazda, while GM snapped up Saab, Daewoo and chunks of Suzuki and, for a time, Fiat. In 1998, Daimler-Benz, best known for its Mercedes line of luxury cars, joined forces with Chrysler to create DaimlerChrysler. Officially a merger, it soon became clear that the German company was the boss. While the relationship had its blissful moments—the Chrysler 300, for example—nine years later the American "partner" was up for sale again. The winning bidder was Cerberus Capital Management, a New York–based private equity firm.

Life hasn't been too rosy for the other two domestic automakers either. While both had popular vehicles in their stables—especially their SUVs and pickups—they also had too many cars that just weren't that appealing. GM, for example, sells over fifty different models. After suffering some huge losses, both companies announced plant closures, massive layoffs and a determination to focus on designing and building better, more exciting cars. In the United States, Toyota roared past Ford in 2007, knocking it out of second place on its home turf for the first time in seventy-six years. Around the world, Toyota sold 9.37 million cars last year, just 3,000 fewer than GM did.

Much is made of the fact that up to $1,500 of the cost of a new American car goes to pay for health care for current and retired employees of GM (or as some people call it, Generous Motors), Ford and Chrysler. Although it's easy to slam the Big Three as reckless and stupid for getting stuck with these "legacy costs," those benefits were the reason the companies were once held up as model employers. Besides, the domestic automakers' problems can really be traced to two long-standing blind spots: good small cars and quality.

For decades, Americans didn't fret about fuel economy or crave better suspension systems. After all, gas was cheap and most of the roads were straight and smooth (even before the government started building the interstates in the late 1950s, the country had a good road system). So the carmakers had little incentive to advance automobile technology except to make vehicles more powerful or to add flashy styling and gadgets. Meanwhile, European manufacturers were saying, "Can we make the car smaller, more fuel-efficient? Can we make it ride better with a more sophisticated suspension? Maybe we should try fuel injection and turbo charging." Most of the advances in American cars after the oil crisis in the 1970s had appeared in European cars years earlier.

The more dangerous threat, though, would come from the other side of the Pacific Ocean. Toyota, which had begun making cars in the 1930s, first started exporting its Crown sedan to the United States in 1957. And within a few years, Datsun (now known as Nissan) and Honda were doing the same, though few paid much attention—until oil prices took off at the same time government demanded emission controls and both government and the insurance industry insisted on safety improvements. As the Big Three scrambled to produce smaller, safer and more fuel-efficient cars, Japanese automakers pounced, taking the opportunity to establish a presence in the North American market. The 1980s were a dreary decade for Detroit, as the domestic companies produced a series of mostly uninspiring cars. But the high gas prices didn't last and by the 1990s, Americans wanted bigger machines than ever.

GROWING UP in a large family—two parents, five kids and a wire-haired fox terrier—I spent a lot of time riding in station wagons. We had several, mostly Fords, over the years and I remember them fondly, but a lot of people my age don't have the same warm and fuzzy memories. In 1984, when Chrysler, then under the leadership of Lee Iacocca, introduced the Plymouth Voyager and the Dodge Caravan, the timing couldn't have been better. Baby boomers were starting to have a baby boom of their own and, being a generation that always wanted to be different from their parents, the last thing these yuppies wanted to do was pack their kids and their proliferating possessions into a dowdy and old-fashioned station wagon. It was not simply a question of style and impotent rebellion, though. The additional interior room and improved fuel efficiency that front-wheel-drive minivans offered over rear-wheel-drive station wagons meant these vehicles actually made a lot of sense.

Other automakers soon created their own versions, and the competition led to many improvements such as more (and more flexible) seating and even entertainment systems for the kids in the back. For carpooling soccer moms, the minivan was a completely practical solution, but not a fun one. Many women who stayed at home with the kids had to suffer the family vehicle while the husband drove solo to work in a more exciting set of wheels. So consumers eventually turned on minivans too. By early 2007, Chrysler was the only American automaker still producing them, as SUVs and crossovers dominated the market. "The rapid growth in SUVs actually would have been slower if it were not for the minivan," said David MacDonald of Environics. "The minivan became the station wagon of the seventies, and it was actually the women who wanted out of the minivan just as they wanted out of the station wagon." Ford dealer Mike Shanahan has heard plenty of his customers say never again to minivans. "They are wonderful when people have little kids and they're going to hockey," he said. "But some people are so tired of driving them they don't ever want to drive another minivan. They don't want to see another one." Instead, they hanker for a sport-utility vehicle.

While our identification with our cars may not be as strong as it was in the past, the success of the SUV is an example of how the industry still manages to create demand out of our expectations and fantasies. SUVs are rugged-looking all-wheel-drive vehicles that have particular appeal to men. But women with children also like them because they offer a big, safe-looking and stylish way to move the family around. Despite the presence of the word "utility" in the name of these light trucks, few of their drivers ever go off-road, and many could get by with a two-door compact; indeed, according to *High and Mighty: The Dangerous Rise of the SUV*, by Keith Bradsher, the sport ute has "a cushy suspension and other features that may even compromise some of its appeal to serious off-road drivers."

The roots of the SUV can be found in the Chevrolet Suburban, which first came out in 1935, and the Jeeps that Willys-Overland started making for the military during the Second World War. The 1963 Jeep Wagoneer didn't sell well but led to vehicles such as the Ford Bronco and the Chevrolet Blazer, big two-door truck-cars that tended to be driven by people who lived in rural areas or actually used them for work. In the mid-1980s, Chrysler's successful introduction of the four-door Jeep Cherokee—which MacDonald considers one of the milestone cars of automotive history—helped people see the SUV differently. And following the release of the Ford Explorer in 1990, these vehicles became a North American obsession. Today, SUV sales outnumber those of sedans, and even Porsche, the high-end sports car manufacturer, makes them.

But if the minivan became boring, the SUV became increasingly controversial. As early as 1999, an episode of *The Simpsons*, called "Marge Simpson in: 'Screaming Yellow Honkers,'" took a run at the behemoths. Homer buys a Canyonero that is, as the jingle promises, "twelve yards long and two lanes wide, sixty-five tons of American pride." Unfortunately, he soon discovers that he bought the model that is "strong enough for a man, but made for a woman"—it even has a lipstick holder instead of a cigarette lighter. So he hotwires Marge's station wagon and takes off in it, leaving his wife with the Canyonero. Initially reluctant, she's sucked in by the SUV's evil charms and soon develops road rage.

Less satirically, Americans for Fuel Efficient Cars, an environmental group dedicated to decreasing the country's reliance on foreign oil co-founded by columnist Arianna Huffington, created a hard-hitting 2003 commercial that intercut among different people saying they did things such as help blow up a nightclub, finance a terrorist training camp and teach children in other countries to hate America. Then, as "What is your SUV doing to our national security? Detroit, America needs hybrid cars now" appears on the screen, a man says, "I don't even know how many miles it gets to the gallon."

Perhaps the most trenchant attack on these machines can be found in Bradsher's *High and Mighty*. In a 2004 article on the dangers of SUVs, *New Yorker* writer Malcolm Gladwell called it "perhaps the most important book about Detroit since Ralph Nader's *Unsafe at Any Speed*." Bradsher's argument is that SUVs are a looming safety, oil-dependency and environmental hazard for North America.

Although most drivers use them as big cars, SUVs are light trucks as far as regulators are concerned, because they are built on pickup truck underbodies. That distinction means little to most people—except that light trucks don't have to meet the safety, fuel-efficiency and emissions standards that cars must. Worse, the size, the height and the four-wheel-drive capability of these well-insulated cocoons give drivers a false sense of safety, a misconception that car companies and their ad agencies have been only too happy to encourage. The truth is that SUVs don't handle as well as cars, so avoiding collisions is more difficult, and they often take longer to stop, especially in slippery conditions; while four-wheel drive improves tracking, it is overrated as a safety feature and makes no difference when braking; the vehicle's weight and the stiffness of the truck chassis mean SUVs do poorly in crash tests; and the high centre of gravity makes them more prone to rollovers. "Sport utility vehicle occupants are at least as likely as car occupants to die in a crash," writes Bradsher, "and SUVs are much more likely than cars to kill the other driver in a vehicle-to-vehicle collision." Despite all these dangers, the sport ute practically taunts its driver to be over-confident.

Most provocatively, Bradsher describes SUV drivers this way: "They tend to be people who are insecure and vain. They are frequently nervous about their marriages and uncomfortable about parenthood. They often lack confidence in their driving skills. Above all, they are apt to be self-centered and self-absorbed, with little interest in their neighbors or communities." The former Detroit bureau chief for *The New York Times* then attributes that profile to "the auto industry's own market researchers and executives."

MacDonald, who does social values research, doesn't agree. When he separates the male SUV drivers from the female ones, he sees some of what Bradsher is saying, but it's no different from the conclusions he'd make about men in general. As an SUV owner himself, he admits these machines are not as green as minivans but argues they are still sensible vehicles. "For me, the packaging works. It's not because I'm insecure in my marriage and a tyrannical driver; it's because it's comfortable, I fit and it doesn't get stuck in the snow," he said. "Look at SUVs and look who's in the driver's seat—a lot of soccer moms and middle age guys with greying hair, not exactly the people you need to be afraid of. And even in the States the profile is not as bleak as he made it out to be. This is quite a sensationalized statement of these drivers."

Bradsher's warnings aren't without merit, though. SUVs are prone to "tripping," a rollover caused when they collide with low obstacles such as curbs and guardrails. And when an SUV collides with a car, the people in the bigger machine usually come off okay, while people in the smaller vehicle are far more likely to be injured or killed than if they'd been hit by another car. Worse, the real danger will come later. People who buy cars and SUVs new are usually fairly sedate drivers, but when neglected, worn-out fifteen-year-old models become three-thousand-dollar "beaters" for teenaged males, we could see a repeat of what once happened with aging muscle cars. "In the seventies, when those cars became cheap wheels for the subsequent generation of teens, it was just mayhem," MacDonald said. "A vehicle that's heavier in mass, easier to trip—laws of physics are laws of physics—and an inexperienced driver or danger-prone driver is something to be concerned about." Already we're seeing SUV resale prices dropping rapidly as gas prices climb. "Nobody wants them because of the fuel economy. Then they become cheap wheels for whoever wants them, and what kind of person wants a cheap big car? An eighteen-year-old guy!"

Many of the people selling their old SUVs are switching to crossovers. Built on car chassis, they are safer and more fuel-efficient, and the lower centre of gravity means they're less prone to rollover and easier to control when doing emergency manoeuvres. The crossover is a blend of the minivan, the SUV and the station wagon. To some people, that's just the least of all worlds, but to others it's the best because it offers the better driving dynamics and safety of a passenger car, the height and comfort of a minivan and the all-weather traction of an SUV.

While environmentalists would like to see all these big gas hogs disappear, MacDonald doesn't see that happening, especially with the aging population. "Older people have trouble bending down low. My wife's car when we got married was a '91 Toyota Tercel, and after we had children I had to drive around in that and it was agony doubling myself over and bending in that little tiny egg. After that, I swore I would never have a small car again," he said. "As the average age in Canada and the United States creeps up into the mid-forties and beyond, and as people want to keep their mobility, I think we're actually going to see more elevated vehicles."

If he's right, that's good news for the domestic automakers, because they have never had much trouble building big cars that appeal to Americans. It's the other end of the market that seems to confound these companies. Neither Ford nor Chrysler, for instance, makes a subcompact along the lines of increasingly popular (though admittedly less lucrative) models such as the Toyota Yaris, Honda Fit or Hyundai Accent (GM does offer the uninspiring Chevrolet Aveo in this class). The problem for Detroit is that the foreign companies can now also make big cars that Americans want while still being able to make the small cars that, with higher gas prices and greater environmental worries, they will need.

AMERICANS HAVE A CURIOUS RELATIONSHIP with the past. They're quick to revel in their history—and yet they're constantly in search of the next new thing. In the 1950s, people wanted a new car long before their old one broke down, so they bought big, powerful cars and traded them in every few years. Needless to say, Detroit executives were fine with that. "If you bought a Cadillac in this country, it didn't mean you were going to keep it for ten years. It meant by God when the models changed, the year after next, you were going to buy another one," said Dressel, which reminded me of the old joke about Caddy owners trading in their rides once the ashtrays were full. "But, boy, in the 1950s in Germany, if you bought a Mercedes, you were scrupulous about the maintenance and you kept it and you kept it and you kept it. Everything about them said, 'We're doing this so it will last a long time and you can fix it when it breaks.'" The lack of emphasis on quality, durability and reliability would soon come back to haunt the Detroit automakers as the Japanese Big Three became household names in America.

Toronto Toyota dealer Ken Shaw's father, who had owned a gas station since 1958, started selling Renaults in 1963. One day, five years after that, Shaw came home from school and his dad showed him a new car.

"What's a Toyota?" wondered the boy.

"Renault is going down and this looks better," his father told him.

Today, Shaw praises his late dad for making the switch, but early on it didn't seem like such a great decision. "In the seventies, it was terrible. I lost friendships over selling friends a Toyota," he admitted, adding that some of the cars even had trouble starting in the rain. "There was a time when 'Made in Japan' was a joke. But in the eighties we moved from poor quality to average quality, and I would say in the last ten or fifteen years we've put together a reputation for quality."

That reputation has made life a lot better for Shaw, and when I met him he was in a buoyant mood about the cars he sells. During the 1990s, the majority of his business came from repeat customers, and he wasn't attracting many people away from other brands. But that started changing five or six years ago. Now, more than half of his customers are first-time Toyota buyers. That's not good news for the Detroit automakers, who've disappointed many customers. "How are they going to get them back? Zero percent financing isn't going to do it forever; cash back isn't going to do it forever. If you've been unhappy with your car and now you're happy with your Honda, why are you going to go back?" he said. "I've never seen anybody pull up to the intersection and say, 'That's a nice deal you're driving.' It's the car, it's the quality and it's the ownership experience, it's not all about the price."

In an effort to make the dealership experience as pleasant as possible, Shaw and his brother Paul host "second delivery" orientation sessions every month. They've found that when people first drive away in a new car, they're too excited to take in much information. At the start of the session I attended, there were about thirty-five people—most clutching owner's manuals—sitting in seven rows of wooden chairs set up in the customer lounge in a corner of the showroom. Shaw, who has an easy manner and relaxed sense of humour and wore a name tag pinned to a grey golf shirt with the dealership logo on it, stood behind a laptop on a podium with a screen off to his right. He asked how many in the crowd were first-time Toyota owners. Only ten or so people put their hands up. He asked about second-time owners and so on until he finally said, "Anybody own more than four?" A man sitting in the front row put his hand up and Shaw asked, "All from us?"

"Yes."

Shaw just laughed and revealed, "Bruce and I play on the same hockey team."

That may have been a bit of a cheat, but the fact remained that the room was full of people who liked Toyotas enough to keep buying them.

Shaw explained that this was an information night and an opportunity for people to ask questions. "We're not here to sell you anything," he assured them, "so I hope everybody left their wallet at home." (Later, he admitted to me that they were in fact selling something: the integrity of the dealership.) Then his brother led a tour of the service department and body shop. Like his older brother's, Paul Shaw's hair was thinning, but he was shorter, had a thicker moustache and longer hair and wore his name tag on a white button-down-collar shirt. Back in the showroom, he answered a question about the roadside assistance program—which Ken had earlier confessed to needing after running out of gas on the highway—by explaining that a version lasting seventy-two months was available.

An older woman raised her hand. "I've had four Toyotas. They last forever. Six years isn't long enough," she said. "Can you extend it?"

A ripple of chuckles swept across the crowd, which had grown to about forty-five people. "I'm serious," she insisted.

"I know you are," Shaw said, producing more laughs.

"My Lexus is sixteen years old—my husband is now driving it—there's nothing really wrong with it."

That's an exchange that hasn't played out in enough North American dealerships that sell domestic cars. Though the Detroit automakers have improved the quality of their vehicles in the past few years, they didn't earn their reputation for mediocrity overnight—and they won't shake it overnight either.

AFTER FIRE DESTROYED his workshop in 1901, Ransom Olds turned to outside suppliers so he could keep his automobile business going. He quickly discovered that along with getting his parts more quickly and cheaply than he could make them himself, the standardized components simplified the process of building his cars. In 1913, Henry Ford refined the idea by adding an assembly line to his Highland Park plant: workers performed the same task again and again as the vehicles moved past them. The efficiency of the system pumped up production levels while reducing costs, and although automakers have introduced many enhancements over the past century, including computers and robots, the classic moving assembly line remains a fixture at most auto factories. But not at the GM Powertrain Performance Build Center in Wixom, thirty-three miles northeast of Detroit. The road into the modern building goes past ponds with fountains—perhaps the first clue that it isn't like other plants. "This is not anywhere near what anyone would ever think about General Motors," admitted plant manager Tim Schag. "Traditionally, people see General Motors as the big ship, and we're fifty-three people out here in the woods of Wixom, Michigan."

Assembling fifty specialty engines a day inside a powertrain factory that churns out thousands every shift would have been more of a distraction than anything else. So the company created this hundred-thousand-square-foot facility, where thirty-two men and three women hand-build 505-horsepower engines for Corvettes and 469-horsepower engines for Cadillacs, which add about twenty thousand dollars to the cost of a car. While there has been some drop-off in demand for the Caddy engines, the plant hasn't been able to meet orders from Vette lovers. The waiting list has been as long as a year and, at the time I was there, the employees were cranking them out at a rate of more than two hundred a week, about 30 percent over the designed capacity of the facility. "Typically on niche products, you have heavy demand in the beginning and then it cools off," said Schag, who noted that people were also paying about fifteen thousand dollars to buy so-called crate engines to put in old models. "This has no signs of that—it appears like it's going on forever."

A friendly, slightly nervous man, Schag is tall and thin with big hands and long fingers and is a manufacturing engineer by trade. He started his career in a Cadillac factory and today, drives a Cadillac SRX, but was thrilled that "in sixty-three days" he was going to get a Velocity Yellow Vette. "I'm a Corvette guy, I love Corvette," he said of the all-American sports car that's been drooled over by kids of all ages since 1953 and has never lost its reputation as a cool ride. "But my heart belongs to Cadillac. There's no ifs, ands or buts." In fact, once he retires, his project car is going to be a 1967 Eldorado. "The styling on them is so magnificent." He was equally enthusiastic about his job, and after twenty-nine years with GM, he couldn't believe his luck in getting it, saying, "I'm going to ride it out into the sunset."

The unnaturally clean plant had a giant U.S. flag on the wall. The clocks that once kept the builders to a schedule now simply show the time of day, an indication of the relaxed atmosphere. Everybody I met in the plant was smiling, and Schag knew all the employees' names and about their families. The thirty-five engine builders move from station to station on one of three lines—two for Corvette LS7 engines, one for Cadillac Northstar engines—instead of staying at one station and repeating the same task. They start with the base block on a rolling stand and move through the eleven stations with it—torquing the bolts with computer-controlled wrenches, for example—and use bar codes to log each step in the process. Once the engine is complete, the builder puts his or her nameplate on it before sending it to a hot-test factory thirty miles away. If the storied heritage of Cadillac and Corvette isn't enough gratification for the workers, then affixing their names is. "The level of pride here is unbelievable," said Schag. "This is the way God intended these things to be." He even had praise for the union, noting that the success of the plant required a lot of flexibility and a willingness to try new ideas. "The union was one of the biggest proponents of doing this," he said. "They saw it as an opportunity for growth. And in the domestic industry—let's face reality here—there's been limited opportunity for growth over the last twenty-five years."

As for the customers, he just marvels at them. More than 500 people have come for a tour after buying an engine built here, most taking the opportunity to get their trim cover autographed and have their picture taken with their builder. And 560 showed up to a July 2006 open house. Schag saves the plant's fan mail and boasts, "I have a shop full of rock stars." Barry Dennis, for one. In his early fifties, he has a greying goatee and shoulder-length hair and wore a white Harley-Davidson T-shirt with "American Dream" in big letters on it. He was about what I'd expect from a Harley rider, though thinner. As someone who has been up to his arms in grease since he was a kid, he loves to tinker with engines even when he's not at work, but he's also been instrumental in the plant's charity fundraising campaigns. Initially surprised by all the attention from the customers—one even took Dennis and his wife out for lunch—he confessed, "It's an odd feeling because I'm just doing my job." He and half a dozen other employees regularly monitor a popular and long-standing thread called "Who built your LS7?" at forums.corvetteforum.com. Some of the thread's content is the silly chatter such sites are famous for—after one poster wrote, "Greg Jones builds the FASTEST ones ..." someone else responded, "Nope, Greg is an apprentice under Chuck [Witmer]. I think your engine was the first that Greg built ... Good Luck!!"— but everyone at the plant gets a kick out of it. And some serious questions do crop up: Dennis has stayed in contact with a Virginia man who is putting one of his engines in a 1967 Stingray.

At this point, it's not logistically feasible to allow buyers to watch the building of their own engines; nor can customers ask for an engine from a specific builder. But Schag figured that when they started getting repeat customers they might have to look at that. Though Dennis wouldn't mind if customers wanted to help build their own engines, he usually builds two to two and a half engines a day on his own. "When I put my name on this, it's my engine," he said, putting his hand on the one he was working on. "They get to use it, but it's mine. That's the way I feel about it." He has been with GM since 1977, and his other friends at the company are envious of his current job. His plan was to retire at fifty-five, but when I spoke to him, he wasn't so sure. "I'm liking it here," he admitted. "I might stay longer."

As a boutique operation, the Performance Build Center is unlike its bigger counterparts, but I wondered if the rest of the company could learn some lessons from it. "Absolutely. Absolutely," said Schag, adding that one of the plant's missions is to develop different products, different processes and different social systems. "We take great care into what ain't broke we're not going to fix. But we've added the people and the simplicity. The way we build engines here is very, very simple. And that is some of the gospel that we can give back to the corporation."

After we toured the plant floor, Schag found a fan letter that a Corvette owner in Houston had written to engine builder Linda

Hooker. He read it to me and then, holding his arms wide as if for a hug, said, "It's like Barney in the car business."

If only thriving in the global auto industry were that easy.

DETROIT IS JUSTIFIABLY PROUD of its architectural gems, including many art deco buildings. So it made sense for the city to try to turn its fortunes around with the Renaissance Center. Dreamt up by Henry Ford II as an ambitious response to the riots and the decline of the city, it opened in 1977. But the gleaming modernist towers, largely financed by the Ford Motor Company, failed to reverse the city's downward spiral as the financial district shrivelled and downtown neighbourhoods decayed.

In the early 1990s, One Detroit Center (now called the Comerica Tower at Detroit Center) opened a few blocks from the Renaissance Center. Designed by the great American postmodern architect Philip Johnson, the building features neogothic spires. And in 2003, after a five-hundred-million-dollar renovation, General Motors moved its headquarters into the RenCen. Meanwhile, in response to the success of the casinos across the river in Windsor, Ontario, three casinos have popped up in Detroit's Greektown, but most of the restaurants and bars in the area have an unappetizing touristy quality. More promising, though, is the Detroit Riverfront Conservancy's attempt to reclaim the waterfront; the centrepiece of the project is a 4.7-mile path called the RiverWalk.

So the city optimistically struggles to revive itself, but great buildings and attractive waterfronts alone can't make a city vibrant and healthy. That takes residents. And Detroit's efforts are hurt by the dismal public transit system. In 1937, the city began replacing its streetcars with buses, and by 1956 the last one went out of service. Today, with the exception of the People Mover, a 2.9-mile light rail loop through downtown that opened in 1987, Detroit relies on buses to move non-drivers in a country without much fondness for buses. An extensive mass transit system isn't feasible with a shrinking population and just eighty-thousand downtown workers, but the Detroit Department of Transportation does want to build some light rail lines or at least bus expressways.

Twenty-five miles northwest, just off Interstate 96, in the overwhelmingly white suburb of Novi where I was staying, inner-city problems such as public transit, poverty and urban revitalization seemed a long, long way away. But the role of the car in shaping the way we live did not. One night, I went to *Talladega Nights: The Ballad of Ricky Bobby*, the comedy about a NASCAR driver. It opens with this text:

America is all about speed. Hot, nasty, badass speed.
—Eleanor Roosevelt, 1936

The First Lady never said anything like that, of course, but it does set the tone for what follows. Let's just say that as Will Ferrell movies go, it was no *Old School*. So the most memorable moment of my evening was my five-minute walk from the mall to my hotel. As I strolled along, I realized that though there were sidewalks, I was the only pedestrian I'd seen on my way there or back.

4 Interstate 69
Amateur Driver on a Crowded Road

I LEFT THE DETROIT AREA at noon on Friday without any tears. I wanted to make it to St. Louis by Saturday night, so with two days to get there I decided to go slightly out of my way and spend a night in Indianapolis. I hadn't gone far before I ran into the first of several construction zones. Signs warning of huge fines and jail terms for killing or injuring a worker appeared, and cars slowed, then slowed again as two lanes scrunched into one. Roadwork is necessary, and usually overdue, though that doesn't make the delays any less annoying for drivers. But I figured I was on a working holiday, and though I was excited to get to my destination and certainly didn't want to dawdle, I relaxed, cranked the tunes and resolved to accept whatever the highway threw at me.

As I crawled along, it occurred to me that in the typical car commercial traffic is just a rumour. Along with this illusory freedom, many ads include fleeting small-print disclaimers along the lines of "Professional driver on a closed road. Do not attempt," as the shiny new car bombs along the empty road or performs flashy stunts. These commercials disturb Cam Woolley, a sergeant with the Ontario Provincial Police's Highway Safety Division: "From my perspective, I can't think of too many where I wouldn't arrest the guy."

All the street racing and aggressive driving he sees have convinced him that "Zoom Zoom"—the Mazda slogan—really should be "Doom Doom." Indeed, a study of 250 commercials from 1998 to 2002 concluded that up to 45 percent showed at least one unsafe sequence, including speeding, aggressive driving or inattentive driving. Woolley spends much of his working life talking to reporters, but his thoughts on the bad example set by such ads rarely make it to air or into print, presumably because media outlets fear losing advertising dollars. After all, carmakers spend more than $11 billion annually pitching their products in the United States, and more than twice that around the world. Auto clients represent about 15 percent of the American advertising industry's revenues. (Domestic manufacturers spend more than $650 on advertising for each of the 16.5 million new vehicles they sell at home each year.) Though the companies use all forms of media, television has been the most powerful tool for decades, and commercials for cars are more expensive to make than for any other product, according to the American Association of Advertising Agencies, which put the average production cost of a thirty-second national automobile spot in 2002 at $578,500. Shooting moving vehicles can be difficult, which adds to the cost, as do exotic locations and special effects. But those costs are small compared to the amount of money it takes to purchase the air time.

People don't buy cars on impulse—in fact, we may spend several months or even years choosing our next make and model—so companies use a variety of messages in different media to take the purchaser all the way from brand awareness to dealer selection. Most television commercials appeal to our emotions, while many print ads work at least partly on logic. But by investing heavily in TV and radio time, as well as in newspapers and magazines and on billboards, automakers haven't just sold a lot of vehicles—they've managed to create and maintain some of the best-known brands in the world. Economic conditions and industry trends mean the message is sometimes more practical than passionate, but it's hard to avoid the conclusion that the automakers have always preferred to play to our feelings. "Car advertising speaks to car culture and societal culture," argued David MacDonald of Environics. "It is all about emotion." While performance isn't the point of every brand, commercials (aided and abetted by movies, television and video games) have convinced us that cars should be big, powerful and, especially, fast—and stoked our obsession with our wheels.

EARLY CAR BUILDERS devoted much of their marketing budgets to promoting public races from one city to another, and the ads they did run tended to be sober, straight-up pitches. Some companies even suggested they were too honourable to indulge in hyperbole or shameless appeals to sentiment. Quality and reliability were early themes in ads, as companies portrayed themselves as working hard to provide excellent cars for Americans. After the success of the Model T pushed down the cost of cars, price became another common selling point.

Text-heavy ads continued to dominate in the 1920s and 1930s. One 1927 example—"The new Ford Car: An announcement of unusual importance to every automobile owner"—included no picture of a car, opting instead for a signed letter from Henry Ford touting the features of the new Model A. That didn't mean that what a car looked like wasn't important in the Roaring Twenties; it was. (Indeed, Ford finally discontinued his Model T because the look of the old car had fallen so far behind the competition.) At the same time, performance and technological developments were emerging as compelling attributes, even if they were only covered in the small print, and advertisers had already begun appealing to—and helping to generate—consumers' fantasies of freedom, power and status.

The companies didn't wait long to start urging Americans to buy two cars. In 1929, GM's "Marooned!" ad laid a guilt trip on any husband who would leave his wife stranded at home without wheels. And few examples were as blatant as a 1950 ad for the Ford Sedan and Ford Convertible that proclaimed: "Think of it! There's not one Ford but two in the garages of over 250,000 American families! Why? Because they have found that nothing else matches two-car convenience. What's more, they've found that owning two Fords costs little more than one high-priced car!"

Women were early targets. Many who'd found the prospect of handling horses daunting had eagerly taken to the independence bicycles afforded them; so, according to *Advertising to the American Woman 1900–1999*, by Daniel Delis Hill, some auto executives reasoned that "women would be even more receptive to the freedom and mobility offered by a car." A 1905 ad boasted that the Oldsmobile "has endeared itself to the feminine heart" and boasted of its ability to "make every woman its friend." Ads often showed women driving alone, stressed ease of use and reliability or explained how a car made shopping more convenient. Later, a few of the sharper marketers realized that in many families, women determined how the money would be spent—and were the ones pushing for a second vehicle.

Typically, the women looked well dressed and sophisticated, but a 1923 ad for the Playboy, a sports car made by the Jordan Motor Car Co., featured "a bronco-busting, steer-roping girl" who "loves the cross of the wild and the tame" and "can tell what a sassy pony, that's a cross between greased lightning and the place where it hits, can do with eleven hundred pounds of steel and action when he's going high, wide and handsome." According to "A look at the 10 best auto-ad campaigns ever," a 1997 article in *The New York Times*, "That targeting was emblematic of a '20s trend in which consumerism was promoted as a way for women to defy convention."

The Jordan example notwithstanding, most ads before the Second World War appealed to the public's rational side. When they plugged styling and performance, they tended to focus on the innovation, technology and craftsmanship that had gone into the car rather than abstract characteristics such as masculinity, sex appeal or status. But that began to change after the war. As more people bought cars, just owning one was no longer the status symbol it had been, and Americans increasingly identified themselves by what they drove. Advertising both fostered this covetousness and took advantage of it. On the surface, 1950s-era commercials promoted the American dream, family values and conformity, but behind that pleasant veneer of the happy suburban life, some serious class jockeying was going on. "Cadillacs and Imperials were cars for managers; Buicks and Packards were for intellectuals like doctors, lawyers and college professors; Pontiacs were for school teachers; and Nashes were for housewives," according to *Cruise O Matic: Automobile Advertising of the 1950s*, by Yasutoshi Ikuta. "People started to upgrade their cars as their social status rose." Even mid-market manufacturers eagerly pushed that button. The photo in a Dodge ad showed a man and a woman standing in a doorway, craning their necks and apparently admiring something, while the copy read: "My, the neighbors sure like our new '52 Dodge!" A 1956 Chevrolet print ad proclaimed, "More people named Jones own Chevrolets than any other car!" and then asked, "Are you keeping up with the Joneses?"

This trend was great news for Cadillac, a brand that had long been about status. The company's first ad in 1903 showed the car driving up the steps of the Wayne County Courthouse and boasted of "new principles of engineering and perfect mechanical construction." A dozen years later, the company ran its "The Penalty of Leadership" ad in *The Saturday Evening Post*, pitching the Caddy as "the standard of the world" and really laying the groundwork for making the brand synonymous with quality and luxury. The ad remains one the ten best auto ad campaigns ever, according to *The New York Times*. In the 1950s, a "Universal Symbol of Achievement" ad featured a photo of two distinguished-looking couples, dressed in tuxedos and evening gowns, walking out of a hotel toward a waiting car. The copy read:

> The New 1959 Cadillac car speaks so eloquently—in so many ways—of the man who sits at the wheel. Simply because it is a Cadillac, for instance, it indicates his high level of personal achievement. Because it is so beautiful and majestic, it bespeaks

his fine sense of taste and his uncompromising standards. Because it is so luxurious and so regally appointed, it reveals his consideration for the comfort of his fellow passengers. And because it is so economical to own and operate, it testifies to his great practical wisdom. The magnificent 1959 Cadillac will tell this wonderful story about you.

Along with striving for the perfect white picket fence, Americans were spellbound by the promise of the future, so advertisers gleefully compared cars to jets and promoted the modern look and conveniences of the contemporary automobile. The photo in the "Magic Touch of Tomorrow" ad for the 1956 Dodge showed a woman effortlessly changing gears by hitting a button on the dash with her gloved fingertip.

Weirdly, regardless of any earlier progressiveness and despite the huge number of women who had entered the workforce during the Second World War, many advertisements displayed a decidedly pre-feminist image of women. "If you look back at the ads in the 1950s, they were in some ways a shameless throwback to earlier attitudes in the ways women were depicted," pointed out the Chrysler Museum's Barry Dressel. "It's strikingly sexist stuff and you always see sexist ads, but it suddenly flowers in the 1950s. It seemed like they were trying to put the genie back in the bottle." Indeed, the "gals" were often little more than glorified hood ornaments. "Since men were the primary purchasers of automobiles, ads of the mid-century invariably featured a winsome female. The code was not hard to crack," notes James B. Twitchell in *Twenty Ads that Shook the World: The Century's Most Groundbreaking Advertising and How It Changed Us All.* "It was the same code that informed the selling of beer or aftershave: buy the product, get the girl."

THE IMAGE of the diminutive Volkswagen Beetle sits in the corner of a vast blank space. The headline is "Think small," and the copy starts off in a self-deprecating manner before extolling virtues such as good gas mileage, the ability to park in tight spaces and the small size of the repair bills. Part of a campaign that started in 1959 and remains one of the most famous and influential in advertising history (making it to Twitchell's list of twenty ground-breakers), such ads took for granted that readers were intelligent. "What is happening here in the VW ads is the effacement of the fourth wall in advertising," argues Twitchell, noting that playwrights and novelists had already used this technique. "You were not being lectured, you were being included." The "Think small" ad, which first appeared in 1962, is probably the most famous example in the black-and-white series, but others included "Lemon"; "It's ugly, but it gets you there"; and "If you want to show you've gotten somewhere, get a beautiful chariot. But if you simply want to get somewhere, get a Bug."

After the social oppressiveness of the post-war era, America was finally beginning to loosen up—a trend the admen of Madison Avenue (and their cousins in Detroit) were eager to both reflect and promote. While ads continued to play to consumers' emotions, transformation and rebellion replaced social status and conformity as dominant themes. A 1968 Mustang ad opens with a woman, her hair in a bun, leaving a lab as the voice-over explains, "They respected Liz in the lab—she was a Ph.D.—but no one knew how much fizz there was to Liz until …" The scene cuts to the woman, her hair now loose and blonder, driving a Mustang to the strains of a jingle that claims, "Only Mustang makes it happen." Another in the series shows a matronly woman leaning down in her convertible, but when she sits up she's an attractive young blonde. If the admen were to be believed, Americans could transform themselves just by buying the right car.

Nothing epitomized the shift from the dream car of the 1950s to automobiles that appealed to the increasing desire for individuality in the 1960s more than the rise of the muscle car, and much of the advertising shamelessly focused on speed and performance. In one example, the copy warned, "I wouldn't stand in the middle

of the page if I were you … it's a Pontiac GTO" while the photo
showed a 1964 model aiming straight at the reader. And an ad for
the 1966 Camaro announced: "A word or two to the competitors:
you lose."

Not surprisingly, the individual remained central to advertising in the 1970s—or, as Tom Wolfe dubbed it, the "Me Decade."
But when the domestic industry began to suffer from a reputation
of poor-quality products in the 1980s, companies looked to ad
agencies to help solve the problem. In 1932, Walter Chrysler's
photo graced ads that urged buyers to "Look at all Three!" The
slogan was an attempt to convince people to compare the new
Plymouth Six to cars from Chevrolet and Ford and led to a
50 percent jump in the low-priced model's market share. Five
decades later, with Chrysler on the verge of bankruptcy, CEO Lee
Iacocca asked consumers to compare the company's products to
the competition's. Pointing his finger at the viewer, he said: "If you
can find a better car—buy it." The line became a trademark for the
celebrity executive and the ads helped save the company.
Meanwhile, Ford tried to rehabilitate its reputation with ads that
boasted, "Quality is Job One."

In the 1980s, the American car hit its design nadir and the
advertising began to mirror that lack of creativity. A 1987 Rolls-
Royce ad in *Architectural Digest* did offer a sniff strip that allowed
readers to smell the car's leather upholstery and, more success-
fully, Nissan tried to tap into the psyche of those who love speed
with a spot for the 300ZX created by Ridley Scott, the director of
Blade Runner, but most campaigns relied heavily on brand recog-
nition and financing deals. "In 1904, the Oldsmobile was urging
the customers to buy it mainly because it was an Oldsmobile,"
according to *Advertising in America: The First 200 Years*, by Charles
Goodrum and Helen Dalrymple. "By the final decade of the
century, ninety percent of the cars were using the same theme."

Even people in the ad business are now unimpressed. Dave
Kelso, a former creative director with Toronto ad agency

MacLaren McCann who spent ten years working on the GM account, praised Volkswagen for fifty years of consistently good campaigns around the world. "The brand is so figured out internally, it doesn't matter who the agency is," he said. "I mean they're the guys who did 'Think small,' which invented good advertising." In general, though, Kelso is disheartened by the state of auto advertising: "As time marched on, all of them got more conservative," he said. "There's nobody doing anything exciting."

At least not in North America. The summer before I left on my road trip, my wife and I visited Argentina. While in Buenos Aires, I met Don Johnson for a drink at the lobby café of the Hilton Hotel in the Puerto Madero section of the city. Originally from Vancouver, Johnson is a twenty-five-year GM veteran who, despite his training as a mechanical engineer, moved over to "the dark side" for the company in 1986 and is now Miami-based regional director of sales and marketing for Latin America, Africa and the Middle East. He brought along Diego Felices, GM's marketing manager in Argentina, and we started off talking about what the car means to Argentines. Felices, a slight man with short reddish hair and a goatee, pointed out that it's difficult to sell cars with automatic transmissions in Argentina, "because people here, they like driving." Even in Buenos Aires, where many residents don't need a car to get to work, they keep one just so they can go for a drive on weekends. "A car is status," Felices assured me. "If you buy here in Argentina, you buy it for the style of the car, trying to show off what you have achieved. It's definitely not an appliance."

Although Johnson had been in his new job for less than a year, he'd already noticed some significant differences between the two hemispheres. "You can be much more subtle here and therefore more creative," said Johnson, who believes South America has some of the most creative art directors and copywriters. It's not just the artistry of the ads that is different, though. "It's a much more emotional message to consumers here. It doesn't mean you don't have rational messages too, but you can reach consumers better when you talk about things that matter to them, whether it's family, friends or what the vehicle means to them in their life," he explained. "In North America, the message to consumers has become much more rational, much more about features and benefits, and prices have become more competitive."

The appeal to the rational is in some ways a throwback to the ads of the 1920s and 1930s, when an automobile wasn't a given for most people and didn't yet possess the entrenched symbolism in the American psyche it does now, so companies spent more effort selling people on the idea of owning a car. Today, a car isn't necessarily the status symbol it once was—and to some people it's just a glorified appliance—so increasingly beleaguered American manufacturers plug benefits such as safety and fuel economy.

Safety hasn't always been the most effective theme to base advertising on (though it has been a consistent winner for Volvo). In *Iacocca: An Autobiography*, the one-time Ford executive admits that when the company pitched safety rather than performance in 1956, "the campaign was a bust." He quickly came up with an alternative approach that promoted a financing deal, and sales took off. But that didn't stop others from trying again. "With SUVs, you see a lot of print ads or TV ads with rainstorms and swerves and stuff like that to impart that sense of safety," noted MacDonald. And GM has promoted the safety features of its OnStar system. In one radio ad, OnStar staff contacted emergency services for someone who has been in a collision; in another, the driver received a "check-in" call after an air bag had deployed. More controversially, children in a 2005 TV ad asked their parents a series of "Would you . . . ?" questions such as, "Would you put my little brother in a car without a car seat?" ending with, "Would you drive me without OnStar?" Some people found these spots offensive because they seemed to suggest that people who didn't pony up for the expensive service didn't care about the safety of their family.

Fuel economy also comes and goes as a selling feature. A print ad for the 1953 Chevrolet touted the car's "sensational new gasoline economy" and opened with: "The smiling people in this picture have been traveling since early morning; and, much to their pleasure, they are having a remarkably *thrifty* trip." It did not, however, cite any mileage figures. During the 1970s, in the aftermath of the OPEC oil shocks, many ads did include those statistics—numbers that may once again become more prominent as gas prices rise and concerns about both the environment and oil dependency increase.

These appeals to practicality aside, many commercials still play on nostalgia or childhood dreams, while others suggest that a car offers a way to control life, brings families together, allows people to escape the chaos of family life, or simply acts as a trusted companion, there through good times and bad in life's journey. And sex is always a temptation, though the European ads tend to be more adventurous in that regard. In one Porsche spot, a beautiful woman in a long coat walks down an alley to a 911 Cabriolet. She admires it, caresses it and then flashes it—revealing nothing but bra and panties and causing the spoiler to rise. The ad did not run in North America. We're not the only prudish people, though. In New Zealand, normally a country with liberal attitudes toward advertising, Nissan responded to viewer complaints by pulling a raunchy 2006 commercial that featured *Sex and the City*'s Kim Cattrall uttering double entendres such as "Why didn't you tell me it was so big? I just wasn't prepared for it," and "The all-new Nissan Tiida makes you feel really, really, really good inside."

Perhaps inevitably, the jingoism of car and country has been another common theme in auto advertising, especially during the Cold War and after September 11, 2001. The famous Chevrolet ads of the 1950s sold both the automobile and the nation: "See the U.S.A. in your Chevrolet, America is asking you to call," sang Dinah Shore. "Drive your Chevrolet through the U.S.A., America's the greatest land of all." In the 1970s, GM employed a jingle about "Baseball, hot dogs, apple pie and Chevrolet." The more the domestic automakers struggle financially, the more likely they are to reach for the flag. In the 1980s, the GM tag line was "The Heartbeat of America." And nine days after the World Trade Centre fell, the company launched its "Keep America Rolling" campaign, complete with zero percent financing: "Now it's time to move forward. For years, the auto industry has played a crucial role in our economy. General Motors takes that responsibility seriously." In 2004, the automaker started using "An American Revolution" as a tag line. GM wasn't the only one playing the patriot card: Ford promoted its own post-attack discount financing deal with its "Help Move America Forward" campaign. And a commercial for the 2005 Ford Mustang told the story of a soldier who had just returned from Iraq. After a melodramatic tale that ended with the father, who owned a classic Mustang, giving the son a new model, white print on a black screen proclaimed, "We at Ford wish everyone in the Armed Forces a safe return home. For your service, you have our gratitude. Brought to you by Ford."

Flying the flag isn't always free of controversy, though. GM may have gone too far when it created a commercial for the 2007 Chevy Silverado that flashed images of Rosa Parks on a bus, Martin Luther King, Jr., preaching, the Vietnam War, Nixon's resignation, the Towers of Light memorial in the Manhattan skyline and Hurricane Katrina while John Mellencamp's "Our Country" played in the background. Finally, a truck appeared from out of a wheat field as the voice-over announced, "This is our country. This is our truck." Some people were upset that GM exploited Parks and King to sell trucks. Others were appalled at the inclusion of September 11 imagery. Still others bristled at the apparent parallel between the country's darker moments and the company's financial struggles. The suggestion seemed to be that once again what was good for GM really was good for America and vice versa. But it didn't matter: the market share for America's Big Three automakers continued to decline.

THIRTY-TWO PEOPLE in a sleepy Swedish seaside town bought Volvo S40s on the same day in 2003. Director Spike Jonze, best known for films such as *Being John Malkovich* and *Adaptation*, even made an eight-minute documentary about it. As hard as it is to believe that anyone would fall for such a hoax, the campaign—which featured an ad, the documentary and a spoof website that purported to debunk the story with a second documentary—worked, and more than half a million Europeans visited the Volvo website.

If car ads on television are increasingly stodgy and predictable, at least the internet offers hope for more innovative campaigns. And with new technologies such as TiVo that make avoiding commercials even easier, the carmakers and their ad agencies have little choice but to try going online to reach existing and potential customers. In what may have been an act of desperation as much as anything else, a floundering Ford launched its "Bold Moves" campaign in 2006. Along with broadcast and print ads, it included a website showing a thirty-part "behind the scenes" documentary series about the company's turnaround attempt. Ford also announced plans to "develop and produce a new reality-driven TV series" that could include "anything from the design of a concept car to the development of a new high-performance Mustang, with unlimited opportunities for everyday customers to participate at one level or another." If auto and ad industry blogs were any indication of the general reaction, most people would rather the company actually built bolder products than create bolder marketing campaigns.

While Ford may not have generated much excitement, at least it didn't face a backlash. Volkswagen was embarrassed when an online British ad that appeared to be for its Polo created a stir early in 2005. The spot showed a man wearing a black-and-white kaffiyeh scarf—obvious shorthand to indicate he was an Arab—who stops his car beside a crowded restaurant patio. When he presses a detonator button, the explosion remains contained within the vehicle. The screen shows the VW logo and the words

"Polo. Small but tough." The video quickly became popular on YouTube, but Volkswagen denied any involvement in the creation of the ad and it soon came out that the spot had been made by an agency hoping to make a name for itself with an impressive show reel.

Volkswagen may have felt burned by the loss of control inherent in online sharing, but others keep trying. In 2006, Chevrolet unveiled a website that offered prizes for creating the best thirty-second commercials for the 2007 Tahoe using the company's video and music. The company hoped the user-generated ads would spread around the internet through email and on video-hosting sites. But many of the homemade ads mocked the SUV as a gas-guzzler. Perhaps GM understood viral marketing well enough to expect the negative ads and didn't care, especially since the campaign generated plenty of publicity in both the mainstream media and the blogosphere. On the other hand, the campaign didn't do much to improve the brand's reputation with the very audience it targeted: young people. Either way, carmakers will likely keep trying to take advantage of the internet, even if it means their ads become more scandalous and offensive—and risky.

IN 1915, TWO MEN on a cliff admire the beautiful gorge below while their car perches beside them and the copy reads, "The Hudson stands at the peak place in its class. It took four years to get there." A 1949 Willys Jeepster ad urges: "Take off from the crowded highway, the mob is not for you. See the unspoiled spots and strange scenes." Cars have always offered the promise of getting away from it all, even if we rarely do. In what must be a bitter irony for many environmentalists, automakers have long sold their products as a way to escape to nature. And now SUV commercials that show the ecologically ruinous behemoths in remote spots, including atop buttes or on the edge of mountains, are common. One spot ends with the driver sitting in front of a waterfall, his Tahoe beside him, while a 2006 Hummer H3 ad—a takeoff on the

Steve McQueen film *The Great Escape*—shows three friends breaking out of their office cubicles and driving around rugged country; the tag line is "Escape Greatly."

I'd escaped the Detroit suburbs—and was happy about it. The fall colours were starting to appear and there wasn't a cloud in the sky, so it was a great day for a long-distance drive. I headed west on Interstate 94, but was soon reminded that rather than freeing us to escape to nature, cars frequently collide with it. I stopped for gas near the town of Parma and exchanged pleasantries with the man behind the register. He seemed slightly awkward or unsettled, and I understood why when he said, "I hope my day ends better than it started." Turns out he'd hit a deer on the way to work, crumpling his front end.

Large animals such as deer are a danger to cars and drivers, but most wildlife doesn't stand a chance. Sprawl and road building destroy their habitats, and pollutants slowly poison their bodies. And if they survive all that, they may end up as one of the estimated one million mammals, birds, reptiles and amphibians killed every day on American asphalt. Sure enough, I began to see a lot of roadkill: people pulled bloody deer to the gravel shoulder, but most of the other lifeless creatures—smushed squirrels and raccoons, for example—just stayed where they had died.

If I was going to spend the next couple of months on the road, I wanted to avoid two things: accidents (with animals or ditches or other cars) and speeding tickets. I've heard so many Canadians, especially those who've driven down to Florida, complain about getting tickets in the United States, and fear of speed traps always adds a smidgen of stress when I drive (though apparently not enough that I'd actually slow down). But with a posted speed limit of seventy miles per hour, and the flow of traffic at eighty or so, I leaned back and cruised down the highway. I was enjoying myself—even if I wasn't a professional driver on a closed course or even riding in a shiny new set of wheels.

5 Indianapolis Road Trips, Pilgrimages and Other Journeys

MY CAR'S ODOMETER, which I'd switched from metric to imperial as soon as I'd crossed into the United States, hit 100,000 about 25 miles north of the Indiana border. As a little kid, I loved to watch when several of the numbers rolled over at the same time, and seeing 99,999 become 100,000 would have been a rare treat. But with the digital readout on today's cars, most of the charm of that experience is lost.

Twin racing stripes running through the vast, flat land, Indiana's part of Interstate 69 is not particularly scenic, so I'm sure many people who often travel it complain of boredom, but it was all new to me and the cornfields, barns and farmhouses, richly lit by the afternoon sun, had a certain bucolic appeal. Having left Detroit and entered the Midwest and a state I'd never been to before, I was starting to feel like I was really on my road trip.

Just one of many rituals, rites of passage and other momentous events in our lives that take place in cars, the road trip is one we're likely to repeat again and again. After all, we can only lose our virginity in a car once. Perhaps the best thing about a road trip is that it's not always clear what's more important or more fun: the destination or the journey.

In some ways, that was true of my current trip. I was on my way to Los Angeles, but I wasn't sure of my exact route or what adventures I'd get into along the way. For now, I was solo, though several friends had promised to join me; in fact, I would be meeting the first one in St. Louis in a few days. But as I sped south, I imagined that many people had travelled this same highway on what were pilgrimages as much as road trips because, for many American race fans, Indianapolis is holy ground.

ABOUT AN HOUR north of Indianapolis, I passed a billboard that proclaimed, "James Dean Country: Where Cool Was Born." Dean, who was born in Marion, Indiana, and grew up in nearby Fairmount, was the poster boy for living fast, dying young and leaving a beautiful corpse. After playing small parts in a few films, he starred in just three—*East of Eden, Rebel without a Cause* and *Giant*—before he crashed his Porsche 550 Spyder and died at the age of twenty-four.

Certainly death by car is not rare, and famous people don't get any special treatment. Big names who've died on the road include author Albert Camus; journalist David Halberstam; painter Jackson Pollock; General George Patton; hockey players Tim Horton, Pelle Lindbergh and Keith Magnuson; musicians Marc Bolan, Eddie Cochran and Harry Chapin; actress Jayne Mansfield; actress-turned-princess Grace Kelly; and the celebrity that our celebrity-obsessed society still mindlessly obsesses over, Princess Diana.

Rebel Without a Cause hadn't even hit the theatres when Dean died on his way to Salinas, California, where he planned to race his sports car, nicknamed "Little Bastard." This was little more than trivia to me when I was younger and going through my James Dean phase, because I was never a race fan. As a thirteen-year-old, I went with a friend and his father to the Canadian Grand Prix at Mosport, where the Flying Scot, Jackie Stewart, won. I enjoyed myself, but watching cars roar around a track was no threat to my love of hockey. In fact, it seemed a bit pointless and I never attended another race. And given that a weekend of stock car racing means burning six thousand gallons of leaded 110 octane racing fuel in machines without emissions controls, hurtling cars around in circles now seems worse than pointless.

Not everyone feels that way. The National Association for Stock Car Auto Racing (better known as NASCAR) is the top spectator sport in the United States and ranks behind only the National Football League in television ratings, while Formula One is an obsession in Europe and elsewhere (just about everywhere in the developed world, except North America). Auto racing has many fans in Canada—I know a few—but it is really just a sub-culture, so I had little sense of its seminal role in the love of the car around the globe.

Humans have always competed to get there first—either on our own (running or swimming or skiing) or in some kind of conveyance (chariot, sled, canoe)—so it was only natural that we would test each other in cars too. Initially, auto races were performance tests to determine who'd come up with the best design, so durability was as important as speed. The first race took place in France in 1894. A year later, Frank Duryea won on a 54-mile course in Chicago. With an average speed of 7.3 miles per hour, he beat three other gas-powered cars and two electrics in ten hours and twenty-three minutes.

Early on, just finishing was an accomplishment, but before long that wasn't enough. From 1900 to 1905, national teams vied for the Gordon Bennett Cup in races between European cities. France won four times and auto racing became a popular spectator sport in that country. So popular that in 1906 the Automobile Club de France held a Grand Prix race at Le Mans. Today, many countries—including the United States—host Formula One races (F1 is the designation of the class of open-wheeled cars in Grand Prix racing) and the cars exceed two hundred miles per hour. Stateside, the first major trophy for auto racing was the Vanderbilt Cup. The inaugural race, held on the dirt roads of Long Island in 1904, attracted a large crowd. The Indianapolis 500, which started in 1911, is a two-hundred-lap race held every Memorial Day. It became a phenomenon of American culture and one of the most popular sporting events in the world, with more than 250,000 fans in the stands on race day and millions more watching on television. Despite that heritage, infighting led to a split within the racing class, and the subsequent dilution of competition means the Indy 500 is no longer the biggest spectacle on the racing calendar.

While many auto sports—ranging from road racing to drag racing to demolition derbies—have their fans in the United States today, none can touch NASCAR. The roots of stock car racing can be found in the bootlegging business that flourished during Prohibition. The moonshine runners tuned their cars so they'd go faster and handle better on the winding Appalachian mountain roads and, if need be, to outrun the cops (and after Prohibition, the tax agents). Inevitably, they started racing these cars. By the early 1950s, stock car racing was catching on with Southern spectators. In "The Last American Hero is Junior Johnson. Yes!" a 1964 *Esquire* story about the legendary whiskey runner turned racer, Tom Wolfe writes: "Here was a sport not using any abstract devices, any bat and ball, but the same automobile that was changing a man's own life, his own symbol of liberation, and it didn't require size, strength and all that, all it required was a taste for speed, and the guts."

At first, the rest of America paid little attention to country boys wildly racing old cars on dirt tracks. "It was immediately regarded as some kind of animal irresponsibility of the lower orders," observes Wolfe. "It had a truly terrible reputation. It was—well, it looked rowdy or something." But once Detroit automakers saw an opportunity to build brand loyalty with this crowd and started pumping money into the sport, stock car racing took off nationally.

Formula One, with its European roots, is all about the glamour, but NASCAR still maintains its rebellious "good old boy" image. Of course, that belies the amount of money involved: in addition to millions of dollars in prize money, the best drivers sign lucrative endorsement deals. The sponsors aren't just auto-related companies either. Despite the Bubba reputation, the sport has a huge following in New York and Los Angeles and about 40 percent of the fans are women, so even the marketers of packaged goods such as Tide want in on the action. Meanwhile, NASCAR merchandise is a multi-billion-dollar business.

As the name suggests, the cars used in this class of racing were originally stock: they were the same Chevys, Fords and Dodges anyone could buy, except that the racers had souped them up so they'd go faster. Today, for reasons of both performance and safety, only cars—some of them (gasp) from Japanese manufacturers—that have been specially designed and built for racing and feature little or nothing in the way of production parts run in NASCAR races. But they do carry the names of models regular folk might check out in showrooms.

A FEW DAYS BEFORE leaving Detroit, I'd gone to the New Hudson offices of Pratt & Miller, an engineering firm that's home to the Corvette Racing team. Steven Wesoloski, GM's road racing manager, wore khakis and a blue button-down-collar shirt, his hair and goatee were going grey prematurely and he looked a bit like Tim Robbins. Armed with a master's degree in mechanical engineering, he'd spent ten years as part of the Corvette production staff, working on projects such as how to make the car stiffer. But after a decade sitting at a computer, he wanted a change. Although he was only a casual racing fan and didn't know that much about it, he was prepared to learn. Soon, he was hooked; in fact, he told me, "There aren't many jobs inside GM that are as fun as mine."

Launched in 1999, the Corvette Racing team competes in the American Le Mans Series as well as at the prestigious 24 Hours of Le Mans. Held annually since 1923, the endurance race takes place on the streets of the French town. Each car has three drivers, who take two-hour shifts behind the wheel. For GM, which aims to go global with its brands, it's a high-profile showcase, especially on a continent where the top two sports are soccer and auto racing.

Close to a quarter of a million fans show up to the event, which is broadcast on television around the world. In 2006, the Corvette Racing team won in the GT1 class for the fifth time in six years.

For 24 Hours of Le Mans, the team sent over forty-seven crates with everything from engine parts to peanut butter, Mountain Dew and Pop Tarts. "The three things you can't find in France," Wesoloski noted. The bulk of the crew stayed for twenty-three days. "So we took a little bit of America with us." An executive chef from a top Detroit restaurant cooked in return for a free hotel room and at each race, roughly thirty people, including management and public relations, support the two cars. Wesoloski and I chatted in one of the team's two tractor-trailers for a while. It had a little office with chairs, a flat-screen TV and desk space for the chassis engineers to set up laptops allowing them to monitor data, plan for the next practice session and decide what to change on the car. The other truck had a similar room where the powertrain guys looked at their data. Each truck also carries one car and every spare part for it, including an engine and a gearbox. Wesoloski was a little coy about the team's annual budget, though he allowed it was in the sixteen- to twenty-million-dollar range.

The racing team program represents the bulk of the marketing for the brand. At one American Le Mans Series race, four hundred Corvettes showed up at the fan corral. That response—and the success on the track—means that unlike some other factory teams, who've pumped a lot of money into a racing program only to pull out a few years later, GM remains committed: "If we cancelled, I think the Ren Centre would be ringed with Corvettes in protest. That's the following we have." Of course, the Vette has long been a revered ride in the United States, so the program's biggest challenge is in Europe, where many people once saw it as an obnoxious car favoured by pimps and drug dealers. "We've turned it around in just the six years I've gone," Wesoloski said. "In 2001 it was still kinda touchy how we were going to be treated. Now we draw the biggest crowd around our pit stall."

On a tour of the Pratt & Miller facility, we stopped in the machine shop, where a yellow Corvette and a red Cadillac were under repair. (GM added the Caddy to the program in hopes of attracting younger people to the brand.) Wanting to control its own destiny, the team makes 90 percent of its own parts, from wheel nuts on up. A Cadillac starts with a piece of the production car, but custom suspension and components go on it; a Corvette C6.R starts with just the frame rails and includes just a couple of dozen production parts. If everything goes well, it usually takes about four months, without too much overtime, to go from an empty bedplate to a completed car.

The team builds two C6.Rs a year, then auctions them off to private racing teams for about $750,000 each, approximately what it costs to build them. In the Race Shop, a man sat on the floor working on a skeletal frame of one of next year's Vettes. Even though the place was clean and tidy, the employees all wore black T-shirts and black pants. "You could do khaki and white," said Wesoloski, "but it would be ugly by the end of the day."

For all the marketing success, the biggest benefit of the program may be the trickle down of technology. Initially, the company had wanted to show off the performance of the Corvette by taking a production car, modifying it and taking it racing. But its competitors—notably the Dodge Viper, at the time—weren't using production models. And once the team took the leap into technology development, it quickly saw the advantages. In the same way that the space program gave us advances in computer technology and medical equipment (not to mention the popular-ization of Tang), some of what GM learns from racing eventually ends up in the cars the rest of us drive. Carbon fibre has started to show up in production bodies, for example, and the racing team shares what it has learned about aerodynamics from wind tunnel tests as well as the ability to get more horsepower without moving to a bigger engine. "That's why we chose the American Le Mans series—it allows the teams to explore the technology," Wesoloski explained. "We can start with very few parts that are Corvette, expand on it and build on it. You've got to maintain a few key components and a few key measurements, but from there, as long as its intent is Corvette, it's good."

After the tour, we popped into the office of Corvette Racing program manager Doug Fehan, which was full of memorabilia, including several photographs. Wesoloski pointed out one taken at Le Mans that showed, from the back, the Corvette team on the winners' podium facing a mass of cheering fans. He has been on that podium and said it was an "unbelievable" experience. "There are almost a hundred thousand people down below and every one of them is yelling, 'Throw your hat,'" he remembered. But there was no chance of that: "Winner's Circle from Le Mans? Forget it. That hat is going on my shelf."

IN THE CLASSIC American film *Animal House*, the fraternity pledge Flounder shows up at Delta House in his brother's car. It's a gleaming black Lincoln Continental with the back doors hinged at the rear (suicide doors, as they were called). Before long, the frat boys declare, "Road trip!"

Properly done, these journeys involve either family or friends. Family excursions tend to produce as many bad memories as good ones. For one thing, there's all that dysfunction to deal with: kids fighting over primo spots in the car; "Are we there yet?"; nagging and odd or fascistic parental tendencies. One friend of mine and his brothers had to pee in a pickle jar because their dad never wanted to stop. Since I was doing an autumn trip, I didn't see many families on long road trips, but Bill Bryson did when he drove around the country for his book *The Lost Continent: Travels in Small-Town America*, and found them easy to spot because they looked as though they'd been in their car so long that they'd turned it into a home, even hanging their wash in the back. "There's always a fat woman asleep in the front passenger seat, her mouth hugely agape, and a quantity of children going crazy in the back," he writes. "You and the father exchange dull but not unsympathetic looks as the two cars slide past."

Once we get older, we get to leave the family behind and do road trips with our friends: to go skiing, to see a band, just to visit another town—the excuse doesn't matter. When I was younger, I had nothing but some easy-to-blow-off classes to worry about. Now, at a more advanced age, I need a reason to pile into a car with pals and go someplace just for fun. But, as my wife regularly reminds me, it doesn't take much.

A road trip is a dangerous experiment in interpersonal relations. At every turn, it seems, dissension looms. There are uncomfortable hours in a car, shared hotel rooms and decisions to make on what to do and where to eat and drink. Throw in obnoxious tics and habits, differing political views and clashing personalities, and a road trip is a donnybrook waiting to happen.

Against all odds, however, most go smoothly. And the ones that don't usually fall into the "someday we'll look back on this and it will all seem funny" category. When I was at McGill, a Montreal car rental outlet advertised a sweet twenty-four-hour deal, so my friends and I picked up a car at six o'clock in the morning and drove to Boston intending to be back by six o'clock the next morning. As soon as we crossed the border, we stopped to buy beer—please, please, don't try this at home—and by the time we got to Beantown we were drunk and in rancorous moods.

We managed to stumble out of a bar not too long after midnight and headed back to Canada. But with his passengers passed out, our designated driver missed a turn and ran out of gas somewhere in the mountains of New Hampshire. The only house with lights on was filled with other college kids on a ski trip. We played cards with them until they served breakfast and sent us on our way. Needless to say, we'd blown the cheap deal on the car.

I'm older now, so the logistics aren't as much of a problem. Getting along isn't necessarily easier, though. On a trip to Cleveland, one guy decided that Saturday dinner was a good time to tell me what he really thought of me. It made for a chilly ride home. Fortunately, inane humour usually comes to the rescue when people are cooped up in a car. In the summer of 2000, four of us squeezed into an old Toyota and drove to Detroit. The excuse: to catch a couple of baseball games at Tiger Stadium before it closed.

The driver was a crazed labour lawyer. He put a tape in the player, but then turned down the volume, preferring to rant against internet porn, dish scurrilous gossip and crow about his sexual prowess. Every now and then, for no particular reason, he'd bellow, "Heeeee struck him out." His blue 1990 Toyota had, until a few months ago, belonged to his mother. Despite its four doors, there wasn't much room in the back, where I, on account of my stubby little legs, sat. But the car did have a handicap-parking sticker. He insisted on its legitimacy because he'd had seven knee operations—the same number, he made sure to remind us, as Bobby Orr. Whenever we swung into a premium parking spot, we broke into gleeful laughter.

I'd travelled with him once before and I was apprehensive about doing it again. Fifteen years earlier, on a trip to Ottawa, he'd driven at unwise speeds in a snowstorm and stopped every hour or so to get something to eat and play video games. But we made it to Detroit with just two stops. The others on the trip were a bond guy with a Henry Fonda–ish demeanour and an eccentric writer with a knack for accents. The bond guy and I had done many trips together, so we shared a room. Since the other two barely knew each other and the lawyer was a compulsive neat freak (his dowdy clothes notwithstanding), while the writer was an absent-minded slob, we eagerly awaited the fireworks. Somehow, though, they bonded quickly.

And so did we all. While looking for the Henry Ford Museum, we ended up at the Henry Ford Estate, where a wedding reception was underway. After the lawyer disappeared into the mansion, we went looking for him, and twice a woman who seemed to be guarding two entrances at once kicked us out. It was the classic road trip moment: three guys standing in the stifling heat waiting for a fourth. We imagined him sipping champagne and chomping canapés—or having his way with one of the bridesmaids.

When he finally showed up, I berated him with a line he'd used so often on me: "There's no I in Team."

"That's right," he barked at me, "There's no I in Tim."

That completely meaningless response became the running joke of our weekend. Something always does. And every time there was a threat of strife, someone said, "There's no I in Tim" and we ended up in giggles. That's the magic of a middle-aged road trip: by driving away from our everyday lives, we are free to act like kids again. And there's nothing a guy likes better than a chance to act like a kid.

INDIANAPOLIS CONSIDERS itself the "Crossroads of America" because four major interstate highways intersect here and half of the population of the country is within a day's drive. I reached the outskirts just before five o'clock on Friday afternoon, but the traffic wasn't too bad, at least in the direction I was going. There were lots of pickups, as I expected, and fewer foreign cars than around Detroit. The city is the twelfth largest in America by population, but the nearly 800,000 residents take up a lot of space; Indianapolis has a density under 2,200 people per square mile (compared to nearly 16,000 people per square mile in San Francisco, which has almost the same number of people). A car-dependent community that last saw streetcars and trolley buses in the 1950s, Indianapolis—unlike many American cities, even smaller ones—isn't investing in light rail. So the only option for transit users is a lacklustre bus system. And anyone wanting a taxi had better not count on being able to flag one down. On the other hand, while even some of the inner suburbs don't have sidewalks, the city is starting to show a born-again commitment to cyclists and pedestrians. The Monon Trail, which runs for 15.2 miles from central Indianapolis to suburban Carmel along an old railway belt line, is now a well-used paved path for cyclists, bladers, joggers and walkers. In addition, the city plans to create the Indianapolis Cultural Trail, a 7.5-mile bike and pedestrian path that will connect several downtown districts as well as the Monon Trail.

Unfortunately, having booked my room online, I was staying farther from downtown than I'd hoped. Just off the highway, which provided an annoying soundtrack of passing cars, the hotel was at the end of a suburban strip that included restaurants, gas stations, a car wash and a GM-Pontiac-Mazda car dealership. No matter. I was on a road trip and even if I was solo, it was Friday night, I'd already put in several hours behind the wheel, and the Yankees and the Tigers were in a playoff series. All I wanted was to sit at a bar, watch a little of the game and wash down my dinner with a couple of cold Rolling Rocks. Normal road trip activities. My options—which included Don Pablo's, a Mexican chain; Bob Evans, a family restaurant with bright lights; a Pizza Hut; and a McDonald's—weren't exactly appetizing. I ended up at an Applebee's, just the sort of corporate operation I'd never go to back home because I live within a short walk or an affordable cab ride of more good bars and restaurants than I could ever hope to sample.

I was the only pedestrian on the street, which wasn't a surprise given that there was no sidewalk, and I could feel the weird looks from people in cars as I walked through parking lots and crossed side streets. But I just couldn't imagine driving that short a distance. The walk back to my hotel, which took only eight or nine minutes at a leisurely pace, was lovely despite the bad urban planning; between the crisp, clean fall air and the big, bright, full moon in the cloudless sky, I sure wasn't rushing to get inside. The folks cooped up in their cars didn't know what they were missing.

6 Interstate 70
The Automobile as Living Room

I WOKE UP ITCHING to get out of suburbia. I just couldn't understand how anyone could be happy living such a car-dominated existence, but it was finally dawning on me that this is where most Americans live. They don't have to, especially when neighbourhoods such as Broad Ripple, just a few miles away from my hotel, offer such an appealing alternative. This gentrified section of Indianapolis is home to art galleries, bars, restaurants, a good indie music store, an independent bookshop with an old-fashioned half door and the Monon Coffee Company (where I sipped my first espresso since leaving Toronto, and a pretty good one at that). My stroll through Broad Ripple took me to the Monon Trail; people were out of their cars, enjoying the warm, sunny day and getting some exercise, so I joined them for an hour. Then, after checking out the largely lifeless downtown, I headed to St. Louis.

Actually, my destination was Fenton, yet another suburb. The members of the Gateway Camaro Club were to hold their annual Fall Colors Tour on Sunday and I wanted to join them. I'd emailed the club president a few days earlier but hadn't heard back, so I planned to just show up at their meeting place: the parking lot of a Drury Inn. I plugged the hotel's address into my portable Pioneer GPS Navigation System and took off.

A GPS is really not necessary for long-distance highway driving, but I had it on anyway. I chuckled at the thought of the grief I gave my friend Mick the first time he brought one on our annual camping trip. As someone who can read a map—and even use a compass, if necessary—I argued that a GPS was not just ridiculous overkill but also counter to his obsession with taking as little as possible to make portaging easier. But here I was, a few years later, driving with one, though I took a while to warm up to it. I hadn't had much time to try it out before I left Toronto, and the few times I did, it suggested routes I knew were teeming with traffic or clogged by construction. So the first time I used it when I didn't know where I was going was after I crossed the border into Michigan. I soon noticed that my trips always took longer than the estimates on the Google Maps website, and I began to wonder why my new guide never sent me on any of the many highways around Detroit. Finally, I checked the settings, and sure enough the gadget's software was set to avoid interstates. Once I'd fixed that, I found it invaluable for the kind of voyage I was on, especially when I had a meeting to make in the suburbs, where I find it easy to get lost.

The downside to using a GPS was that I became lazy and rarely looked closely at a road map. I started to think small—turn right in two miles was about as big picture as it got—instead of having a good sense of my larger route in my mind. When travelling from one Detroit suburb to another, I had only a vague idea of what direction I was headed in. And once I'd decided to go to Indianapolis rather than through Gary, Indiana—which would have been more direct—I just let my GPS tell me where to go instead of studying maps and choosing my own, possibly more interesting, route. I found it an odd sensation to know what my destination was but to have little sense of how I would get there or even where I was.

As I drove to St. Louis, there was another reason I had my GPS on: time. My GPS projected a travel time of four hours and twenty minutes from downtown Indianapolis to the hotel in Fenton, and I wanted to beat it. Making good time is an irresistible game for many drivers. Sometimes it's an individual pursuit to, say, beat a personal best from one place to another, but when several people are driving to one location—a cottage for the weekend, for example—it becomes a competition. Before even offering drinks to the just-arrived guests, the host invariably asks how long the drive took. It's not enough to simply drive fast—making good time requires choosing the right departure time and selecting the best route with the least traffic and fewest construction zones. There are no prizes, of course, and no one even acknowledges that it's really a competition, but everyone knows that drivers who made good time can take pride in having the right combination of speed, strategy and luck. (Even with a stop for gas on my drive to Fenton, I beat my GPS by nearly forty minutes—and felt strangely proud about it.)

Navigation systems are just one of the many high-tech devices that are increasingly finding their way into cars. This technology is part of a long-running trend of transforming the car into a living room. Before leaving for my trip, I got a crash course in telematics and other gadgetry from Tom Odell, a technology planner with GM Canada. I met him at the company's headquarters in Oshawa, Ontario, about sixty kilometres east of Toronto. Known as Mr. Gadget around the office, Odell is an engineer and nineteen-year veteran with the automaker, and his job combines technology with marketing. Dressed in a light lime green shirt with a pen in the pocket, he had a little grin that made me wonder if he wasn't more mischievous than his clean-cut look suggested—the kind of guy who despite his quiet demeanour raised a lot of hell in engineering school. "More and more," he observed, "people see their vehicle as their cocoon, as the last vestige of privacy and solace from the outside world."

That may explain why some buyers now consider a car's interior more critical than the exterior. For decades, there was a lot of continuity between the way a car looked on the inside and the outside. Even in the 1950s, interiors were mostly sheet metal and appeared to be one with the exterior. In the 1960s, while the design still took a lot of cues from the exterior, the interiors started to get a little softer. Finally, in the 1970s, with the new emphasis on safety, interiors began to look completely different from the outside and continued to develop in their own direction. Wayne Cherry, who was vice-president of design for GM, saw interiors grow in importance during his more than forty years with the company. He still believes that people experience an emotional reaction to the external look of the vehicle, but admits, "You buy the exterior; you live in the interior."

I appreciate comfort as much as the next guy, but in the same way that I found the desire to live in the suburbs baffling, I couldn't imagine the thrill of spending a lot of time in a car—unless, of course, I was on a road trip.

AMERICANS AREN'T THE ONLY ONES who spend a lot of time on the road. While in Argentina during the summer, I noticed two things: people loved their cars and it was a huge country with varied and gorgeous landscapes—in other words, it was a place that offered many reasons to jump in a car and go for a drive. When I asked some members of an Argentine car club if there was a connection between geography and car culture, they dismissively pointed out that people who live in small European countries love their cars too. But Chrysler Museum manager Barry Dressel had a more nuanced take: pointing out that Australia, another big country, has a car culture that's similar to the one found in the United States and Canada, he noted a difference between the European love of cars and the American one. A European likes to steer tight hairpin curves and dreams of being in a Formula One race car while an American wants to cruise on four lanes of open road at eighty-five miles an hour in a big, luxurious car. I was on the open road, finally, and I was digging it.

No clouds marred the sky when I left Indianapolis, and just a few wisps made an appearance as I headed west. All that sunshine was great at first, but it would soon leave me squinting. A westward road trip across the continent in the fall has a lot of advantages—less traffic, lower room rates at hotels and temperatures that are neither too hot nor too cold—but because the sun sets in the late afternoon, it also means a lot of driving into a blinding ball of fire, though that seemed a small price to pay for the chance to take a journey like mine. Robert Sullivan is a guy who has driven across the country dozens of times and in the process figured out that the road is not just a path but also a place. It's also relentless in the way it compels drivers forward. "The America that I see is an America that tells you to keep moving, to move on to something better, to get on the road and keep going, to stop only briefly to refuel your car and yourself but then to keep pushing toward the place that is closer to where you should be, or could be, if only you would keep going. America says move, move on, don't sit still," he writes in his 2006 book *Cross Country: Fifteen years and 90,000 miles on the roads and interstates of America with Lewis and Clark, a lot of bad motels, a moving van, Emily Post, Jack Kerouac, my wife, my mother-in-law, two kids, and enough coffee to kill an elephant.* "When I am on the road, I see the America that is a continual expedition, the never-ending race to the last frontier, rural or suburban or exurban. In other words, America is the road."

If the road is a place, then I was at I-70. It runs from Maryland to Utah, and sections of the highway in Missouri and Kansas were the country's first completed interstates. In 1956, President Dwight D. Eisenhower signed the *Federal Aid Highway Act* into law after a dozen years of political wrangling. Sometimes called the *National Interstate and Defense Highways Act*, the legislation was enacted as much for military reasons as economic ones. Eisenhower, who had travelled on the Lincoln Highway as a soldier in 1919 and had later seen Germany's autobahns, realized that a good highway system was essential for defending America. (Similarly, during the Cold War, the Pentagon and the RAND Corporation, then a military think tank, were worried about defence when they dreamed up the electronic network that would eventually become the economic superhighway called the internet.) But most businesses—including automakers, trucking companies and the oil industry—were thinking of profit, not war (though these lobby groups weren't as keen on the idea of paying for the expansion with taxes on gas, tires and other vehicle-related goods, which explains many of the political machinations).

The plan called for the federal government to pay 90 percent of the cost to build a network of forty-one thousand miles of super-highway. The states would pick up the remaining 10 percent and then own and operate the roads. The original spending estimate of $25 billion over twelve years turned out to be a little optimistic: the system ended up costing $114 billion and took thirty-five years to complete—the largest public works project in the nation's history

Today, Americans spend a lot of time on the more than 42,700 miles of interstates, using them to move goods, get to work and go on vacation. These freeways carry about sixty thousand people per route-mile a day, but for all their efficiency, they killed small towns and bankrupted mom-and-pop diners, motels and tourist attractions. In his 1982 travel memoir *Blue Highways: A Journey into America*, William Least Heat-Moon travels around the country on secondary roads, which are known as blue highways because on old maps the main routes were red and the smaller ones were blue. He starts and ends his adventure in Columbia, Missouri, and leaves town on I-70 then cuts down to I-64 and across Illinois and Indiana. "The interstate afforded easy passage over the Hoosierland, so easy it gave no sense of the up and down of the country; worse, it hid away the people," he realizes. "Life doesn't happen along interstates. It's against the law."

The new interstates also meant that more and more companies shipped their products by truck rather than by train, which wasn't good for the environment; public transit suffered as governments stopped investing in it; and people moved to the suburbs after the destruction of inner cities. Though they diminished downtown life for everybody, these new roads typically went right through poor neighbourhoods because the land was cheaper and the residents didn't have the clout to put up much of a fight. Noting that interstates were "white men's highways through black men's bedrooms," architecture and planning critic Jane Holtz Kay argues in *Asphalt Nation: How the Automobile Took Over America and How We Can Take It Back* that the roads actually helped to create ghettos. "The blight and traffic they cause, the ceaseless noise and fumes, sack the weak. The visual detritus of the motorized world is dropped on their doorsteps. Their mean streets hold the repair shops and car washes, the spray paint services and tire marts, the muffler stores, auto parts dealers, and glass vendors." Worse than unpleasant, it's actually unhealthy. After discussing the carcinogens and other environmental toxins the people who live in these neighbourhoods are exposed to, she writes, "This is the classic case of rich people polluting unto poor, spurred by the auto age's pollutants and spatial segregation."

Given that legacy, some of the original enthusiasm for the expressways seems almost comical now. Although they were conceived as a way to move people and goods between cities, in 1965, when many interstates were still under construction, author Frank Donovan contended that the most vital sections were in and around cities. The only problem was that the country wasn't building enough of them. "If much of urban America—where eight out of ten Americans will soon live—is not to become a permanent traffic jam, a great deal more is needed," he insisted in *Wheels for a Nation*. We now know that more roads just beget more traffic, and that means more pollution, more collisions and more time devoted to commuting. Bizarrely, Donovan also believed that highways would improve urban planning because they used significantly less land than a network of secondary roads. In addition, since commercial activity would cluster around the access points, we would need fewer local streets than "were necessary when the housewife had to walk to the corner store."

Along with making the country safer and the economy stronger, highways promised to give Americans the freedom to never walk again. And that was the optimistic view.

RATHER THAN CRUISING the open road on our way to a new city, too often we're stuck in traffic as we do various chores, including shopping and chauffeuring the kids to their games and classes, or making our way to and from our jobs. Even for those who like their jobs, commuting by car is frustrating, time-consuming, expensive, unhealthy and bad for the environment. It is also more popular than ever: our society has voted with its feet—its right foot, more accurately. The one on the gas pedal. Although most people support the *idea* of public transit, our crowded highways suggest that people prefer the comfort of their cars to the inconvenience, overcrowding and potential uncertainty of trains, streetcars and buses. In fact, U.S. census data from 2000 suggest that despite substantial investment in public transit in cities across the country, only 4.7 percent of people took it in 2000, down from 5.3 percent a decade earlier. Northeasterners were the most likely to be transit users, and just under a quarter of the people in New York State were. (The percentage of users drops off dramatically outside New York City.) Meanwhile, just 2.9 percent of Americans walked to work, down from 3.9 percent in 1990.

Drivers may rationalize their choice by saying they don't have the time to take transit or walk, but their journeys to work take up more and more of their day. In 2005, the average Canadian commuter spent 59 minutes a day driving to and from the office, up from 51 minutes a day in 1992, according to a 2006 report from Statistics Canada called "The Time It Takes to Get to Work and Back." The situation is only slightly better in the United States: the average American spends 25.5 minutes for the one-way trip to work, though that number includes all commuters, not just drivers. And it's probably even worse than those studies suggest, according to Nick Paumgarten, author of "There and Back Again," a 2007 piece in *The New Yorker.* "But commuting is like sex or sleep: everyone lies," he writes. "It is said that doctors, when they ask you how much you drink, will take the answer and double it. When a commuter says, 'It's an hour, door-to door,' tack on twenty minutes."

One reason for the longer and longer commutes is that rather than just travelling from the suburbs to downtown, more and more trips are from one suburb to another, and neither the road infrastructure nor the transit infrastructure is in place to make doing that fast and easy. Another reason is the increased traffic congestion. "Rush hour used to be an hour," according to Sgt. Cam Woolley of the Ontario Provincial Police. "Now we've got two rush hours: all day and all night."

Nor is commuting cheap. A study of long-distance commuters in the Greater Toronto Area in the fall of 2006 found that while these drivers thought they were spending between one hundred and two hundred dollars a week to get to work, the actual cost was closer to four hundred dollars. One way to save money is to carpool, but 76 percent of the 128.3 million workers in America drive to work by themselves. Sharing a ride can provide convivial company for the long ride and mean getting to work in less time if the route includes high-occupancy vehicle (HOV) lanes. Sometimes called diamond lanes or carpool lanes, these have been controversial ever since the California Department of Transportation first reserved one lane of the Santa Monica Freeway for cars with three or more people in them. Author Joan Didion called the pilot project "a foray into bureaucratic terrorism" in a 1976 essay called "Bureaucrats," collected in *The White Album.* She complained that Caltrans was devoting 25 percent of the highway to 3 percent of the cars and argued that the lanes led to more collisions.

Three decades later, HOV lanes have cropped up across the continent. And they're still contentious: now, though, car fans are increasingly positive about them, while much of the criticism is coming from environmentalists. Carpoolers enjoy being able to zoom down the highway beside solo drivers stuck in thick traffic, but even the latter benefit because the new lanes mean fewer cars on the rest of the road. New lanes around Toronto in 2005 meant that Highway 403 commuters saved eight minutes and those on Highway 404 saved eleven minutes. But by adding lanes rather than converting existing ones, transportation departments are actually encouraging people to use cars rather than switch to public transit. A smarter approach would be to convert existing lanes, but rare is the politician with the guts to do that. Meanwhile, for all the investment and hullabaloo, the increase in ridesharing has been small; since the number of Americans driving alone grew, the percentage of commuters who carpooled actually fell from 13.4 percent to 12.2 percent between 1990 and 2000. Apparently the lure of HOV lanes can't overcome the disadvantages of ridesharing: carpools are a pain to organize, passengers don't like giving up the freedom and flexibility of their own car and some people find the company more annoying than convivial.

As our travel time stretches, we prefer to suffer alone. To celebrate its fiftieth anniversary in 2006, Midas International held a contest to find the person with the longest commute in America. The winner was Dave Givens of Mariposa, California, who drives 186 miles to San Jose, where he works as an electrical engineer with Cisco Systems, and another 186 miles back home. The round trip, which he has been doing since 1989, takes seven hours and he survives it by drinking a lot of coffee, listening to the radio and keeping his eyes on the road. "I have a great job and my family loves the ranch where we live," he told the company. "So this is the only solution."

Well, obviously not the only solution, just a trade-off he's willing to make. But according to Paumgarten, "Commute time should be offset by higher pay or lower living costs, or a better standard of living. It is this last category that people apparently have trouble measuring. They tend to overvalue the material fruits of their commute—money, house, prestige—and to undervalue what they're giving up: sleep, exercise, fun."

I work out of my house or, when I teach, I walk two and a half miles to Ryerson University, so the concept of spending seven hours a day commuting by car seems ludicrous to me. When I am out on the road during rush hour, I always wonder why the poor sods with daily commutes put up with the frustration. I know that there are a lot of people who claim their car is the only place they can enjoy some "alone time," but I find it more than a little pathetic that fighting traffic for hours a day is the best way for some people to seek tranquility.

AT GM CANADA, Odell and I climbed into a red 2007 Avalanche and he gave me a demonstration of the pickup's rear-view camera, and then, as we drove to the regional engineering centre, of the navigation system. Determined to make the point that unlike products from outside companies—the so-called aftermarket—GM makes sure all these new technologies work together with the car; he cited remote car starters as an example. Aftermarket versions had been available for years, but GM was concerned about the warranty problems created when owners had to disable the security system and change diagnostic codes to install these gadgets. The company decreed, "Thou shalt not install remote starters," and wanted dealers to insist that owners remove the devices before running diagnostic programs on the cars. The dealers, who knew their customers liked remote starters, responded that if GM wanted to ban them, then the company had better make one of its own. Odell's job was to sell the idea to head office in Detroit—not an easy task given the environmental concerns about idling and the fact that modern cars don't need to be warmed up. He succeeded in part because some Americans live through cold winters, and even among those who don't, some liked the idea of "pre-conditioning" their car in the heat.

Originally launched on the 2004 Chevy Malibu, the remote starter is now a popular option on several models.

As Odell was showing off his high-tech toys, I asked him to define telematics for me. Strictly speaking, it's the transmission of information from a distance. The ability of GM's OnStar system to remotely unlock the doors of a subscriber's car is a good example of what the term originally meant. GM liked "infotainment" to cover a lot of the goodies that didn't fit that definition, but the moniker didn't catch on and the use of telematics has since expanded to include any technology in a vehicle that conveys information or provides entertainment. "It's basically gadgets," he explained, "though some gadgets, like rear parking aids, aren't considered telematics because there isn't a communications element. But then when we start to integrate these things, they start to blur." And Odell is big on integration, both because it means the technology is safer and because when various features—air bags and OnStar, for example—are combined it makes the technology even more powerful. Still, he responds "in-vehicle technology" when people ask him what he does. "I don't tell them I just do telematics."

After a drive across Oshawa, we arrived at the engineering centre. One of the five hundred engineers who work in this building is Pablo Carvacho, a senior control systems engineer with a goatee and two earrings in his left ear. He took us to a large cabinet that housed four banks of electronics; it had blue sides, a silver front with a black frame and a maze of wiring in the back. "Basically what you're looking at is an '05–'06 Equinox," he announced. "As we see it."

The Chevrolet Equinox is a mid-size crossover designed and built in Canada. The engineering bench, one of four in the room, contained every electrical module in the vehicle. "Every single signal that you would find in the car, the vast majority never seen by the driver, is available to us," Carvacho explained. He'd never counted them but estimated there were between three hundred and four hundred signals, although the driver of a real Equinox might see only ten or fifteen.

All of the car's electrical systems—from the transmission control to the power steering to the sound system—were here and integrated with a simulator. "We fool all of these modules into thinking they're in a car," he said. Once, the engineers deployed the air bag module only to receive a call from OnStar through the speakers saying, "We've detected your air bag, but we're seeing you inside a building. Is everybody okay?"

Carvacho, whose background is in mechanical engineering and who was part of a team that created the bench, said it allows the company to do pre-production testing, work on problems that pop up during production and later re-create problems customers encounter, especially in cases where testing on a real car would be impossible or exceedingly dangerous. "We can reproduce anything we want," he said. For example, the bench can re-create skids—or, as Carvacho called them, "wheel speed events," because the wheels spin at different speeds—that would be too dangerous for a driver to re-enact in a real vehicle. And the feedback is available immediately.

After Odell and I left the engineering centre, we got back in the pickup and drove to where he'd parked his 2006 Buick Lucerne. We got in and he turned on the seat coolers. As my butt chilled and he gleefully drove around Oshawa showing off OnStar, I asked him what was fuelling the telematics boom: the technology or consumer demand. Odell said the carmakers generally trailed the consumer electronics industry, relieving them of the pressure to not bet on the next Beta as the rest of the world goes VHS. Bluetooth wireless technology, which allows gadgets to share information over a short-range radio frequency, is an example: for seven years, GM kept an eye on its development and tried to figure out when consumers were going to want it. "It's just happening now," he said, noting that GM has started introducing the feature. "For a technology like that, you want to react to demand in the marketplace. You don't want to lead." Similarly, the company is monitoring the three leading options for delivering video to cars' back-seat screens. An on-demand service would allow consumers to download the movies they want when they want them, but that would be expensive. A subscription-based system would make only certain movies downloadable at certain times, resulting in less choice, and the kids might have to wait until half an hour into a trip, but it would be cheaper. A third possibility would let consumers download video from their homes to hard-drive storage systems in their cars through a Wi-Fi network or some other short-range communication system. But since the winning solution will likely be decided by the consumer electronics industry, the automakers can wait and watch, rather than gamble.

GM learned the hard way about the risks of introducing technology for technology's sake. In the late 1990s, it developed a product called "infotainment radio," which was essentially a Windows CE–based system that allowed people in cars to surf the web. The idea, back in the days of the dot-com boom, was that people would be able to check stock quotes and sports scores. The development was a learning experience in itself. "What we learned was that Microsoft doesn't think the way the auto industry thinks, so they were frustrated with the way we do things and we were very frustrated with the way they do things," said Odell. "We cannot afford to have a blue screen of death happen when you're driving down the road. And they were willing to put patch after patch after patch on their system. We call those recalls." By the time the product was ready for launch, the dot-com bubble had burst and the last thing most people wanted to do was check stock prices. "We delivered it," admitted Odell. "And we shouldn't have."

A more cautious approach can mean being a few beats behind—as the automakers were after being tone deaf to the popularity of the iPod. The sound system in Odell's new Lucerne included an AM radio, FM radio, XM satellite radio, a CD player that reads both regular audio and MP3 files and a jack for an MP3 player, such as an iPod. The next stage will be to let the driver navigate through iPod menus using steering wheel controls. Still, it's all a little late in coming for some music lovers. In 2004, BMW was the first carmaker to respond to the iPod's ubiquity by offering an adapter, and other companies now offer their own versions, but the roads are filled with people in late-model cars and trucks who must suffer through the hassle and poor sound quality of connecting their MP3 players via aftermarket FM transmitters.

As fun and handy as a GPS can be, my favourite gadget, in or out of a car, is the iPod. Some people like to listen to books while they drive, but my twenty-gigabyte iPod holds more than 5,400 carefully chosen songs, so I like to plug it in, leave it on random and drive away. When I got my first iPod back in 2001, I used a cassette adapter in the car. But in the fall of 2005, the cassette player ate the adapter and I switched to an FM transmitter, which I endured until I knew I was going to drive my car to California. That's when I bought a new car stereo—one with a jack for an MP3 player.

Even without an expensive sound system, music is such a pleasure in a car, especially on a road trip, because we have a chance to actually listen to music—a rare treat these days. When I was younger, I would go to a store, buy an album, go home and put it on my turntable and sit down and listen. Other than reading the liner notes, I didn't try to multi-task. Instead, I concentrated on actually hearing the music. Nowadays, I buy CDs—or, increasingly, download songs—and then play them while I do my email or surf the web. But in a car travelling down a highway, I can finally listen again. In fact, for many people, that's one of the best things about the automobile. As one friend, who had just completed a road trip to a wedding, wrote in an email: "After driving a total of twenty-four hours in the past week (to and from Vermont) I have one main thought: music is better in the car than almost anywhere. Other than that, I kinda hate cars."

INSTEAD OF PLEASING iPod owners, GM opted to focus on OnStar. First introduced in the United States in 1996, OnStar combines GPS and communications technology to offer a growing range of goodies. It will notify emergency services at the touch of a button; call to offer assistance when an air bag deploys; run a monthly diagnostic of the car and email the results to the owner; allow hands-free phones calls; remotely unlock car doors for drivers who've locked themselves out; help the police locate stolen vehicles; activate the horn and lights for drivers who can't find where they parked; and provide directions. OnStar was originally an expensive dealer-installed option with fewer features, and early on it didn't have many takers, but it is now standard equipment. "What do you really want to offer? Those debates go on," Odell said. "If we want to lead the charge, it's got to be something vehicle-centric. We don't sell iPods, so we want to find something that enhances the value of the car and also meets either pent-up needs or develops needs by coming up with a breakthrough product."

Another technology the company hopes to play a leading role in is XM NavTraffic. At one time or another all of us, usually while cursing stop-and-go traffic, have thought, "If I'd only known then what I know now, I would have taken a completely different route." Traffic updates on the radio sometimes help, especially with major tie-ups, but Intelligent Transportation Systems, or ITS, promises to offer so much more than Arnie Pie in the Sky, the traffic reporter on *The Simpsons*, could ever hope to. ITS takes advantage of computers, sensors and communications technology to save lives, time, money, energy and environmental damage because drivers receive immediate, up-to-the-minute route-specific information, including the traffic speed on a route; reports of accidents, disabled vehicles and bad weather; and news of construction slowdowns and road closures. First launched in 2004, NavTraffic is available in luxury cars from various manufac-turers and works with several aftermarket navigation systems.

Dozens of metropolitan areas in the United States already provide the necessary ITS data.

If drivers find this information worth the money, then the technology will eventually follow the well-worn path to becoming standard equipment. Since the first cars hit the road, owners have eagerly snapped up add-ons to enhance the appearance, safety, speed and comfort of their automobiles. Horns, tail lights, speedometers, radiator temperature meters and hood ornaments all started out as accessories. Over time, they stopped being luxuries and became necessities. Ford dealer Mike Shanahan's customers no longer come to his showroom looking for cars with air conditioning and power windows. Now they take those features for granted and ask about the number of air bags.

Rather than more horsepower, most buyers want comfort and safety. And the more time we spend in our cars, the more we demand. So far, automakers have been good at meeting our demands. We wanted better seating and the designers gave it to us. We wanted more places to put our stuff and many new cars have additional glove compartments, storage areas under seats and even umbrella holders. We wanted good sound systems to help us survive long commutes, and sure enough we got them. (Ford has also developed Sync, a voice-activated in-dash communications and entertainment system for cell phones and MP3 players.) We wanted to keep the kids occupied in the back seat—playing I Spy, Punch Buggy and other car games doesn't cut it anymore—so automakers started offering video screens. David MacDonald of Environics showed a profile of minivan owners to an auto parts executive who looked at the data and said, "These people are low on the spectrum when it comes to technology, so why is it that every one of these things I see on the road has one of those screens in the back?" The father of three kids under the age of ten, MacDonald laughed and said, "That's not enthusiasm for technology, that's crowd control." Shanahan agrees. "If you're driving a car, you'd rather your kids are watching a movie than screaming and yelling and throwing food around and hitting you in the back of the head when you're driving," he said. "So it's actually a safety feature."

Most of all, we demanded cup holders. The stories of people picking their new car based on the number and design of the cup holders are too numerous to just be urban legend. Americans have enjoyed eating in their cars at drive-in restaurants since the 1920s. Of course, drive-in patrons usually finished what they were eating before they left. Drive-thru windows—which first appeared in the 1940s and have proliferated in recent decades, especially at fast-food joints—made noshing on the go more popular. Trying to scarf down a burger while driving is dangerous, but most people were more concerned about drink spills, so cup holders first started showing up in the 1980s, especially in minivans. They weren't just for Slurpees and milkshakes; as American society's obsession with coffee grew deeper—and there's probably a bit of that proverbial chicken-and-egg thing going on here—the cup holder became a beloved feature in domestic cars.

Almost everyone agrees that foreign automakers schooled the Big Three on interiors for years. Not on cup holders, though. European designers were slow to pick up on the trend for two reasons. First, they couldn't imagine why anyone would want to gulp coffee in a car when the civilized, and sensible, thing would be to enjoy it at a café. Second, Europeans tend to take a more focused approach to driving, and manual transmissions are far more common there, so they couldn't imagine drinking anything while driving. Apparently, Japanese designers were equally baffled because my 1991 Maxima had no cup holders, which meant my otherwise tidy car invariably had water bottles rolling around in it and I have to admit I hoped my next car would have at least one of the handy little cavities.

Now that cup holders are a given in most cars, the race to design better ones is on. Several vehicles come with adjustable cup holders; others offer ones that can keep drinks hot or cold and, with ambient lighting starting to show up in cars, the Ford Focus now has an option for LED lighting inside the cup holders while the Dodge Caliber has glowing rings around them.

So, as we drive around in cars with cushy interiors, we eat and drink, listen to tunes or audiobooks, talk on the phone and let the kids watch movies on rear-seat DVD players while we get directions and up-to-the-minute traffic information from a GPS navigation system instead of pulling over to read a map. Depending on the car and the living room, the car—especially if it comes with a sophisticated sound system, seats that heat and cool, and mood lighting—may be better. There's nothing wrong with wanting to be comfortable, especially for commuters, and cool gadgets are fun, but by turning our vehicles into cushy living rooms, we're only making it more inviting to spend even more time in our cars. Unfortunately, that means many of us will.

7 St. Louis Sedentary Behind a Steering Wheel

"HAVE FUN SITTING in a car and getting fat for two months," my eighteen-year-old nephew taunted me before I started my trip. Now, I'm far from a health food fanatic, but I did resolve to avoid fast food as much as possible during my journey. In truth, I was worried about surviving the road food. Interstate highways encourage making time and discourage getting off to seek a good place to eat. Besides, many of the independent diners that once served real, though not always particularly healthy, food to travellers are now shuttered because of the success of the fast-food industry. When I'm on the road back home in Canada, the only place I can handle is Tim Hortons. Once a coffee-and-donut chain co-started by the great National Hockey League defenceman— who died in 1974 after crashing his De Tomaso Pantera sports car—the company has expanded its offerings to include soups and sandwiches and now has more than 2,750 stores across Canada. A friend who has toured the United States as a musician emailed me before I left: "Say hello to interstate service stations for me. It's been too long. My only advice: Subway (y'know, the sandwich place)." And so, here I was on a Saturday night in what I now realize were the outskirts of Fenton, Missouri, with nothing appetizing within walking distance. Not even a Subway. So I reluctantly climbed back into my car to search for some dinner. Foolishly, I drove around for half an hour, not really sure where I was or where I was going, and still nothing caught my fancy. Sometimes there's really no choice: I ended up at a Steak n Shake for the first and, I really, really hope, last time in my life. At least the name was funny. I could actually see the place from my hotel, though reaching it by foot would have meant jaywalking across several lanes of fast-moving traffic—risking my life, in other words. The suburbs were killing me.

Whining downtown snobbery aside, cars really do kill people. Or at least make them sick, because even when drivers can avoid crashing into each other or mowing down pedestrians, our vehicles are not good for our health. Traffic noise isn't just annoying—according to a report by the Toronto Board of Health, it may increase blood pressure, disturb sleep patterns, impair learning in children and can even lead to depression. But the assault on our ears is mild compared to what the air is doing to us. The bad news starts with that delightful new-car smell: some of the plastics and other materials, as well as the paints, glues and sealants in an automobile's interior give off chemicals that may cause throat irritation, kidney or liver damage or even cancer. But the air outside is an even graver concern. In addition to emitting greenhouse gases, cars and trucks spew carbon monoxide, nitrogen oxides, sulphur oxides and fine particulate matter. After Atlanta limited traffic during the 1996 Summer Olympics, the resulting 28 percent reduction in the concentration of ozone led to a drop of between 11 and 14 percent in the number of children who needed medical attention for acute asthma symptoms. Similarly, hospitals near Buffalo, New York, and Fort Erie, Ontario, saw fewer people with respiratory diseases in the days following September 11, 2001, because of a 50 percent cut in traffic across the Peace Bridge. And a Toronto Public Health study linked 440 deaths and 1,700 hospitalizations in the city each year to air pollution generated by cars and trucks.

As bad as the air is, our "car first, exercise last" attitude is worse. Just as it's healthier to eat an apple that might have been sprayed with pesticides than to scarf down a Krispy Kreme donut, for most people it's better to stroll in bad air than to get no exercise at all. And yet we're raising a generation of kids that never walks or cycles. They take it for granted that, as the title of the popular parenting guide *Get Out of My Life, but First Could You Drive Me and Cheryl to the Mall?* suggests, the only way to get anywhere is by car. Children who walk or cycle short distances become more active and less automobile-dependent. Aside from increasing stamina, alertness and academic performance, physical activity improves kids' overall health and fitness while reducing the chances they will be obese.

Since 1979, obesity has more than doubled in the United States. The rate is now over 32 percent and cheap gas is one of the culprits. When fuel prices rise, more drivers opt to walk, bike or take transit, expending more calories than if they'd simply sat in their cars. People also have less disposable income to eat in restaurants, most of which overserve their patrons. (Some fast-food burgers contain close to 2,000 calories, while the average homemade one comes in at about 420 calories. In addition, restaurant meals are often much higher in fat and sodium, which most of us are already getting too much of.) When Charles Courtemanche of Washington University in St. Louis looked at the relationship between obesity and gasoline prices, he concluded that a one dollar per gallon increase in the cost of gas would lead to a 15 percent drop in the American obesity rate.

Unfortunately, bad urban planning means that some people will have no choice but to drive no matter what the cost because the distances between home, work and shopping are so huge. To take advantage of cheap land, some schools are so far away from where families live that no kid can walk or cycle to class—the only way to get there is by bus or car.

And sitting sedentary behind a steering wheel is no way to go through life. Aside from packing on the pounds and inducing back and neck pain, some drivers suffer psychological damage. Cruising down an open highway may be a blast, but crawling along in bumper-to-bumper traffic sure isn't. A tense commute is, at best, dispiriting and exhausting; at worst, it can lead to road rage.

The term became popular in the 1990s after a spate of violent incidents, some involving guns, made the news. The trend coincided with an increase in aggressive driving—including following too closely, driving at excessive speeds, weaving through traffic, and running stoplights and signs—and a general drop in civility on the road. After being cut off in traffic or frustrated by a slowpoke, some drivers become incensed and seek revenge. It can start with swearing and bird-flipping, escalate to intimidating driving and end up in fisticuffs, assault with a weapon (such as a golf club or tire iron) or gunplay. Some road ragers have even used their automobile as a weapon.

The phenomenon may not get the media attention it once did, but it certainly hasn't gone away. One study suggested that up to sixteen million Americans experience what psychiatrists call "intermittent explosive disorder." Not everyone agrees that the problem is medical, arguing instead that it's cultural, but there's little debate that as the traffic volumes increase and commute times grow longer, people become more impatient and less forgiving. Some experts speculate that drivers behave differently (read: more irrationally) in a car, which—especially if it's a big SUV—can create a sense of isolation and invincibility. The anonymity of riding in a living room on wheels, an extension of the anonymity of suburban life, can weaken common sense and self-discipline so much that even upstanding citizens with responsible jobs do things they'd never do in a grocery store lineup. "They aren't all Charlie Manson look-alikes," Sgt. Cam Woolley, of the Ontario Provincial Police, told me. "They've timed their commute down to the last second, and if anybody goes too slow or doesn't drive the way they'd like, they go nuts."

ON MONDAY, when I fled Fenton for St. Louis, I was relieved rather than filled with rage. Back home, everyone was celebrating Canadian Thanksgiving, but I wouldn't be feasting on turkey and fixings for several more weeks. Instead, I made a detour to the Whole Foods Market in Brentwood, a low-density inner suburb that includes several shopping malls with well-used parking lots filled with more Japanese cars than American ones. Then I drove to the Central West End. I'd found a cheap hotel there, but since it wasn't check-in time yet, I walked over to Forest Park, which is one of the largest urban parks in the United States and about five hundred acres larger than New York's Central Park.

The Central West End is a gentrified neighbourhood near St. Louis University, Washington University in St. Louis School of Medicine and Forest Park. I walked around some of the residential streets and saw plenty of lovely homes, particularly to the north, while lofts were going up to the south, closer to the hospital and the medical school. In the middle, restaurants and bars drew people out of their houses. Even on a Monday night, people were out and about, taking advantage of the restaurant patios. It all seemed good.

The Central West End's pleasures aside, St. Louis is a car city—and by that I mean one ruined by the car. At the turn of the last century, the Gateway to the West was the fourth-largest city in America, and by 1950 the population had grown to more than 850,000. Since then, as more and more residents headed for surrounding suburbs, the population has fallen below 350,000—about what it was in 1880. Unlike some American cities, St. Louis has not had much luck attracting many people back downtown again despite the presence of the big park, a healthy arts and cultural scene and Metrolink, the region's light rail system. A few neighbourhoods—notably the Central West End and Lafayette Square—are doing well, but residents are still clearing out of other areas, particularly North St. Louis, and the high crime rate hasn't helped. The region has also lost economic power, and though railway car manufacturing, some Boeing operations and Big Three plants are still up and running, it's not the major centre for transportation manufacturing it once was.

On Tuesday afternoon, I rode the Metrolink down to the Gateway Arch. The Central West End is about twelve miles from the arch, and as I looked out the window of the train, I saw a lot of industrial desolation. The Metrolink has the airport at one end and has stops by the domed stadium, the hockey arena and the baseball stadium, which are all close to downtown, the arch and the waterfront. And yet, it wasn't busy. Even returning to my hotel after four o'clock in the afternoon, I had no problem getting a seat. The trains heading to East St. Louis were a bit more crowded, but they were a claustrophobe's dream compared to the cattle cars on rapid transit at that time of day in more dynamic cities.

Except for some gambling riverboats, the banks of the Mississippi River offer nothing to attract people to them; indeed, the St. Louis waterfront makes the pathetic one in Toronto look good. Laclede's Landing, an old warehouse district with cobblestone streets that's now home to shops, bars and restaurants, is nearby. But on a Tuesday afternoon, it had all the vibrancy of a morgue. I got the impression that rather than living or working there, people popped in to party, especially before a game since Busch Stadium and the Edward Jones Dome are close by. The city is trying to revitalize its neighbourhoods, so there is hope, but without people living downtown, St. Louis lacks the energy a great city needs.

On my way back to my hotel, I got off at Union Station. Once an important railway terminal—after it opened in 1894 it was the largest and busiest passenger rail terminal in the world—and an impressive piece of architecture, it's now a shopping mall and entertainment complex, which surely says something about our current attitudes toward train travel, on the one hand, and shopping, on the other. But in the late afternoon on a Tuesday, the place was all but empty and I wondered how the retailers stayed in business. When I went outside and walked around the old station, I found that, as is so often the case with such malls, it had failed to generate any nearby development.

That didn't surprise me, but the light traffic at a time of day when most cities are chock full of cars did. It also dawned on me that in the two days since I'd escaped the suburbs, I'd seen hardly any taxicabs. Obviously, I hadn't expected St. Louis to be like Manhattan, where cabs seem to outnumber private cars (except when it's pouring rain, of course), but I had assumed that someone on a busy St. Louis street would have little problem flagging one. Taxis flourish in dense cities where there's effective public transit and plenty of pedestrians—places where people might walk partway and then hail a cab or take a taxi to their destination and walk back or, at night, take transit there and a cab home. One thing's for sure: car drivers don't flag taxis. So pedestrians go where there are taxis and taxis go where there are pedestrians. As I thought about this, I figured that I'd stumbled on a new way to measure the walkability and livability of an urban centre: simply count the number of cabs driving around looking for fares.

8 Route 66 (Part One)
Kicks, Flicks and Tailfins

AS SOON AS MY FRIENDS heard about my road trip, they wanted to join me. I didn't invite them, they just said, "I'm coming." Naturally, when it came down to it, work or family or a lack of cash intervened for some of them, but not for all. And so, just eight days into my adventure, I picked up Chris Goldie at the St. Louis airport. A self-described "history buff," Chris wanted to drive Route 66 with me.

The highway, created in the 1920s, ran from Chicago to Los Angeles and quickly became not just the country's most famous road but also part of popular culture, inspiring hit songs, bestselling books and even, in the early 1960s, a popular television show called *Route 66*. The series featured two drifters driving a convertible Corvette around the country in search of "a place to put down roots," though they had more luck finding adventure with different characters, ranging from a Nazi hunter to a dishonest beauty contest promoter to a heroin junkie (played by Robert Duvall). Shot on location, though only a few shows actually took place on *Route 66*, the show captured the restlessness and hunger for meaning many young Americans were feeling at the time. Chris and I are well past our youthful restlessness, but we were searching for meaning, or at least a better understanding of the history of America's love affair with the road and its influence on popular culture.

Despite decades of mythmaking, Route 66's kicks couldn't last forever. As soon as the interstates offered more efficient ways to travel across the country, most drivers forgot about the old road. Fortunately, many individuals and organizations remain dedicated to promoting and preserving this part of American history, and 80 to 85 percent of Route 66 is still driveable. But it's a bit trickier than simply getting on the road and stepping on the gas pedal.

Having decided to start at the Chain of Rocks Bridge, which isn't far from Lambert International Airport, I keyed it into the GPS and off we went. Built in 1929 as a private toll bridge, it took Route 66 travellers across the Mississippi River between Illinois and Missouri. The trussed steel girders on concrete make it appear assembled from a giant Meccano set, but the really notable feature is the curious twenty-two-degree bend in the middle that was a compromise between the limits of the geology and the demands of river navigation. Closed to automobile traffic since 1968, it would have been demolished in 1975 except that a collapse of the price of scrap steel meant that it was cheaper to let the bridge stand. Today, the rusting mile-long structure is open to pedestrians and cyclists and, on special occasions, to car clubs.

After walking across the bridge to the Illinois side and then back again, we drove through St. Louis, remarking on the light traffic and laughing as we followed a dancing lowrider. Particularly popular in Latino communities, lowriders are cars and trucks with suspension systems modified so they ride low to the ground. Some owners—who often add flashy paint jobs and graphics, custom interiors and powerful audio systems—install hydraulics, allowing them to adjust the suspension at will and even raise and lower different corners of the vehicle as they drive. While cars from the 1940s, 1950s and 1960s are favourites, the lowriding scene, which involves a lot of cruising the main drag after dark, wasn't around during the heyday of Route 66. So seeing the big white Cadillac in front of us bouncing up and down, sometimes one wheel at a time, in a gleeful ballet was a reminder that car culture is alive and well—and mutating.

EVEN THOUGH CHRIS had brought along a couple of guidebooks for the old road, it soon dawned on us that this might be more of a challenge than we had imagined. We stopped at a gas station and bought a map—and then promptly hit a dead end. Right in front of us was a large concrete barrier overgrown with bushes. We turned around and drove back to the information centre at Route 66 State Park near Eureka. The volunteer staffer working the place, and presumably repeating the same spiel innumerable times a day, wore a name tag that said read "Jerry." He was already busy talking to another struggling road tripper, a man who spoke with a Southern drawl and wore cowboy boots and a weather-beaten trucker's cap. Outside, his wife—a gargoyle with a peroxide-blond beehive hairdo, ruby-red lipstick and so much makeup she must have used a trowel—hauled on a cancer stick as she sat in a Ford F-350 pickup with a crew cab and Alabama plates. Although she looked terminally bored, I assumed she was secretly delighted to have a husband who would actually ask for directions.

Our wives were back home, and the GPS couldn't help us, so we were two men with no choice but to seek guidance. We left the centre with another map and some directions. But it was already mid-afternoon and we weren't even thirty miles west of downtown St. Louis. At this rate, we would never get to Albuquerque. Undaunted, we took off with renewed purpose and followed the road through a series of sleepy towns with names such as Pacific and Bourbon and Cuba, but after accidentally finding ourselves on the interstate again, we decided to stay with the rest of the world and take the superhighway into Springfield. Although it was a minor defeat, the sun was dropping on the horizon, so we soon wouldn't be able to see much anyway. Besides, it was only the first day and we were confident we could redeem ourselves on the second. Arriving later than we had hoped, we checked in to a hotel surrounded by parking lots. Inside, we discovered a five-storey atrium featuring a ten-foot sculpture by Dale Chihuly, the renowned American glassmaker known for his vibrant colours and abstract designs—we were definitely no longer on Route 66.

Tonyea, the front-desk clerk, told us about the nightmarish road trip she took with her family when she was a teenager. The plan had been to drive to Alaska, across Canada and then home, but she bailed out on her parents halfway through and vowed never to go on any trip like that again. Her story reminded me why I'd never want to be a teenager again, but failed to dent my enthusiasm for our expedition.

Springfield considers itself "the birthplace of Route 66" because that's where Cyrus Avery, the road's biggest proponent, settled a dispute over what number would designate the road; although he and his supporters originally wanted 60, they finally agreed to 66. With a population of just over 150,000, the Queen City of the Ozarks is the third-largest city in Missouri, and while the density is a meagre two thousand or so people per square mile, the downtown, which was a short walk from our hotel, had lots of bars and restaurants and a lively feel to it. We enjoyed an excellent meal with a rather unnecessary, though much enjoyed, second bottle of wine and then found a fun place full of college students enjoying a good bar band. And I was thrilled to be in a town with the same name as the one Homer Simpson lives in. But a cool name and a few good blocks of downtown can't make up for all the sprawl and woeful urban planning—or lack thereof—that goes into creating too many cities just like Springfield.

ALTHOUGH IT REMAINS America's most celebrated national highway, Route 66 wasn't the first. One of the earliest efforts at creating a cross-country road was the Lincoln Highway. The brainchild of Carl Fisher, the man behind the Indianapolis Motor Speedway, it offered drivers a 3,400-mile route from New York City to San Francisco in a more or less direct east–west path through thirteen states. But a trip from one end to the other meant spending up to a month on bad roads. Despite Fisher's hope of covering it with concrete in time for San Francisco's 1915 Panama-Pacific

International Exposition, little progress had been made by 1917 when the United States joined the First World War. Indeed, even by 1920, as the car was becoming a machine for the masses, the vast majority of the close to three million miles of road in America was better suited for travel by horse and buggy than by automobile. The *Federal Highway Act* of 1921 offered matching construction funds to states and led to the creation of an interstate system, but it took Avery, a Tulsa businessman, to make a truly car-worthy national highway happen.

As the leader of several highway associations, Avery championed the idea of a route from Chicago to Los Angeles (one that, naturally, would go through Oklahoma). In 1926, when the plan became official, only a third of the 1,648-mile, eight-state route featured pavement. The remainder, according to *Route 66: The Mother Road*, by Michael Wallis, "was either graded dirt or gravel, bricks covered with asphalt, or, in a few stretches, nothing but wooden planks." But by 1937, Route 66 was completely paved from Chicago to Santa Monica, California, mostly with either Portland cement or compacted layers of broken stone called macadam.

The path took travellers through the middle of so many small towns that, as early as 1927, supporters called it the Main Street of America in maps and promotional material. And tireless promotion from boosters—whose successes included the Bunion Derby, a 1928 footrace from LA to New York—was one reason the highway resonated with the nation so quickly. Despite plenty of bad road and some dangerous sections, it was an immediate hit with travellers and truckers and many of the almost two million American migrants to Southern California between 1920 and 1940. Not even the Great Depression could kill the buzz. Many Midwestern farming families, having lost everything in the dust bowl, saw the road as the way to salvation and prosperity in California. Suddenly, Route 66 wasn't just a busy highway—it had symbolic meaning.

During the war, when gas rationing and tire shortages reduced travel for most people, the road was vital for moving troops across the country. After the war, the road flourished as Americans eagerly bought cars. The gas stations, restaurants and early motels, called motor courts, that survived the Depression and the Second World War, began to thrive. Curio shops and tourist attractions joined the increasingly crowded roadside, as Route 66 became popular with holiday travellers. Some drove it as part of a trip to California, especially after 1955, when Disneyland opened in Anaheim; some were on their way to the Grand Canyon; some even saw the road as its own destination.

But just as the Main Street of America was hitting the height of its popularity in the 1950s, states started to bypass the old road by building four-lane highways. And in 1984, the opening of Interstate 40 in Arizona replaced the last stretch.

ROUTE 66 OFTEN RUNS along beside the interstate. At points, the two roads are within spitting distance of each other. In the wooded hills of the Ozark Plateau, the modern highway is mostly straight and as flat as possible given the terrain, while the old one curves and undulates. The stark contrast between the two is a testament to advances in civil engineering over the decades, but it's also a potent reminder that the two roads were built for two different purposes. One takes drivers past everything and gets them to their destination with as few stops as possible; the other invited travellers to visit towns along the way and to stop at motels, diners and other businesses. One is anti-social; the other was decidedly social—and a lot more fun.

So we stopped. In Halltown, a village with 189 residents in the southwest corner of Missouri and long known for its antiques, we pulled up in front of Whitehall Mercantile. The lopsided clapboard building, which sits just steps from the road and dates from the turn of the last century, was once a lodge and general store. The white paint has now started peeling, the concrete steps are cracked and inside, past the rusty horseshoe nailed over the red door with the jingling bell, is a dimly lit, stale-smelling room filled with Route 66 memorabilia, political campaign buttons, old farm implements, kerosene lamps, chipped plates, worn furniture and a few books. I guess the owners knew what they were selling because they'd put up a sign that read, "This is not a museum. This junk is for sale."

Eventually, Thelma White, the proprietress, appeared from the back. A frail old woman in a white cardigan and blue slacks, she was struggling with Parkinson's. She moved slowly and with the help of a cane and had to hold the counter when she adjusted her glasses. But that did little to diminish her eagerness to chat, and she urged us to sign her guest book, which already bore the names and hometowns of people from all over Europe, Asia and across North America. Originally from Indiana, she'd moved to Joplin, Missouri, to go to college in 1949 and later settled in Halltown. She told us about how bustling the place had been back before the interstate; in fact, people had to run across the road because the traffic was so thick. It's not like that anymore, of course. Less than a mile away, tens of thousands of oblivious cars stream by on I-44 every day, but on a Wednesday afternoon in early October, we were the only tourists in town. And to make things worse, the area was in the midst of a drought so bad her husband had just decided to sell his cattle.

Before I left, I bought a fiftieth anniversary–edition copy of *The Grapes of Wrath* in good condition and with a dust jacket—in other words, a significant upgrade on the old jacketless copy I'd owned since university. White filled out the receipt by hand. Chris was peeved that I'd snagged it, but as I later pointed out, "It's not my fault you went right to the junk and I went to the books."

A classic of American literature, John Steinbeck's 1939 novel tells the story of the Joad family, dirt-poor sharecroppers who drive from Oklahoma to California to escape the Depression-era dust bowl. Many of the Okies who took Route 66 called it the

Glory Road, but Steinbeck called it the Mother Road. "66 is the path of people in flight, refugees from dust and shrinking land, from the thunder of tractors and shrinking ownership, from the desert's slow northward invasion, from the twisting winds that howl up out of Texas, from the floods that bring no richness to the land and steal what little richness is there," he wrote. "From all of these the people are in flight, and they come into 66 from the tributary side roads, from the wagon tracks and the rutted country roads. 66 is the mother road, the road of flight."

Though they are usually pursuits of happiness rather than matters of survival, road trips are common in American writing. The most celebrated example is *On the Road*, the Beat Generation bible by Jack Kerouac. I'd started to read the novel in my early twenties, but soon gave up, cheerfully (if a little arrogantly) explaining my decision to friends by quoting Truman Capote, who'd famously dissed Kerouac's work when he pronounced, "This isn't writing, it's typing." I started it again in Indianapolis and this time managed to fight my way to the end. Although the back of my paperback edition claims it is the book that "turned on a whole generation to the youthful subculture that was about to crack the gray façade of the fifties wide open and begin the greening of America," I regret to say I found the typing neither enjoyable nor an inspiration. Perhaps the book just didn't age well. But I admit that Kerouac does capture a time when young people really did have a freedom that no longer seems possible. Travelling around the country was cheap, jobs were plentiful and cars offered unprecedented independence.

Among more recent road books, many people cite *Blue Highways: A Journey into America*, by William Least Heat-Moon, as a favourite. Though I found that travel memoir well written, and even compelling in places, Bill Bryson's *The Lost Continent: Travels in Small-Town America* is much funnier. Best of all, though, is the laugh-out-loud-funny road trip to Sin City in Hunter S. Thompson's *Fear and Loathing in Las Vegas*.

After I returned home, I opened up my new copy of *The Grapes of Wrath* and saw an inscription made out to Thelma White in 1993. I wondered if business had grown so dismal that she had been reduced to selling her own possessions.

AFTER HEADING WEST from Halltown to Paris Springs, we completed an older stretch of Route 66 and then drove Missouri Highway 96, a newer, wider version of the old road, that led us through Heatonville and Albatross, Phelps and Rescue, Plew and Avilla. The biggest of the bunch was Avilla, with a population of 137. There were plenty of good signs in this area, so we started off making good time. The countryside is not dissimilar to what we were accustomed to back in Ontario, but when we almost drove over some armadillo roadkill we knew we weren't in Canada anymore. We were, in fact, almost in Kansas.

After Avilla, we saw a sign promoting the 66 Drive-In Theatre, but instead of announcing a double bill, it said, "Closed until April." I was still keen to stop and check it out except that coming out of Carthage, home of the Boots Motel and the Civil War State Park, the road gave us the slip and we missed it. Once we found our way again, I insisted we drive back to the theatre, which is just west of Carthage. Chris grumbled a bit, but later agreed it was well worth the backtracking and lost time because the place, which originally operated from 1949 to 1985, is a real gem, especially the ticket booth. The grounds were in immaculate shape, even though it was closed for the winter and despite having served as a junkyard for several years.

America's first drive-in theatre opened in Camden, New Jersey, in 1933, but it took the development of an in-car speaker by RCA in 1941 for the concept to really catch on. The craze began after the war and peaked in the 1950s. By 1958, there were more than four thousand drive-in theatres in the United States, and they were as controversial as they were popular. Parents and other prigs from the *Leave It to Beaver* era condemned them as passion pits.

And it was true that for many young people—who wanted to hang around with friends and take advantage of the privacy a car offered at night to smoke, drink and make out—the movie was the last thing on their minds.

Though moralistic outrage had little to do with it, drive-ins would never again be as popular as they were in 1958. By the late 1970s, after two decades of decline, the industry fell into deeper trouble because of cable television, VCRs and other entertainment choices; trouble getting first-run pictures from the studios; soaring land values; aging owners looking to retire; and perhaps even concerns about the growing amount of nudity and sexual activity in movies. More than 1,000 screens closed between 1978 and 1988. Since the late 1990s, though, there has been a modest revival, with a number of restorations and even some new theatres. Still, by the summer of 2006, there were only 651 screens at 398 theatres in the United States.

While people may not go to drive-ins as often as they once did, car movies remain popular. In *Cars*, an animated feature from Pixar and Disney, a cocky hotshot racecar named Lightning McQueen, on his way to a speedway in California, ends up in Radiator Springs on Route 66 instead. *New Yorker* reviewer Anthony Lane didn't think much of the movie and bristled at the message: "With the price of oil gurgling upward, and even the President conceding that the nation's fuel consumption could use a trim, Pixar has produced a hymn to the ecstasy of driving." The movie-going public didn't mind, and *Cars* topped the box office for the first two weeks of its run in June 2006—and the DVD gets a workout in many homes with small kids. (Friends of mine had to stop referring to the movie by name for fear their two-year-old son would hear them and demand to see it yet again.)

Movies have been influential in car culture at least since the 1950s, at once reflecting and stoking our love for the automobile. Road trip movies are a Hollywood staple and a few of them are actually watchable, including *Rain Man*, about a pair of brothers who drive across the country in an inherited Buick Roadmaster convertible because the only airline the autistic one will fly is Qantas; *Hard Core Logo*, about a punk band on a cross-Canada reunion tour; and *Sideways*, about a middle-aged man who takes his old college roommate, who's about to be married, to Napa Valley wine country with hilarious, and sometimes touching, consequences. I can only imagine how many road trips such movies inspired.

Despite Lane's umbrage at *Cars*, questionable messages are nothing new. *Rebel Without a Cause*, James Dean's 1955 sophomore effort, wasn't his best film—that would be *East of Eden*—but it did become his best known and the one that forever linked him to teenage angst. The film glamorized chicken runs because a central scene shows Jim Stark (Dean's character) taking on Buzz, a local bully, in a "chickie run." The pair race stolen cars toward a seaside cliff and the first to jump out is a chicken, but while Stark gets out safely, Buzz's black leather jacket catches on the door handle and he goes over the bluff with the car. Meanwhile, movies with car chases—and they are legion—encourage driving fast and furious. They may seem clichéd now, but that wasn't the case back in 1968 when Steve McQueen in a 1968 Ford Mustang GT-390 Fastback, two villains in a 1968 Dodge Charger R/T 440 Magnum and the streets of San Francisco set the standard in *Bullit*.

Rather than promoting dangerous driving, some car movies are content to wallow in nostalgia. *American Graffiti* takes place on a Saturday night in the late summer of 1962 in a small town based on Modesto, California, where director George Lucas grew up. Several teenagers—two of whom are college-bound—cruise the strip, listen to Wolfman Jack on the radio and look for action. One of the characters becomes obsessed with a beautiful blond woman in a white Thunderbird; another must drive a preteen girl around in his yellow deuce coupe; and a third borrows a friend's ride and meets a girl, but can't quite live up to all the possibilities promised by the car. When the movie came out in 1973, it filled theatres, earned five Academy Award nominations and sparked a revival of music from the late 1950s and early 1960s as well as a renewed interest in cruising.

TO ME, THE 66 DRIVE-IN was not just another roadside attraction on a route that had more of them than we could ever hope to visit. Drive-ins have always been more about the car than what was on the giant screen. After all, from the beginning they offered poor picture quality, worse sound and a dubious lineup of movies. Even now that the picture is better and the sound comes through short-range FM radio, going to the drive-in often means sitting in an automobile on a hot, mosquito-filled night and watching a movie through a windshield—not exactly the ideal conditions for the film aficionado. On the other hand, a car offers a level of privacy and freedom no indoor theatre can match.

I'd gone to a drive-in for the first time the previous June, which I guess is a weird thing for someone my age to admit. Shortly after 7 p.m. on a Saturday, the cars were already lined up when Paul Peterson, the owner of the Mustang Drive-In, swung his battered black Toyota T-100 pickup onto the ten-acre property just outside Picton, Ontario, a town of about 4,500 people a couple of hours east of Toronto. Summer solstice was only a few days away, so nothing would be showing on either of the theatre's screens for at least two hours, but no one seemed worried about that as they waited for the box office, which is actually an old bus, to open.

The cargo bed of his truck was jammed with tools, supplies and junk, and the cab was an even bigger mess. Peterson, who admits to being "a bit of a slob," looks the way Jerry Garcia might have if he'd been a member of ZZ Top instead of the Grateful Dead. A big guy with long grey hair and a grey beard, he wore blue shorts, a large blue shirt, a paint-splattered blue Tilley-type hat and white socks with his running shoes. Normally a gregarious showman, he was suffering mightily from the flu, so he wasn't out mixing it up with his customers—many of whom he knows by face, if not by name—or helping out in the canteen. We sat in the new projection room for the back screen on the just-added second floor of the white building that sits in the middle of the property. The drywall remained unpainted and film spools were scattered everywhere. A weak and weary Peterson sat on a stool as he rewound the films from the night before.

The Mustang opened in 1956, the same year Peterson was born. He and his wife Nancy bought it in 1988 when they were still social workers with the Children's Aid Society. "I had always gone to the drive-in, but this was not *Cinema Paradiso* or anything," he told me, making a reference to the 1990 Italian film about a boy who befriends a projectionist and falls in love with the movies. "We were going by this one and saw it was for sale and I thought, 'Man, that would be so cool.'"

The property was in bad shape and the theatre had a reputation as a place for young people to get drunk and, he learned later, there had been a small riot on the last night of the 1987 season. Worse, the Petersons knew nothing about running a drive-in. "We painted the screen and put some money into the place," he said, "but it still looked awful." Fortunately, he had a knack for promotion and an ability to entertain people. He also realized he had to convert the party palace into a place that would attract families. At first, instituting a "zero tolerance on alcohol" policy didn't seem so smart because the theatre made a lot of money from the partiers, especially during the all-night shows. But he'd worked with kids in crisis and what he saw disturbed him, especially because so many were actually arriving drunk. Revenues fell fifteen thousand dollars the first year, and attendance at the all-nighters plunged from as many as 700 people down to 150 on a good night. "It would have been easy to second-guess myself," he admitted, "but I knew it was the right thing to do—ethically, professionally and all that. It was hard for a seasonal business, but it worked because word got out: it's not a dump anymore."

Today, the all-nighters—when four movies run—regularly attract a thousand people. His adult children help run the drive-in and the two indoor theatres the family now owns in nearby towns. In 2002, he added the second screen, giving the place a capacity of four hundred cars and increasing his programming flexibility, but he refused to follow advice to play his best movie second to increase concession sales because he didn't think that was fair to his customers. "It should be fun," he said as the rewinding film slapped around the reel. "These movies aren't going to change your life. Go to the drive-in, get eaten by some mosquitoes, eat way more stuff than you should and then go home."

During intermissions, he leaves the front-screen projector on so children can make shadow puppets; on some nights, there are thirty or forty kids up there. He shows three movies on Saturdays in the summer, holds all-nighters on long weekends and hosts special events, such as the popular annual pyjama night. "We're branding with memories."

Apparently, some of those memories will be the same as they were back in the heyday of drive-ins. When a young couple drives up to the ticket booth and asks what a movie is about, Peterson is tempted to say, "What difference does it make?" Sure enough, the morning light invariably reveals condoms and bits of clothing on the ground, especially in the back row. He knows a drive-in is "a cheap room for the night," and just laughs about it. "To me, the one thing that is sacred is what you do in your car is your business. If it spills over and starts to offend people or get in the way of them enjoying what they're doing, then I'll step in, but until then ..."

Downstairs, there was a long line at the canteen. It's the kind of place that proudly displays a sign that says, "Fudge. Not just for breakfast anymore." Outside, cars, vans and pickups—mostly from GM, Ford and Chrysler—were covering the lawn in the rows that are still marked by bent and tilting speaker stands even though the theatre moved to radio sound several years ago. Some teenagers lounged in the back of a pickup while a family dangled their legs over the back of a van with the rear door up. Nearby, a man used Windex to clean the windshield of his Montana van. Some people listened to the sixth game of the Stanley Cup final on their car radios; others walked their dogs, while still others just hung out. Children played on the swings and slides at the playground; soon some of the younger kids would be in their pyjamas.

The mercury had hit thirty degrees Celsius that day and even though the air was cooling as the sun dropped in the sky, it was still warm and humid, so the inside of a car wasn't the most comfortable spot. Facing the main screen, where *The Breakup* and *The Fast and the Furious: Tokyo Drift* would soon play, four teenagers sat in camping chairs beside a rusty white Cutlass Supreme. Seasonal campers at a nearby campground, they visit the Mustang every second week in the summer. Fifteen-year-old Josh has been going to drive-ins all his life and, even though he can't drive yet, said it's more about the car than the movie. Nineteen-year-old Caitlin, who has been a regular for six years, agreed: "I'm more likely to see a movie at the drive-in because it's a better experience."

Meanwhile, in front of the second screen, which would soon show *Over the Hedge* and *The Da Vinci Code*, Rob and Shana watched their four kids play beside a Safari van. The family, from Trenton, about thirty miles away, goes to the Mustang at least four times a summer. They especially enjoy the all-night shows, though the two youngest stay home for those. Rob first went to a drive-in when he was three or four and has been going ever since. As a teenager, he and Shana spent a lot of time there. "We didn't watch the movies too much though," he said as they both laughed. Rob added that they would always go to drive-ins. "As long as we've got a car," he declared, "we're coming."

By 9:25, the sky had grown dark enough to start and Peterson got on the public address system. He greeted the crowd, announced some birthdays and talked about the movies, admitting that *The*

Breakup falls apart about two-thirds of the way through. Then, as usual, he asked his patrons to make some noise with their horns. Some also flashed their lights. According to regulars I was with, this wasn't exactly a vintage performance from the showman. But he did have an extra treat in store for them: he passed the mic to a young blond man named Scott, who proposed to his girlfriend Emily. "We've had a lot of special time together at the drive-in and it's a part of our life," he said in his preamble. There was another round of honking, and then Peterson wryly warned Scott: "Once you get married, you come to the drive-in to watch the movie." Scott left the projection room and Peterson finished up by saying, "Here's the movie. Thanks for coming, folks. Have fun. We'll see you at the intermission and, remember, there's no point taking money home with you."

I asked him, "Do you get a lot of proposals?"

"Well, I do, yeah," he deadpanned. "I mean, look at me."

We all found out at the intermission that Emily had said yes. Later, Peterson, who was having projection problems on the second screen, was hand-feeding *The Da Vinci Code* onto the film reel. "Hopefully they'll have a happy life together," he said, "and we'll have the next generation of drive-in kids."

CHRIS AND I TRAVELLED beside the interstate and mocked the drivers who had to contend with the huge trucks and heavy traffic. When I took a turn at the helm, I was tempted to see if I could go as fast as the people on the superhighway; Chris, on the other hand, was wiser because he relished the opportunity to slow down to the pace of a Sunday driver. Either way, we'd figured out that driving Route 66 is part road trip and part road rally, so while one of us took the wheel, the other juggled our growing collection of guides and maps to figure out our next move.

Sometimes our route just ended in the middle of nowhere. Sometimes we needed to be on the north frontage road, running along the interstate; sometimes we needed to be on the south road. Sometimes the way all but disappeared, or so it seemed, as we drove into towns. And since what was Route 66 is not called that anymore, the name of the road we wanted to be on changed frequently. Whenever we saw the distinctive brown-and-white "Route US 66" sign, we felt triumphant, but too often we couldn't see one when we needed it most. (Theft and vandalism, particularly graffiti tags, mean volunteers are always playing catch-up in the battle to improve the signage.) And because the route changed in places over the years, we occasionally had to contend with different alignments. Navigational errors, which were unavoidable, usually meant we had to double back or ended up on the interstate or actually had to ask for directions. We'd figured out that between our mistakes, the slowdowns in towns and our stops to take photos or visit a point of interest, a distance that would take an hour to cover on the interstate took us twice that. We called it Route 66 time and happily settled into it. The sun came out as we left the 66 Drive-In, so we opened the sunroof and cranked up the iPod.

From the earliest days of the automobile, musicians have sung about cars and what people do in them. After the publication of the first car song—"Love in an Automobile"—in 1899, almost two hundred others appeared in the next decade. The most popular one was "My Merry Oldsmobile," but others included "The Automobile Kiss," "In Our Little Love Mobile" and "Let's Have a Motor Car Marriage." The connection between cars and sex would become more explicit: in 1936, blues legend Robert Johnson released "Terraplane Blues," a double entendre–filled song in which an inexpensive sedan made by Hudson is a metaphor for a woman. When the "car "won't start, Johnson assumes she has been unfaithful and sings, "Who been drivin' my Terraplane for you since I been gone." Johnson may not have been the first to use this literary device—and he certainly wasn't the last because nowadays cars and sex often seem like pretty much the same thing in popular music.

It's not all sex, though. When folksingers such as Woody Guthrie and Pete Seeger started singing about Route 66 in the 1930s, their interest was primarily political. Guthrie, in particular, travelled the Mother Road frequently, but the most famous song about the road is Bobby Troup's "(Get Your Kicks on) Route 66." A 1946 hit for Nat King Cole, it helped build the legend of America's Main Street. The simple lyrics—which mention St. Louis, Joplin, Oklahoma City, Amarillo, Gallup, Flagstaff, Winona, Kingman, Barstow and San Bernardino—advise taking "the highway that's the best" to California. An unabashed romanticization of car travel, the song became a pop standard covered by many artists, ranging from Bing Crosby to the Rolling Stones to Asleep at the Wheel.

When rock 'n' roll first crackled onto the airwaves in the 1950s, car culture was also exploding, so perhaps the strong connection between the two was inevitable. Sex continued to be a major theme, but musicians weren't afraid to sing about automobile tragedies; two of the best known are Mark Dinning's "Teen Angel," which topped the charts in 1960, and "Dead Man's Curve," a huge hit for Jan and Dean in 1964. The Beach Boys had a more upbeat message, with infectious good-time pop tunes about wheels, girls and surfing that sold young people around the world on California's car-filled endless summers. At the same time, with the gathering storm of generational rebellion, a ride and the road also began to represent a new kind of freedom. In the 1970s, New Jersey's Bruce Springsteen began singing darker songs about cars, but even if the mood was more desperate, that didn't mean he wasn't glorifying the automobile just as much as the Beach Boys did.

While popular car songs may not be as common today, anti-car songs haven't taken their place on the average iPod. Protest music is a great tradition and musicians have been singing about the environment for decades—and in 1970's "Big Yellow Taxi," Joni Mitchell did sing about paving paradise for the sake of a parking lot—but I'm baffled that more songwriters don't think the downside of car culture is worth confronting.

IT'S NOT JUST the obvious arts of literature, film and music that find inspiration in the automobile. Peter White is a curator who put together a show called "It Pays to Play—British Columbia in Postcards, 1950s to 1980s" that opened in Vancouver in 1997 and then travelled to several other Canadian cities. White was interested in how the car and the road helped to define how we viewed and even understood the landscape, and decided that postcards were a good way to look at that topic because they were designed for people who were travelling and wanted souvenirs—either for themselves or to mail to those stuck back home. "Postcards are related to leisure and there was far more leisure time, new leisure time," he explained, adding that his parents drove to Los Angeles along Route 66 on their honeymoon in 1947. "People were far more mobile and they were using the car to take advantage of this leisure time."

One postcard in the exhibit featured a woman and a Nash next to the world's tallest totem pole in Victoria, B.C.; another showed two women sitting in chairs beside their car as they enjoyed the view of a lake. "Cars were placed in postcards as basic props," White explained, adding that motels also published postcards, usually with carefully chosen attractive cars parked in front. "The car was a central part of the experience." But he also admitted that the problem with nostalgia, especially because we romanticize cars so much, is that the past suggested by these images never really existed.

In a few days, Chris and I would visit a Route 66 attraction that offers another idealized take on the car. Just west of Amarillo, Texas, we pulled over to the side of the road and walked two hundred yards into the middle of a field where ten old Cadillacs were half-buried—nose down, fins up—in the ground. In 1973, local helium tycoon Stanley Marsh 3 invited Chip Lord, Doug

Michels and Hudson Marquez, part of an art collective called Ant Farm, to come up with a proposal for an installation. If he liked the idea, he'd let the group use some of his ranchland. The Caddies stayed there from 1974 to 1997, when they moved two miles west because Amarillo's sprawl was getting too close for comfort. They remain surrounded by what seems like infinite stretches of flat pastureland in every direction except back to Amarillo. In a neat twist, the cars are arranged at the same angle as Egypt's Great Pyramid of Giza. And they are, of course, heading west.

One of the best-known public art installations in the country—its fame aided and abetted by Springsteen's 1980 song "Cadillac Ranch"—it is, according to Lord, "a monument to the rise and fall of the tailfin." The distinctive styling feature first appeared on the Cadillac V8 in 1948. Harley Earl, the GM designer credited with the innovation, had been inspired by the look of Second World War planes, notably the Lockheed P-38 Lightning. From Caddies, tailfins spread to other GM cars and those made by its competitors and reached their height of excess—the fins on the 1959 Cadillac were forty-two inches off the ground—and popularity in the late 1950s. By the mid-1960s, they had all but disappeared from the American automobile. Lord and his colleagues found the ten Cadillacs they wanted, plus a spare, for an average price of two hundred dollars per car, in just two weeks. Each of them is a different model—the oldest is a 1949 Club Coupe; the newest is a 1963 Sedan—and today they are covered in graffiti, a practice encouraged by Marsh and the artists.

To Michels, it is the "hood ornament of Route 66," and Chris and I agreed it was one of the highlights of the old road. But we could see no antipathy—or even ambivalence—toward the automobile in the installation. If even the artists won't challenge it, our obsession with cars will never topple.

9 Route 66 (Part Two)
Oil, Booze and Automobiles

FROM CARTHAGE, Chris and I pressed on through Carterville, Webb City and into Joplin. We'd entered the Tri-State Mining District, a region that was once the world leader in lead and zinc production. The base metals helped several towns in the area prosper for many decades starting in the early 1870s. But unlike many neighbouring towns, greater Joplin has continued to grow instead of shrivelling up. Now, with I-44 just to the south and a diverse economy, almost 170,000 people call the metropolitan area home. But like many other towns that have grown a lot in recent years, it reminded us of every other suburb we'd ever been in. Such places may have survived the interstate, but they had certainly lost their Route 66 charm—a few buildings, motel signs and other leftovers notwithstanding.

By the time we reached the Missouri–Kansas state line, we'd noticed that the sky and the horizons had grown bigger. We stopped at a gas station with original pumps and asked a man dressed in blue jeans, a jean jacket, cowboy boots and a baseball cap how to get to Galena. He seemed to us the picture of the archetypal God-fearing, patriotic, rural Republican from Middle America—except that his pickup was a Toyota Tacoma. He pointed straight ahead, grinned and said, in a friendly way, "If you can't find it, there's something wrong with you."

Turned out there was nothing wrong with us, but the economy of Galena, Kansas, didn't look too healthy. After the discovery of lead in 1877, the town boomed, and by 1904, more than thirty mining companies operated here. Eventually, the town had 15,000 residents and plenty of places for miners to spend their money on alcohol and women. Route 66 made the economy even stronger for a while, but after a decrease in mining activity that began in the 1930s and the closing of all the mines in the 1970s, Galena now has a population of just over 3,200. We kept going, past Riverton, and stopped for lunch in Baxter Springs, which bills itself as "the first cowtown in Kansas" because it was the end of the Shawnee Trail, an early cattle-herding route. It's another place crushed by the closing of the area's mines. Then, because Route 66 just grazes the southwest corner of Kansas, doing a thirteen-mile right angle, we crossed into Oklahoma. After Quapaw, we drove through Commerce, another one-time mining town and the hometown of Yankee great Mickey Mantle. On we went into Miami (pronounced My-am-uh rather than My-am-ee), with its Spanish Revival–style Coleman Theatre. Originally a 1,600-seat vaudeville stage and movie house that opened in 1929, it has never gone out of business and the local community is in the process of restoring it.

South of Miami, we took a dirt road to the Sidewalk Highway, which actually predates Route 66. Faced with a choice between paving two lanes for half the route and paving one lane the whole length, the county chose the latter. Today, the little-used road remains a single eight-foot-wide strip, so that when we met a pickup coming the other way, I kept one wheel on the paved section and one on the gravel shoulder. When that ended, we continued on Route 66 to Narcissa and into Afton, where I stopped to aim my camera at the delightfully dilapidated sign in front of the ruins of the Rest Haven Motel. We kept on through towns, villages, hamlets and named crossroads until we reached Tulsa.

We were hitting our Route 66 stride, and Toronto seemed a long way away. So far on my trip, I'd seen lovely countryside but also sprawling suburbs and towns such as Joplin that might as well have been suburbs. What struck me the most, though, were all the small towns left to die by the interstate and the downtowns the car had killed.

HEADING INTO TULSA, we plugged the address of a downtown hotel into the GPS. Nestled among the forests and rolling hills between the Great Plains and the Ozark Mountains, and split by the Arkansas River, the city boasts 140 parks and was the self-proclaimed Oil Capital of the World in the early part of the last century. But when we got there, it looked desolate. Not dangerous, just dead. We saw plenty of beautiful art deco buildings and no human activity, even though it wasn't quite six o'clock on a Thursday evening. Wondering if a neutron bomb had gone off, we spent the next half hour driving around in search of a hotel that might be close to something resembling a lively neighbourhood. At one red light, ours was the only car at the intersection.

America first struck oil in western Pennsylvania in 1859, shortly after the invention of the kerosene lamp had created a huge demand for the fuel. Discoveries in Ohio, West Virginia, Louisiana, Texas, Oklahoma and California followed. Initially, gasoline was just a kerosene by-product with little value, though it was sold as a treatment for lice, and once Thomas Edison developed effective electric lighting in the 1880s, oil was no longer so valuable. Suddenly, the country—which produced the majority of the world's supply—had an abundance of a natural resource and no overwhelming way to deplete it.

Internal combustion engines, which several people were working to refine at the time, provided a possible solution to this dilemma. But it took the automobile makers—who put the engines in their horseless carriages and found them more effective than battery power—to ensure that we would one day be addicted to the environmentally ruinous, geopolitically fraught black gold.

At the end of the Second World War, the United States was the source of three-quarters of the world's crude—far more than its citizens could consume. By the early 1970s, the country had to import about a third of its oil, but few people worried about where their gas would come from or how much it would cost. That changed in 1973. First, Americans faced brownouts and rising prices; then, in October, the Arab members of the Organization of Petroleum Exporting Countries, along with non-members Egypt and Syria, announced an oil embargo to punish the Western countries that were supporting Israel in the Yom Kippur War. Some gas stations ran out of fuel while long lineups at others led to frayed tempers and even violence. The government reduced highway speed limits to fifty-five miles per hour and instituted a rationing system that allowed owners of cars with odd-numbered licences to buy gas on odd-numbered dates and those with even-numbered ones to buy on even-numbered dates.

The country went through a second oil shock in 1979 during the Iranian Revolution. With oil prices quadrupling in the early part of the decade and then doubling again at the end, the 1970s were marred by high inflation and low growth, or as we called it back then, "stagflation." But by the mid-1980s, the price of a barrel of crude had plummeted. And despite a mild six-month increase during the first Gulf War, the cost of gas fell even farther in the 1990s and didn't rise sharply until 2004.

The experience of the 1970s could have been an opportunity for Americans to adjust to smaller, more efficient automobiles. With the introduction of Corporate Average Fuel Economy regulations, better known as CAFE, the average American car started to go farther on a gallon of gas. But the rules had many loopholes, and much of the improvement took place at the expense of safety as manufacturers made vehicles lighter to reduce fuel consumption. This would have been a great time to get good at producing appealing small vehicles, but domestic automakers just couldn't pull it off. Indeed, when Car Talk, the popular National Public Radio show, held a Worst Car of the Millennium contest, four of the top five were small American models from the 1970s: the Chevrolet Vega, the Ford Pinto, the AMC Gremlin and the Chevy Chevette. Only Yugoslavia's laughable Yugo was worse. While most foreign automakers, notably the Japanese, had success with their small offerings, the Detroit automakers couldn't wait for the return of cheap oil. When it did, they concentrated on increasing the horsepower of their engines instead of worrying about fuel efficiency. That was fine with many Americans who would eventually make the SUV the It ride—and under CAFE, SUVs were light trucks that had to meet less rigorous fuel efficiency and emissions standards than passenger cars. Not that today's fuel regulations are that severe anyway: just 27.5 miles per gallon. (They've been stuck there since 1984, though I suppose that's better than the 15 miles per gallon we were at in 1975.) For light trucks, an average of just 22.2 miles per gallon is good enough. New standards will require a fleet-wide average of 35 miles per gallon by 2020, but while the improvement is welcome, it does seem too little, too late.

Along with heaps of burning disco records, gas station lineups are just another weird image of 1970s nostalgia, but we'd be foolish to think we could never see them again. America now has only 3 percent of the world's known petroleum reserves and, in 2006, the country produced more than 8.3 million barrels a day—and consumed 20.6 million. Though oil now has many uses, from home heating oil to plastics manufacturing, cars are the thirstiest customers: "The typical North American driver consumes his or her body weight in crude oil each week, and the automobile engines sold this year alone will have more total horsepower than all the world's electrical power plants combined," according to Richard Heinberg, author of the 2003 book *The Party's Over: Oil, War and the Fate of Industrial Societies*. "Globally, cars outweigh humans 4 to 1 and consume about the same ratio more energy each day in the form of fuel than people do food."

By the time he had to give his February 2006 State of the Union address, even President George W. Bush, the former oilman, was admitting, "America is addicted to oil." But when it came to policies, not much changed. The Bush administration wouldn't even make a serious effort to encourage conservation, let alone try more drastic measures such as higher gasoline taxes. Instead, it eyed reserves in Alaska's Arctic National Wildlife Refuge with bad intent, even though the amount of oil there would put only a small dent in the amount the country has to import, while drilling would be done at an unconscionable cost to a fragile ecosystem.

The government also maintained its steadfast defence of the Iraq War. Though the weapons of mass destruction weren't there and the putative ties between Saddam Hussein and Osama bin Laden were a complete canard, the anti-war chant "No Blood for Oil" is too simplistic. The United States gets far more of its oil from Canada and Mexico than from the Middle East. But while America's neighbours, especially the northern one, seem politically stable, many oil-producing nations in the world aren't so lucky: civil war looms in Nigeria, nationalization threatens in Bolivia, nutty demagogue Hugo Chavez rules in Venezuela and oil is a political football in Russia. All of which suggests the United States may become more reliant on Mideast oil rather than less. So it seems likely that petroleum was part of the rationale for the invasion of Iraq—or at least a nifty ancillary benefit. But little has worked out well over there, and oil production in the country has remained lower than it was before the war. Nine months after Bush's "addicted" speech, New York Times columnist Thomas Friedman wrote: "And what could possibly be more injurious and insulting to our men and women in Iraq than to send them off to war and then go out and finance the very people they're fighting against with our gluttonous consumption of oil?"

High gas taxes long ago forced Europeans and others into smaller, more efficient cars and made them think about how much they drive. Even in Germany, a country with a robust auto industry and an abiding love for fast, well-engineered cars, the government raised gas taxes by three cents a year for five years in an effort to reduce greenhouse gas emissions. Any such policy would be a tough sell in the United States, with its powerful oil and automobile lobbies, tax-averse population and succession of politicians who, since Jimmy Carter was run out of Washington, haven't had the guts to ask the American people to make any sacrifices. (In the aftermath of the September 11 terrorist attacks, when the country might have been willing to make sacrifices, asking people to go shopping was the best the Bush administration could do.) Even without increased taxes, though, the price of gas is likely to stay high. Additional geopolitical tensions aside, the demand created by the roaring economies of China and India could make oil even more expensive. And if climate change means we'll endure more hurricanes like Katrina—or even if we're just entering a period of more and more severe tropical storms—we may find ourselves at the mercy of hard-to-predict and painful shortages and price spikes.

Perhaps spooked by what high gas prices might do to the sales of some of its least-efficient vehicles, in 2006, as gas headed to $3 a gallon (and, in some places, higher), GM launched a promotion to woo Californians and Floridians to buy certain models, including Hummers and other SUVs, by pegging the cost of a gallon of gas at $1.99. Under the scheme, the company refunded the difference between the average price at the pump in the state and the $1.99 cap for one year. Maybe GM got the idea to adopt a standard drug pushers' ploy after hearing the president say the country was addicted.

THE DISCOVERY OF OIL in Red Fork, now part of West Tulsa, in 1901 led to an economic boom in what was then Indian territory, especially after the massive Glenn Pool oil field strike of 1905. By 1914, Oklahoma produced more than a third of American oil, and by 1920, the city had a population of seventy-two thousand and was home to hundreds of oil companies. The output started declining in the 1930s, and by the early 1980s, Tulsa's status as an oil capital was just a memory—and today Oklahoma pumps just 3 percent of the nation's crude.

The brief prosperity did leave Tulsa with a solid cultural legacy, including the Philbrook Museum of Art, and the fruits of an ambitious building boom from the first third of the 1900s. And since art deco was the style of the time, that's what Tulsans built. The stunning Boston Avenue Methodist Church, completed in 1929, is perhaps the city's most dramatic example of the style, but there are impressive buildings throughout the central core. Those charms are apparently lost on the more than 900,000 residents of the metropolitan area, most of whom seem determined to live anywhere but downtown, and that means the greater Tulsa area inevitably suffers from sprawl. Even the city itself, with a population of almost 400,000, has a density of just 2,150 people per square mile.

Eventually, we gave up looking for a hotel in a cool part of town and checked in at our original destination. At the front desk, a cheerful young woman with a pixie cut and freckles sympathized with our plight. She couldn't recommend anything within walking distance and suggested we take a cab up to Brady Village. She also offered to call us one because we'd be wasting our time trying to flag anything. (Along with taking us to our destination, our Lebanese taxi driver explained that the people who worked downtown started emptying out of their offices at four o'clock and the afternoon rush hour was over by six o'clock. We'd just missed it.)

As a bar district, Brady Village was hurting. Once again, that shouldn't have been the case. Located near a cross-town expressway and not far from college campuses, it's a section of town dominated by old warehouses—just the kind of area being transformed into entertainment districts in cities all across the continent, including just down Route 66 in Oklahoma City. Plus, the area is home to two popular entertainment venues, the Brady Theatre and Cain's Ballroom. Though it has since hosted a variety of acts, including Bob Dylan, Elvis Costello and Wilco, Cain's is a seminal site in the history of Western swing music because during the Depression, Bob Wills and His Texas Playboys—best known for their signature song, "Take Me Back to Tulsa"—recorded their popular radio show there. Later, in 1978, Cain's was one of the few places the Sex Pistols played during their disastrous and short-lived U.S. tour.

Apparently, location and history aren't always enough. When we got to Brady Village, the cabbie stopped on a deserted, dimly lit street and admitted he didn't know much about the area and so could offer us no suggestions. When we got out of the cab, we saw only a few bars and restaurants and, even though it was a Thursday night, they weren't busy. Nor did we see people on the streets. The most appealing option of an uninspiring lot was a place called Lola's at the Bowery, which had two rooms—one with a sloppy jazz trio and one with a long, polished wooden bar. We sat at the bar and ordered dinner and drinks.

The bartender was a small, thin, fey man with bleached blond hair who had lived in several U.S. cities before returning to Tulsa. When he told us he lived in a downtown condo, we were surprised to hear the place had downtown condos. He admitted he'd lost his original optimism for Brady Village—slow nights will do that to people who rely on tips—and wasn't even sure Tulsa would make it: "I'm so frustrated." He sounded as though he was about to cry.

Later in the evening, before he called us a cab, he told us about a conversation he'd had with a woman on the next treadmill at his fitness club. Recognizing him, she asked where he was working now; when he told her, she said, "Oh, I love the martinis there." What she didn't like was the location; the problem was that if she and her friends went downtown, they needed a designated driver. The implication was that if they went to a bar near where they lived, they could drink and sneak home on back streets and not have to worry about cops.

As I thought about this story, it dawned on me that sprawl encourages impaired driving. People heading out for a night on the town, or even a dinner that includes a bottle of wine, don't want to take a cab because they can't flag one at the end of the night—and they have to travel so far they couldn't afford the fare anyway. So they drink and drive.

10 Route 66 (Part Three)
The Long and Lucrative Road

BURMA-SHAVE SIGNS—displaying jingles promoting a brand of brushless shaving cream—first appeared along a Minnesota road in 1925, but they may be best remembered as part of Route 66 lore. Spaced about one hundred feet apart in sets of five or six, the small wooden signs were easily readable by people in cars going thirty-five or forty miles an hour. The rhymes were corny—"This cream makes the/Gardener's daughter/Plant her tu-lips/Where she oughter/Burma-Shave," or "A Man A Miss/A Car A Curve/He kissed the Miss/And missed/The Curve/Burma-Shave"—but wildly popular, boosting the shaving cream to number two in the market. By the time Phillip Morris bought Burma-Shave in 1963 and started taking down the signs, more than five hundred jingles, many written by the public, had appeared on roadsides across the country. Perhaps they were too hokey for the marketing department at a big corporation, but it's also true that interstate speeds made the little signs all but unreadable. Now, huge billboards put up by businesses—hotels, restaurants and attractions, for example—and evangelical Christians fight for the attention of highway drivers.

Ever since Cyrus Avery used his influence to bring Route 66 by the front doors of his tourist court, café and service station, the Main Street of America has been about making money. That's just one more reminder of how central the car is to the world economy. For decades, General Motors was the largest corporation on the planet, while Ford, Chrysler and several oil companies weren't far behind. Steel, rubber, glass and plastics industries also benefited from automobile manufacturing, while many other businesses grew rich catering to drivers.

Even though a lot of the old motels, diners and other enterprises have closed, nostalgia tourism may be the last great hope for the Mother Road. Brad Nickson, a small, dark-haired man who wore running shoes and jeans without a belt, is the Tulsa County representative for the Oklahoma Route 66 Association, a group of more than three hundred people dedicated to promoting the past and present of the old road. Born on the thirty-eighth anniversary of the birth of Route 66, he moved to Tulsa from Texas in 1997 to work for a software firm. Chris and I met him for lunch at the Metro Diner on Eleventh Avenue. Now mostly a busy but otherwise unremarkable strip of light industry, fast-food joints and used car lots, Eleventh is dotted with the occasional gem from the past, including the Desert Hills, a renovated 1953 motel with rooms lined up diagonally to save space on the lot and a gorgeous neon sign featuring a giant green cactus. But most of the past is gone: Nickson's organization had planned to help a Tastee-Freez outlet repaint its sign and building, but the franchise closed. "Sometimes," he admitted, "we don't get there in time."

The state has just over four hundred miles of the old road, the most in the country, but the Oklahoma Department of Transportation, which needed some convincing just to allow the city to erect a sign at the exit to Eleventh Street, remains reluctant to put up Route 66 signs. "I've heard their reasoning is they don't think it is a safe highway," said Nickson. But the bureaucrats finally designated the old road a scenic byway, and if the association can obtain similar status from the feds, money from Washington is a possibility.

Small towns struggle to attract travellers to their Route 66 legacy, but so do bigger centres. "Tulsa's had a long-term problem," explained Nickson, "because once you hit Catoosa, it's real easy just to take the interstate all the way through Tulsa and suddenly you're on your way to Oklahoma City and you have no clue of what all you're missing here." But in 2004, the city hosted the International Route 66 Festival, which pumped nine million dollars into the local economy—and spurred the Desert Hills to refurbish its sign.

Tulsa County also launched a fifteen-million-dollar project to revitalize its twenty-four miles of Route 66. The money, raised through a voter-approved one-cent increase in the sale tax, will improve streetscapes; add decorative gateways; erect a sculpture of Avery and a Model A Ford meeting a horse and wagon from the oil fields at the Cyrus Avery Route 66 Memorial Bridge; and build the Route 66 Experience, which, though Nickson avoids the word "museum," will be an interactive museum. In addition, the city saved a sixty-foot sign for the old Meadow Gold dairy in 2004, when the building was being demolished to make room for a car dealership. The restored sign will go up somewhere else. The long list of ideas to revive Route 66 would have cost eighty million dollars, he explained, "So there were some tough choices to make."

After lunch, Nickson invited us on a tour, put on oversized aviator sunglasses and led us to his black PT Cruiser Limited Edition. When I asked if he was much of a car guy, he demurred. But I noticed that he kept his six-year-old PT Cruiser in immaculate condition—most days he drives his Chevy pickup—and had added an eight ball to the top of the gear selector and hung black fuzzy dice from the mirror. "It's one of the most fun cars I've ever owned," he said, and it later came out that he was a founding member of the Tulsa Area PT Cruisers, a local car club. He'd also sold a beloved two-door 1953 Ford Ranch Wagon so he and his wife could buy their first house in Tulsa, and his father had been a hot rodder. More than that, though, Nickson's demeanour changed noticeably once we were in the car. In the diner, he'd seemed reserved, nervous and a little nerdy, but behind the wheel he loosened up, laughed at our jokes and revealed his own dry sense of humour, teasing me about my old car and suggesting I take advantage of one of the many used car lots in town.

Used car salesmen may suffer from a reputation as cartoonishly shady characters with slick patter, but more than twice as many people buy pre-owned vehicles as new ones. It may not be as lucrative as manufacturing automobiles, but there's still a lot of money to be made selling cars. Or renting them. Nickson showed us the building where Thrifty Car Rental started in 1958. With a thousand locations in sixty-four countries, the company is now one of the largest in an industry that started in 1918 when Walter L. Jacobs, at the age of twenty-two, started renting a dozen Model T Fords in Chicago. Within five years, his revenues had reached one million dollars. In 1923, Jacobs sold the business to John Hertz, who changed the name to Hertz Drive-Ur-Self System and then sold it to GM in 1926. It later had a great rivalry with Avis, which started when Warren Avis opened up shop at Detroit's Willow Run Airport in 1946. In response to being the second-largest rental agency, Avis launched its celebrated "We Try Harder" advertising campaign in 1963—and tripled its market share. The original businesses on Route 66 were mom-and-pop operations, and though most of them are now gone, Nickson is convinced there's a growing fascination with the old highway. He suggested that different people are drawn to different elements of it, including the architecture, the history, the economics or even the music. (As he drove us around, he played a recording of the *Bob Dylan Theme Time Radio Hour* show. It was the episode about places, which I thought was a bit calculated, though I appreciated the effort.) Taking a trip on the old road is also a great excuse for people to slow down a bit or simply enjoy a great drive. His main interest is the history, but Nickson, whose grandfather ran a Holiday Inn in Gallup, New Mexico, is increasingly fascinated by the economics. "Route 66 has always been a commercial road," he said. "It's still a commercial road and it will probably always be a commercial road."

EVEN CHARITIES TRY to make money off Route 66 nostalgia. Shortly after noon on Saturday, we hit the first annual Depew Route 66 Auto Show, a fundraiser for the Depew Education Foundation. Sixteen gleaming classic cars, including a black 1954 Buick, a blue-and-white 1957 Bel Air and a red 1959 Chevrolet Impala, sunned themselves in the parking lot of the local high school's gymnasium. Buddy Holly's "That'll Be the Day" blared from the loudspeakers as we introduced ourselves to Bill Inman, one of the show's organizers and the president of the foundation. A tall man with broad shoulders, and dressed in a denim shirt, polished cowboy boots and a white Stetson, he urged us to buy some raffle tickets, boasting that one of the prizes was a .30-06 rifle.

About halfway between Tulsa and Oklahoma, Depew is one of those towns the interstate forgot. The discovery of oil nearby in 1911 spurred growth until the 1940s, but today, the oil and the Route 66 traffic are gone and Depew has a population of a little over 560. That can make life a tad uninteresting for the teenagers who live there, according to the members of the high-school debating team who were selling hot dogs and barbecued bologna sandwiches to raise money so they could travel to Indianapolis for national championships sponsored by the FFA, the youth organization formerly known as the Future Farmers of America.

"Nothing ever happens here!" insisted a tall, giddy debater.

"We had three funerals this week," one of her friends corrected her. "Two on Wednesday and the other yesterday. It was a car accident, and they say he was under the influence."

"And there was a murderer a few years back," pointed out another. "Yup, he shot his girlfriend and her mother right here in town, then he holed up in the church tower, and they walked right by him for three days!"

"And there's a nudist camp about five miles outside town!" squealed another young woman, but as the others sniggered, she quickly added, "But nobody here goes there."

"Other than that, it's dull, dull, dull," she continued. "Nobody comes here except to take pictures of Spangler's." The kids laughed at the thought of anyone wanting to photograph the old general store on what was once Route 66.

Along with wanting to grab a hot dog and hear the town gossip, I was curious about the students' relationship to the car. The debating team had already won the state championship by arguing that ethanol was good for the environment, created jobs and helped the war on terror by reducing oil imports. One of the debaters was Evan Newpher, a seventeen-year-old junior. A small, wiry kid with a few freckles, he was also a running back and linebacker on the school football team. He wore blue shades, flip-flops and a grey FFA T-shirt that read "Characters Under Construction." Eighty percent of his classmates drive to school, he estimated, and 90 percent of those arrive in pickups. Newpher gets around in a 1993 Chevy pickup, a hand-me-down from his sister. But he really wants a Honda Element. "It's a little bit fuel-efficient," he explained, "and it's a different-looking car, so it's something that fits my personality."

Young drivers aren't the only ones who've severed their bonds with Detroit. Several members of the Guthrie Flashbacks car club were lounging under a canopy in the middle of the show. One of them, Dennis Doughty, was there with his 1960 Chevy Impala. A retired attorney who lives in Edmund, Oklahoma, he also owns a 1959 Impala, two Ford trucks and a Mazda Millennia that his wife drives. He bought his first import, a Honda, after he was disappointed with a 1977 Chrysler Cordoba. "I couldn't keep it out of the shop," he said. "It wouldn't run half the time." Now, his loyalty is to older Chevys. "It seems like General Motors has forgotten about styling and what the customers want. We'd like to have something that looks nice and drives nice and is dependable and economical," he said. "The Japanese are providing the kind of cars that people want."

As for loyalty to Detroit, he drawled: "GM doesn't give me a paycheque."

"But isn't what's good for GM good for America?" I asked.

"That's what GM says, I guess."

Actually, no one at General Motors ever said what's good for GM is good for America—at least not publicly. What GM president Charles E. Wilson, who later became secretary of the Department of Defense, did say was: "What's good for the country is good for General Motors, and vice versa." Today, most people toss around the bastardized version, perhaps because they assume that's what he really meant. Regardless, the Big Three, with their shrinking market share, do not power the economy the way they once did.

Whatever happens to the American automakers, it's hard to imagine cars not being a central part of the lives of the people who live in this part of the country. One of the locals at the show was Blackie Farris, who was showing off a black 1954 Buick. Wearing a plaid shirt, black jeans that were torn at the knee and a brown cap covering his bald pate, the seventy-seven-year-old rose out of his chair with the help of a cane and told us he did all the restoration work himself. Chris asked him how many cars he owns. "Eight to ten altogether," he said, "plus those that don't work."

After the prize ceremony—there were sixteen piston trophies, which worked out well for everyone—the owners got in their cars and started their engines, creating a loud and thrilling rumble.

Chris, who collects old people the way crazy ladies collect cats, was saying goodbye to Farris and remarked, "That sounds even better than it looks."

"It's supposed to."

And then we watched all the old cars drive away.

Later, Chris told me I had to stop saying I was researching our relationship with the car because people were not so much confused as nonplussed. "It's like saying you're writing about our relationship to air."

WE FINALLY FIGURED OUT that we'd been doing it all wrong—at least when it came to hotels. We were spending our days desperately trying to stay on Route 66, and then as soon as it was time to find a place to sleep, we'd gone looking for a big, new high-rise hotel off the Mother Road in the hope we'd be near some action. That had worked out fine in Springfield, but in Tulsa we'd ended up in the middle of a ghost downtown and we both deeply regretted not staying in the Desert Hills motel. Then, in Oklahoma City, we'd ended up next to Bricktown, a tourist-infested bar district.

Fortunately, we're just slow, not completely stupid, and it took us only four nights to realize we should have been staying in old Route 66 motels. So on Sunday our destination was the Trade Winds Inn in Clinton, Oklahoma, if for no other reason than that Elvis Presley stayed there when he drove between Graceland and Los Angeles. After doing some big-city stuff—visiting an art gallery and a good independent bookstore, where Chris bought a copy of *The New York Times* and I bought yet another Route 66 guidebook—we headed west again. The torrential rain took some of the pleasure out of the sightseeing, but we made our way through Yukon and El Reno, over the Canadian River on the Pony Bridge and on to Weatherford and into Clinton. As we checked in at the Trade Winds, I asked the clerk about the restaurant next door. "It's good," he said. "It's not fast food, but it is good food." He was half right.

As Eric Schlosser makes clear in *Fast Food Nation: The Dark Side of the All-American Meal*, the automobile helped to create the fast-food business. Decades later, we know that aside from its generic banality, the fare must share at least some of the blame for our obesity epidemic with the car culture it's part of. But the two industries continue to feed each other: in 2006, GM and McDonald's cooked up a deal that saw the fast-food giant distribute forty-two million toy Hummers in Happy Meals and Mighty Kids Meals. Back in Baxter Springs, Kansas, we had wanted to have lunch in a Route 66–era diner, but couldn't find one. The sad fact is that chains have killed off most of them. So we stopped at a Sonic Drive-In, which had a menu board with speaker system at each of the car bays. We ordered and a young woman brought our food before we could even figure out whether or not we were supposed to go inside to get it. In fact, there was no seating or service inside. (Many drive-ins and drive-thrus refuse to even serve pedestrians and cyclists.) Sonic bills itself as "America's Drive-In," and despite the modern—dare I say, ersatz—look, the chain of 3,200 restaurants in the United States and Mexico has its roots in the Top Hat drive-in that opened in Shawnee, Oklahoma, in 1953. The company adopted the Sonic name in 1958.

A&W, which started in 1919, was one of the first restaurants to offer curb service. Drive-in restaurants, which began appearing in the early 1920s, featured carhops—often young women on roller skates—delivering hamburgers and similar fare on trays that hung from a car's window. By the 1950s, these places had become ideal hangouts for teenagers. "The drive-ins fit perfectly with the youth culture of Los Angeles," according to Schlosser. "They were something genuinely new and different, they offered a combination of girls and cars and late-night food, and before long they beckoned from intersections all over town." But as the demographic bulge aged and became pressed for time, more and more people wanted to be able to eat while on the move. And so the drive-thru, which had first appeared in the late 1940s, became increasingly common.

Cars waiting in long lines at drive-thru windows increase emissions, but that isn't the only worry. When a McDonald's franchise wanted to replace its existing restaurant on a busy Toronto street with a new one that would include a drive-thru in 2001, area residents—using the slogan "A live-in community ... not a drive-thru"—fought the plan because they didn't want more traffic, more danger to pedestrians, more noise, more garbage, more smell or more pollution. Joe Mihevc, a city councillor who helped pass a by-law forbidding drive-thrus within thirty metres of a residential neighbourhood, found one more reason for stopping these sops to drivers: "If you have to eat the stuff, at least get out of your car and move your gut around a little bit."

It's not just food anymore. Drive-thru banks and drive-thru pharmacies are commonplace, and we now have drive-in churches—the first one opened in 1955—and drive-thru libraries and even drive-thru wedding chapels in Las Vegas. Some people are so in love with their cars that they don't want to get out of them for anything.

AFTER DINNER IN CLINTON, we found the second-floor room with the plaque on the door saying the King used to sleep there. It was the high point of our stay because the Trade Winds turned out to be less than we expected. A two-storey motel, it had become part of an international chain, but it was still a dump. Our room—which looked out on a depressing inner courtyard with a filthy, all but waterless swimming pool—had heavily stained brown carpeting, dirty orange bed covers and grey sheets. We sipped beer and read *The New York Times*, laughing at the thought of reading the great big-city paper in a seedy small-town motel. Then we went to sleep with most of our clothes on.

During my road trip, I stayed with Best Western, Courtyard by Marriott, Days Inn, Doubletree, Drury Inn, Embassy Suites, Hilton, Holiday Inn, Holiday Inn Select, Kimpton, La Quinta, Loew's, Ramada Limited, Wyndham and many independents. Travelling in the fall, I avoided peak-season rates and paid as little as fifty dollars a night and as much as two hundred dollars, but the connection between the rate and the quality of the hotel was often fuzzy. Not at the Trade Winds, though—it was the cheapest and the worst.

Arthur Heinman opened the first motel in 1925. The Milestone Mo-Tel, later known as the Motel Inn of San Luis Obispo, proved to be a much-copied concept. But Kemmons Wilson improved on it twenty-seven years later when he opened the first Holiday Inn. Wilson, a real estate agent and developer, had taken his family to Washington, D.C., but was less than impressed with the accommodation along the way. In the corporate lore, this was "the road trip that changed the world." He found the motels he stayed in cramped and uncomfortable, most lacking air conditioning; the restaurants were inadequate or non-existent and, most galling of all, they all charged an extra two dollars per child. So Wilson built his own on the outskirts of his hometown of Memphis. Each of the 120 rooms had a private bath, air conditioning and a telephone, the hotel offered a swimming pool, free ice and dog kennels and, of course, children stayed for free—and it launched what would become the largest hotel group in the world and one of the best-known names in American corporate history.

The best thing I can say about the Trade Winds is that at least it was directly across the road from the Route 66 Museum. An excellent example of how to create a small, focused museum, it presented the social and cultural history of the Mother Road—from the Okies fleeing the dust bowl to the hippies hitchhiking or truckin' down the highway in VW microbuses—in a way that was as entertaining as it was informative. As teachers led classes through, we noticed the students didn't seem bored. Our visit there put us in a good mood as we opened the sunroof and left for Texas and the Big Texan Steak Ranch in Amarillo. The landmark first opened on Route 66 in 1960 but moved to its current location just off Interstate 40 in 1970. Outside the massive restaurant, a huge sign with a long-legged cowboy makes sure no one misses the bright yellow building while a huge steer advertises a free seventy-two-ounce steak. It's true: there is no charge for anyone who can eat a dinner consisting of four and a half pounds of top sirloin steak, a baked potato, salad, dinner roll and shrimp cocktail in under an hour. Over the years, forty-two thousand people have attempted the feat, but all but eight thousand of them had bigger eyes than stomachs. (Those who fail to eat the whole thing must pay $72, up from $9.95 in the 1960s.) Since it was lunch—and because we're wimps—Chris and I ordered nine-ounce steaks, which was more than enough. We were amazed at how easily we'd been sucked into a routine of overeating, even though we did nothing all day but sit in a car.

IF THE TRADE WINDS had been a disappointment, Tucumcari's Blue Swallow Motel made up for it. Set amid the mesas and plains of New Mexico, the town once erected billboards on Route 66 that proclaimed, "Tucumcari Tonight! 2000 Rooms." Now primarily a ranching and farming community, it was originally a railroad centre—with a roundhouse, a depot and a water tower—and later, as the largest town between Amarillo and Albuquerque, a popular stopover for Route 66 travellers. After the interstate went in, the number of rooms shrank to about 1,200 and the population of Tucumcari has fallen below 6,000. But that didn't stop Bill Kinder from resurrecting the Blue Swallow.

Built in 1939, the old motor court, which features a small garage for each of the thirteen rooms, eventually became a wedding present for Lillian Redman in 1958. She ran it for forty years. At the end of 2005, when Kinder and common-law wife Terri Johnson bought it, the hotel was tired and had been closed for a year. "It needed some help," admitted Kinder with what I imagined was quite a bit of understatement. But the oft-photographed neon sign was in good working order, and Kinder and Johnson had already restored eleven of the rooms. Our room featured twin beds covered in colourful quilts, a 1940s-style rotary telephone and a new television sitting on top of an antique one. All the other rooms have different themes and colour schemes. "It's really hard to find the fine line between fixing it up nice and going too commercial and losing your Route 66 flair," he said, adding that too many other places do a great job on the outside, but inside, every room looks the same. "I don't think it should be done that way—it wasn't done that way back then."

Now sixty, Kinder looks younger; he has reddish hair and a beard and blue-grey sweatpants and a grey T-shirt. A Vietnam vet, he spent many years working in construction in Las Vegas before taking early retirement in Florida. But after seven or eight years, even golfing—he trimmed his handicap to an impressive six—and fishing every day began to lose its charm. Johnson had worked in the hotel business and they'd driven Route 66 on Harleys several times ("It's the only way to do it. The wind in your face, the solitude, not a lot of traffic. You can take it nice and slow and enjoy everything"). And as far as Kinder is concerned, the Blue Swallow was the most famous Route 66 hotel. While the challenge of restoring and running the old place appealed to him, he pointed out, "Working is a lot more fun when you don't have to do it." He also liked the thought of opening eight months of the year and closing for four. In fact, he just bought a camper with solar panels on the roof and "Born Free" written on the side. In four days, he and Johnson would begin a three-month trek to visit friends and family.

The motel office is part souvenir shop, part museum jam-packed with Route 66 memorabilia as well as a coins from foreign guests, a copy of *Moby Dick* (his favourite book) and a picture of a British car club whose members had had their cars shipped over for their road trip. Kinder pulled an old Route 66 atlas out from under the counter; he'd found it on eBay for forty-seven dollars and described it as his pride and joy. While Johnson calls him a pack rat, he considers himself a nostalgia buff. "I just like the good old days better than the new days."

He showed Chris and me one of the two as-yet-unrenovated rooms. He was using it to store junk, but from what we could see, it looked as though he had a lot of work to do to bring it up to the standard of our room. Then, he opened one of the garages to show us his blue-and-white 1958 Chevy. As he lifted the hood, he said, "This is why everyone tries to buy it from me ..."

Chris said: "Oh, you've got a stock ..."

"This is totally stock. This is the original engine, rust-free. This is the way they used to come. That's why I won't get rid of it. This is as stock as you can get it." Kinder has repainted and reupholstered the car in the original colours, but that's it. Just two days earlier he'd put it away for the winter, but throughout the summer, he takes his hotel guests for rides in the car, which has ninety-six thousand miles on it. "As soon as it gets dark," he said, "we cruise the strip and they take pictures of the neon."

Most of those guests are members of car clubs or from Europe. While he hopes more baby boomers will want to drive Route 66, so far most of the people who've stayed with him have been from other countries. "Europeans pay more attention to our culture than we do, I guess. They know more about it." Many of the Americans he does see come to photograph the hotel and the neon sign but stay down the road at the Hampton Inn. In fact, after we'd checked in the night before, several people had done just that. "They won't even give me a chance to show them how nice the rooms are," he complained. As for Americans slowing down and enjoying the journey, he was doubtful: "I don't know if they will. Everybody in this dot-com generation wants to get there now. So it's hard to say. I run into so many people who say they're doing Route 66, but they're still in a damn hurry. You just can't see it all if you do it quick."

WE HAD NO CHOICE but to speed up as we approached Albuquerque, because for about seventy miles, Route 66 disappears under Interstate 40. Chris and I had fallen instantly in love with New Mexico, and yet once we were back on a modern highway, we quickly realized we were both focused on the engineered road ahead of us instead of the beautiful arid mountain scenery that surrounded us.

The idea that interstates changed the way Americans see their nation—or, more accurately, what they see of their nation—was, as I later discovered, not exactly an original thought. "These great roads are wonderful for moving goods but not for inspection of a countryside," John Steinbeck complains in *Travels with Charley: In Search of America*, a book about a road trip he took with his French poodle in 1960. Gone are the vegetable stands, the antique stands and all the other roadside attractions. "When we get these thruways across the whole country, as we will and must, it will be possible to drive from New York to California without seeing a single thing."

Fortunately, for the past week we'd taken the road less travelled. But while we would have loved to have followed Route 66 all the way to Los Angeles, we had to get off in Albuquerque. Chris was flying back east and I was driving north. In a way, that was fitting because we'd finally reached the new America. We'd left St. Louis, an old rust-belt city declining in both population and economic might, and for a week travelled through dying small town after dying small town—and a few places such as Tulsa and Oklahoma City trying to recapture past glory—before finally ending up in the booming Southwest. Though Albuquerque was founded in 1706 and later benefited from being on Route 66, only two hundred thousand people lived there in 1960. Today, with a population of close to half a million, Albuquerque is growing—and sprawling—rapidly.

Aching for some food that was healthier than what we'd been eating for the past week, we set the GPS for the Whole Foods Market in the northeast quadrant of the city. We saw plenty of pickups but also many imports, especially out at the mall where the Whole Foods was. That's when Chris—who shares a Honda with his wife and would buy a fully loaded Volvo if he could afford one—told me his theory about American cars: to a lot of urban professionals in Toronto, anyone who buys a Detroit product is a chump. There are exceptions, of course—notably SUVs, and iconic cars such as Mustangs and Cadillacs—but most of the people we know drive Toyotas, Hondas or BMWs and look down their noses at anyone in a Chrysler LeBaron or a Chevrolet

Impala. Maybe, he suggested, it's the same in a place like Albuquerque.

As we pondered the meaning of that bit of car snobbery, we headed south to Central Avenue to look for a hotel. We crawled along in thick traffic—the worst congestion I'd seen since leaving Toronto. Now the eighteen-mile spine of Albuquerque's sprawl, Central Avenue was once part of Route 66. Driving through the Nob Hill neighbourhood, past the University of New Mexico and finally into downtown, we saw many remnants, especially motels, of the past. Most of them look pretty seedy now.

My sister Molly had told me that she and a friend had once unsuccessfully tried to find Albuquerque's downtown, and I could see why it would be difficult: it's small, and tall buildings are shockingly scarce for a city of this size. But then, Albuquerque, like many Southwestern cities, has grown into an urban area with many centres rather than expanding in the radial pattern common in older Northeastern cities.

After much deliberation, we checked into the Hotel Blue. It was an unremarkable building despite some art deco touches, but it did offer a cheap rate and a good location on Central Avenue. Since Chris had a flight at 6:30 in the morning, and we were planning a night on the town, he wasn't going to insist that I drive him to the airport. But we hadn't seen many cabs while driving around, so we asked the woman at the front desk about arranging one for the next morning. She explained that it would take anywhere from five to twenty minutes to get a taxi—possibly longer, in other words, than it would take to get to the airport once it arrived. And we were in a downtown hotel.

True, the city's core did fall to ruin in the 1960s and 1970s, as the downtowns of so many American cities did, but recently Albuquerque has been trying to revitalize it. One sign of success was that the strip of Central Avenue between First and Eighth streets, where we were staying, does offer an urban, rather than suburban, feel with a good concentration of funky cafés, restaurants and clubs. In addition, the city converted one-way streets to two-way streets, which are safer and more inviting for pedestrians; built an extensive system of bike lanes and routes; and installed bike racks on city buses. What will likely make a bigger difference is that Mayor Martin J. Chávez is determined to bring streetcars back by the fall of 2009. The first phase would run along Central Avenue from the Albuquerque Biological Park to Nob Hill, and the mayor hopes the project will reduce traffic while spurring infill development and encouraging pedestrian-friendly neighbourhoods.

Those laudable efforts aside, this remains a city built for drivers, not pedestrians, as we found out when we went out for dinner. We'd read good things about a restaurant called Artichoke, and though it was on the other side of the train tracks, it was less than a mile away, so we headed out on foot. The walk was pleasant enough, even if there weren't a lot of other pedestrians. We couldn't get a table for another twenty minutes, so we decided to go for a stroll and kept going along Central Avenue toward the university. We were the only walkers, and while some blocks seemed prosperous enough, others felt a little dodgy, with empty storefronts and litter blowing around the dimly lit empty sidewalk. As it turned out, we might have read the Stay Safe section on the Wikitravel web page devoted to Albuquerque, which warned, "The section from the train tracks (eastern edge of downtown) to University Blvd. can be a little scary in the evening." We turned around before we got to the university and walked back to the restaurant, where we were impressed, though a little surprised, that our waitress hadn't had a car for a year and happily travelled around town on her bicycle.

11 US 285
Drivers Wanted

AS A SMALL BOY, Scott Tomenson, my second road trip partner, liked to sit in the family car and imitate his father. He stuck his left elbow out the window, put his right hand on the steering wheel and, as he moved it back and forth, pretended he was driving down the road. His parents got a kick out of this cute performance until the day he put the car in gear and it rolled down the driveway.

I also played in the family station wagon as a boy. I remember the sheet metal dashboard that came to a rounded point and the steering wheel that had no padding. Back in those days, cars did not have ABS brakes, air bags or even headrests. Seat belts were optional. Fortunately, car safety has come a long, long way in the past few decades. Much of the credit, at least for the early improvements, goes to Ralph Nader, the consumer advocate and author of *Unsafe at Any Speed: The Designed-In Dangers of the American Automobile*, who pushed the automakers to build safer machines. (When the car companies hired private detectives to shadow him, the gadfly sued and, in a fitting bit of irony, funded his watchdog work with the multimillion-dollar settlement.)

The industry no longer needs Nader and his ilk to push as much. Safety sells, especially to the suburban parents who spend so much time ferrying kids around to soccer games, ballet lessons and other activities. That's why automakers are in a frenzied arms race to come up with new and better ways to protect people in cars. Already electronic stability control, which senses when a driver loses control and applies the brakes to individual wheels to reduce the chance of a rollover, is becoming standard in more and more cars. We're also starting to see sensors that monitor tire pressure; side obstacle detection, which is similar to the systems that beep when there's an obstacle behind a vehicle in reverse and will indicate that it's not safe to make a lane change; adaptive cruise control, which adjusts the car's speed to keep it a safe distance behind the vehicle ahead; warning systems that alert drivers with a rumble strip–like shudder when they stray from their lane; and monitors that alert drivers who aren't paying attention that a collision is about to happen. In addition, some manufacturers have guidance systems that help people park with the help of a dashboard screen, while Lexus goes a step further by offering hands-free parking at the push of a button, though it's not clear to me whether this technology really serves a safety purpose or just provides an out for people who are too lazy to learn how to parallel park properly. Other advances in the works could mean vehicles will immediately start applying the brake after sensing the driver's foot coming off the gas pedal quickly; read speed limit signs and reduce the car's speed to match it; detect cars entering from hidden entrances; and alert drivers about yellow or red lights if they don't slow down. And by combining sensors, GPS technology and short-range vehicle-to-vehicle communications, automakers will someday be able to offer a system that will allow a car that hits a patch of black ice and engages its stability-control system to transmit a signal to following cars about the hazard.

Not every invention sticks. Night Vision was an option on Cadillac DeVilles starting in 2004, but the infrared technology, which detected heat-emitting objects in the dark, was expensive and not enough customers wanted it, so GM no longer sells it. The automakers always have to balance what's possible with what people are willing to buy. There's also the danger that drivers will simply disable these features if they feel overloaded with flashing lights, warning messages and beeps.

And even when people do want them, these gizmos can't improve bad driving habits, which have always been with us. The first recorded traffic collision in America took place just two months after Charles and Frank Duryea started selling their cars commercially in 1896. Henry Wells of New York City hit a cyclist; the biker broke a leg and Wells spent a night in jail. In 2006, more than 42,642 people died and another 2.5 million were injured in nearly six million police-reported crashes on U.S. roads. Cars have killed more Americans since 1900 than have died in all the wars in the country's history.

New technology may actually aggravate the problem. The danger is that this new equipment will just make drivers more complacent or even more reckless. Armed with side obstacle detection technology, for example, some people might simply stop bothering to check their blind spot before switching lanes. "When we put a new safety feature on a vehicle, we're trying to build a safer vehicle," GM Canada technology planner Tom Odell told me. "But what we find is drivers turn around and say, 'Well, I have ABS so I can drive faster.' They start to expect that their vehicle is going to perform so much better that they can drive more aggressively."

Researchers who looked at drivers in Washington State confirmed this fear when they found that while safety-conscious people were the most likely to buy cars with air bags and antilock brakes, these devices had little effect on the rate of collisions and injuries, suggesting that drivers trade off enhanced safety for speedier trips. The study's authors weren't optimistic that the new generation of safety features, including sophisticated collision detection and avoidance technologies, would end up enhancing drivers' safety. "Vehicle manufacturers and Federal policymakers may attempt to promote these systems to the public on safety grounds," they concluded, "when, in fact, drivers may respond to them by traveling closer to other vehicles at higher speeds or paying less attention to their driving."

No matter what futuristic technology the manufacturers come up with, the weak link in car safety will always be the people operating the machinery. Carlos Tomas has been teaching people how to drive since 1977 and started Shifters, a manual shift driving school, in 1987. He would rather see better drivers than better cars. "We're relying too much on technology to fix these things up for us. If we screw up, the car will take care of it for us. But at some point that's bound to have some dire consequences."

All the technology is separating the drivers from the driving. Bare-bones cars once demanded that the person behind the wheel stay actively involved in operating the machinery. Now, vehicles with automatic transmissions, power steering and power brakes, and bursting with safety equipment and protective armour make driving seem easy—so easy that some drivers talk on the phone, check their email on their CrackBerrys and attend to personal grooming even though greater congestion and higher speeds are actually making the roads more dangerous.

"THERE'S SOMETHING about a man who is a good driver: calm, good reflexes, knows where he's going, gets in and out of situations gracefully, knows when to speed up and slow down," according to "12 Things You Don't Know About Women," by actress Dana Delany in the December 2006 issue of *Esquire* magazine. "Invariably, he's good in bed." Even before I read that, I wanted to be a better driver. Specifically, I wanted to relearn how to drive stick before I started my road trip.

Like most sixteen-year-olds, I took driving lessons, but I never bothered to take the test to get my licence. I obtained four year-long learner permits and spent some time behind the wheel of the manual transmission Volkswagen Rabbit my mom owned as well as in some beat-up pickups when I worked for my cousins' farm-fencing business. I finally got my licence, but I knew I'd be at a total loss if I were ever to find myself in a car with a stick shift again. I certainly didn't want to be like my friend who rented a car in France. Although he'd actually learned on a manual transmission, it had been a couple of decades since he'd driven one and, well, to make a long story short, let's just say he ended up returning the lurching and smoking car to one of the rental company's outlets in another city, much to the embarrassment of his teenage children, who insisted on walking the last few blocks. When he told the staff there was something wrong with the car, they suggested he might want to take an automatic. I wanted to avoid that fate but couldn't remember much more than that there was a clutch involved.

Bernard Doerner promised to change all that. A former Formula 3000 racer in his native Germany, he had curly white hair and a trim moustache and had a hearty laugh. Twenty years ago, while he was working as a structural engineer, his employers sent him to Canada to check out a company they wanted to buy. He met a woman and stayed. When the company closed the Canadian operations, he began teaching people to drive stick.

He showed up at my house in a blue Mazda 626 LX with a "Shifters" sign on it, and I hopped in the passenger side and he drove to Rosedale, a ritzy residential area that's not too busy. After he pulled over to a curb and stopped, he reached into the back seat of the car, grabbed a shoebox, opened it and pulled out a LEGO model, which he used to show me how the gears, the clutch and the flywheel work.

The model could have been just a gimmick, but I found it quite helpful. And if he hadn't told me he'd been an engineer, I might have guessed because he also liked to pull a little pad out of his pocket to draw, for example, a graph showing how torque increases, then plateaus, then declines as the revs increase. He relished the opportunity to cite studies such as the one that found that people driving manuals make four times as many decisions as those who drive automatics. By the end of the first lesson, I was starting to get the hang of it, but stalling the car is just part of the learning process. In my second lesson, I stalled after stopping on a slight hill at a red light. The guy behind me started honking at me, though he could obviously see the driving school sign on the car. I wondered why he was in such a rush to get on with his no-doubt dreary existence. As Doerner said, "There's something wrong with his life."

For my third lesson, I drove down to an industrial area near the waterfront where I could work on downshifting and handling curves. That's when I understood why it's so much fun to drive stick. There was little traffic, and as I downshifted before entering curves, accelerated after the apex and then zoomed along the straightaways, I started to become one with the car in a way I never had before. It reminded me of something I'd heard in Argentina, a country where automatics are rare. Manual transmissions are better, a man told me, because, "the car needs the driver."

A week later, when I met Doerner and his boss Carlos Tomas at my favourite espresso place, I learned that my reaction to my third lesson was not uncommon. One Shifters student, who was feeling a lot of peer pressure to buy a Porsche but was reluctant because he didn't know how to drive stick, was totally stiff and clearly not enjoying himself for the first two lessons. But when they drove down to the docks, everything changed. "All of a sudden he lit up," said Doerner in his thick German accent. "He grew a foot that day."

Both men teach about thirty-six hours a week, but while Doerner enjoys helping good students get better, Tomas prefers working with students who are struggling because then he has to use his wits, his knowledge and his creativity—and he learns more about teaching. The two instructors also have different reasons for recommending that people master a clutch. Tomas cited greater control and cost-effectiveness (cars with manual transmissions are less expensive and cheaper on gas and maintenance if driven properly). Doerner simply said: "If you want to have fun, then learn stick."

After ten years with the same driving school, Tomas became dissatisfied because his bosses wanted to standardize all in-car lessons. "The problem I found is there's nothing standard about people," he explained. So he started Shifters. Lately, he's seen interest in driving stick grow and believes that manual transmission cars are increasing in North America while automatics are increasing in Europe. Forty percent of his clients want to buy a manual car or already have. In some cases, people seek lessons after burning out a clutch. The day after one father gave his son a new Celica, the car was in the shop and the father was on the phone to Tomas. About 10 to 15 percent of his students are travelling or moving abroad; one Ford executive who was transferring to Europe flew to Toronto to do five lessons in one weekend. Sixty percent of his clients are women, in part because machismo prevents some guys from seeking lessons. Even those who do can sometimes have trouble checking their egos at the curb. When Doerner pulled out his LEGO model for a Ferrari-owning student in his mid-thirties, the man said he just wanted to drive. So Doerner let him. After the student stalled the car in the middle of heavy traffic, and became the victim of a lot of impatient honking, he said, "Okay, show me the model."

Although Tomas previously offered courses for beginners, he now focuses on in-car instruction for licensed drivers. Sometimes, though, it's hard to tell the difference. "It boggles my mind that someone with a driver's licence has to be treated like a beginner," he said. "We shouldn't be having to re-teach steering skills, how to turn, how to change lanes, how to use mirrors—those things you would assume a licensed driver would already know."

"So you have to do major remedial work?" I asked.

"Major, major," chimed in Doerner.

Tomas, who believes that too often the government issues death certificates rather than driving permits, explained that people aren't being taught proper decision-making skills or how to obtain the necessary information to make good decisions—problems that will only worsen as the population ages and drivers' eyesight and reflexes deteriorate. "If their driving skills are weak to begin with," he worried, "they're going to be really, really weak in the future."

As someone who was a passenger for a long time, I've had a chance to see a lot of my friends behind the wheel. Some are very good drivers, even if they do speed more than they should; others follow too closely, are prone to jackrabbit starts and other errors and sometimes engage in what can only be called aggressive driving. But if I was skeptical of most people's driving skills, these two instructors were completely pessimistic. Doerner said the major difference between driving in North America and in Europe is that people follow too closely here. Tomas attributes this to poor observation skills; not looking far enough ahead is rampant and leads to poor lane changes, bad turns, loss of control in slippery conditions and failure to recover after losing control. "The number one sin of people who are following too closely is tail-watching," he said. Instead of looking down the road, too many drivers look only at the bumper in front of them, and once they become fixated on that car, their mind begins to wander and too often that ends badly. "The most common crash is the rear-end collision and it's the most easily preventable crash."

Just as driving skills are deteriorating while automobile technology improves, drivers are becoming more discourteous as the roads get more crowded. Tomas compared the situation to hockey, a game that saw a lot less stick work before players wore helmets and face shields. "There was a certain level of respect on the road. Perhaps people sensed there was a certain vulnerability." As more cars feature more safety equipment, we forget how vulnerable we still are in a car. So many people seem blind to just how dangerous cars really are; in fact, although plane crashes are rare, far more people are afraid to fly than drive, and even many of those who are afraid to drive think little of getting in a car as a passenger.

Nor does Tomas find it encouraging that nine out of ten drivers rank their skills as above average, meaning that a lot of them think they're better than they really are and presumably aren't working too hard at improving. "The general population basically handles their cars like baboons," he said. "There's very little thought involved, and most of the time they're just upset that there's somebody in the way."

AFTER SPENDING TWO DAYS eating, drinking and hiking in Santa Fe, Scott and I left for Denver. If we took Interstate 25, we could make the trip in as little as five hours, but we opted to drive a blue highway, US 285. We immediately detoured to Abiquiú and the area that bewitched painter Georgia O'Keeffe. As the passenger, Scott got to fully enjoy the breathtaking views of the arid mountain country; as the driver, I had to devote at least some of my attention to the road, but all the curves and steep inclines, combined with little traffic, made the driving a lot of fun.

After Abiquiú, we headed to Taos, but as soon as we crossed US 285, we hit a road trip turning point. Since we were going to a Denver University hockey game that night, we could check out Taos, but then we'd have to take I-25 after all. Or we could turn around and head north on 285. I kept driving east as we debated the pros and cons. Scott said he'd be happy either way, but I've known him since grade nine and could tell he was really keen on a good lunch in Taos. After my Route 66 experience, though, I was pumped for 285. And since he wasn't adamant, I turned the car around.

North of Alamosa, Colorado, the traffic and the trucks increased, and Scott took the wheel. We had the sunroof open and were travelling through the broad, flat San Luis Valley between the San Juan Mountains on our left and the Sangre de Cristo Mountains on our right. We made a detour to the impressive Great Sand Dunes National Park and Preserve, home of the tallest dunes in North America, but we calculated that we didn't have time to do a hike. So we drove back to State Highway 17 and north again. We passed a UFO watchtower just north of Hooper and then, by the tiny town of Moffat, Scott asked, "Do you want an espresso?"

Of course I did, though I thought that was a weird question to ask out in the middle of nowhere. But Scott, who is one of the few people I know who is more serious about his espresso than I am, had spotted a sign for the Mirage Trading Co. that advertised, "Antiques, Espresso, Gallery." (It was also a Wi-Fi hot spot.) We weren't expecting much, especially since homemade jerky was the only food the place appeared to sell, but the espresso was great. Turns out the guy behind the counter had worked in a coffee bar for ten years and knew what he was doing with his machine.

After 17 merged into 285, the valley narrowed, and as we approached Poncha Pass, the blue skies gave way to some flurries. For a long time we skirted a snowstorm, but at Fairplay, the model for the town in the *South Park* cartoon series, we drove right into it and noticed lots of Jeeps and pickups—good mountain vehicles—on the road, which quickly became treacherous.

Rather than a car guy, Scott is a Jeep and truck guy. As a boy, he lusted after the Corvette Stingray. At sixteen, he learned to drive from an obese and unpleasant instructor in a Ford Maverick with a three-speed gearshift on the steering column, otherwise known as "three on the tree." His first car was a Honda Civic hatchback, followed by a Honda Prelude, but since then he's had five Jeeps (including a Golden Eagle, a YJ and a CJ), three Ford Expeditions, one Land Rover Discovery and one Land Rover Defender 90. His favourite vehicles were the Defender 90 and the Ford F-150 King Ranch he drives now, though he also has a soft spot for an old orange Jeep he owned for many years. "I don't drive for fun, but if I have to drive, I'd like to do it in something that's enjoyable," he insisted, adding that he wished we were in his wife's convertible Thunderbird. "It's a fun car. Perfect for this drive."

We talked about our love–hate relationship with the automobile, and at first he said the only thing he hated was paying the insurance premiums. But it didn't take much prodding before he was giving me a longer list. "I hate traffic. And construction. I hate rush hour," he groused. "I hate other drivers. I think the majority—a great majority—of them are shitty drivers." People who are too lazy to use their turn signals to indicate a lane change disgust him, but few things enrage him as much as those who sit in the passing lane and make other cars overtake them on the right or not at all. Left-lane hogs are indeed rude and dangerous scofflaws—and shockingly common. In the more than nine weeks of my road trip, the drivers in Minnesota were the worst I encountered for this transgression. True, I wasn't in the state long, and it was a Sunday, but as I skirted Minneapolis-St. Paul, I saw more cars in the left lane than even the middle lane, let alone the right lane. And north of the Twin Cities, I saw an old black Saturn nearly cause a collision as it moved into the left lane without looking and then stay there for more than half an hour. (We all have our own ideas of where to find the worst drivers, but rather than rely on anecdotes and curmudgeonly opinion, in 2005, Allstate analyzed two years' worth of crash and claim data from 196 U.S. cities. The insurance company discovered that Cedar Rapids, Iowa, was the safest city in the nation, while Washington, D.C., was the most dangerous because, on average, drivers there are involved in one collision every 5.2 years.)

"I also hate speed limits," Scott concluded. "I think they're stupid because I don't think it's the speed that you're travelling that's the problem, it's how you drive and your ability as a driver." Let's face it: going fast is fun. In fact, part of the reason we love cars is the sense of speed and power we feel as we roar down the road. That's why so many North Americans with a little lead in their right foot talk about the German autobahns with a certain reverence because stretches of these roads have no speed limits and other drivers know their lives depend on staying in the right lane.

And yet, while the autobahns are no more deadly than other European highways, it's a mistake to argue that speed doesn't kill. I asked Sgt. Cam Woolley about speeding, because it seemed to me that with modern cars on modern highways, Ontario's top speed limit of 100 kilometres an hour (62 miles per hour) was too low, especially since several states have speed limits of 75 miles per hour (120 kilometres an hour).

"I've studied that whole issue internationally, and basically the problem is the speed differential," he said. "There's a theory that 85 percent of the traffic will find a safe speed."

"So if it's a clear day, good weather, good road conditions, and 85 percent of the people are going 130 kilometres an hour, that's fine?" I asked hopefully.

"Well, no, I can't say that. We're not allowed to give permission for anybody to break the law. What I can tell you is we have lots of days out there where there's good weather and good traffic conditions, where the average speed is higher than the limit and there are no collisions." While new technology may make ideas such as variable speed limits possible, the problem is that with higher speeds, stopping distances increase, and given the huge range in the ability of drivers, something as simple as a wide-load truck taking up a lane and a half would result in people making sudden lane changes at speeds they can't handle. Even curves are more difficult at higher speeds: a third of all the fatal crashes on U.S. roads involve speeding, and about 40 percent of these take place on curves—double the number for non-speeders.

Unfortunately, the laws of physics mean that the higher the speed, the worse the crash and the higher the fatality rate: the chances of being killed in a vehicle travelling at 120 kilometres per hour are four times higher than at 100 kilometres per hour. Crash at 200 kilometres per hour and it's all over but the funeral.

THE CAM WOOLLEY SHOW started at six o'clock on a Friday morning. Easily the best-known member of the Ontario Provincial Police, the sergeant had gathered all the props to attract reporters and crews from local television and radio stations at a service station on Highway 400 north of Toronto for the OPP's long-weekend kick-off. A couple of days earlier, when I'd met him in his cluttered office, he'd told me, "It'll be like O.J.'s trial." Not quite, but along with lots of local media, the scene included fire trucks, a police boat on a trailer, paramedics with a dummy to be rescued, a driver who'd hit a moose and an officer who'd seen the collision and had some advice for how to avoid such crashes, representatives from the Ontario Safety League and the Ontario Trucking Association, and a booth with anti–drinking and driving bumpf. Even Elmer the Safety Elephant, who has been teaching kids for six decades, showed up.

Officially, May 24 (or the closest Monday before it) is a holiday to celebrate Queen Victoria's birthday, but to most Canadians— many of whom can't understand their country's anachronistic colonial ties to a foreign country's royal family—the long weekend in May is the start of summer. Often called the May Two-Four Weekend because a "two-four" is a case of beer, it's an opportunity to open the cottage after the long winter, go camping or just get out of the city to party. In all the excitement, some drivers also see it as an invitation to do stupid things, so the OPP held its first highway blitz of the summer to nab people for everything from improperly installed child seats to speeding and aggressive driving to operating unsafe vehicles (including what Woolley calls "Fred Flintstone cars" because they have no floors). Highway 400 is the most heavily travelled route for people heading to cottage country—up to a million cars drive it over a long weekend—so it's the logical spot for a command post.

Six foot two inches tall and weighing in at 280 pounds, Woolley is really just a super-sized version of Tom Hanks in *Big*. He's got an eager grin, a goofy sense of boyish humour and a tendency to call everybody Buddy. A self-confessed car nut, he attended Upper Canada College, a prestigious private school for boys that churns out far more investment bankers, hedge fund managers and other lucre-chasers than cops. Since his father was a corporate lawyer who owned an interest in some GM dealer- ships, he drove demos—or, as he referred to them, demolitions—

to school. His first one was a Chevy Vega he called The Veg-o-matic. Later, he had a Nova, a Camaro, a Buick wagon, a Cadillac Eldorado and, in his last year of high school, a Corvette. After graduation in 1976, he bought a blue-and-white Blazer "when SUVs were still utility vehicles, not a fashion statement." Over the years, he has owned about 150 cars. And he's a partner in a company that rents cars for film and television productions (he also moonlights as a movie consultant and occasionally acts). Today, he's the proud owner of close to twenty vehicles, including a Rolls-Royce, a convertible Mercedes, a Range Rover and a Porsche 928—all of them purchased used, and usually with some story behind the sale. The walls of his messy office are filled with awards and photographs, including one of his wife, a service manager at a GM dealership, on an armoured military vehicle called a Ferret. "It does a hundred kilometres per hour off-road and it's bulletproof. It is all one hundred percent, except the machine gun is welded up. But the grenade launchers work good." He buys hundreds of dollars' of European car magazines every year, hasn't taken public transit since high school and believes, "You are what you drive."

A cop since 1978, Woolley put in many years as a traffic accident investigator but now spends as much as 90 percent of his time doing media work. And this was the sixth year he'd helped make the highway blitz a high-profile event. As if fines, demerit points and lost plates weren't enough of a deterrent, part of the sergeant's strategy was to get the force's message out to the public by gleefully dishing details on the miscreants for reporters. His anecdotes were just too good to make up, and they would have been hilarious if they weren't so scary, so naturally the media lapped them up: several broadcast outlets showed up at the kick-off, and all four Toronto papers ran articles based on his stories.

Even with such widespread coverage of the increased police presence on the roads, the close to two hundred officers who took part in the blitz never had trouble finding drivers to ticket or material for Woolley's colourful cautionary tales. Some people drive right into the service station parking lot breaking the law. "We've had people pulling in smoking dope and drinking and"— here he made the sound of someone drawing on a joint and adopted a stoner voice—"'Whoa, the cops, man.'"

Television reporters frequently introduced him as someone who has seen it all, but the fact is he's constantly amazed at what people do. Some of the more memorable Woolley chestnuts include the teenager who was trying to impress his girlfriend by doing 212 kilometres per hour in his mom's Lexus and ended up having to take his date home on the bus; the man clocked at 180 kilometres an hour who claimed he'd forgotten his wife's birthday and was rushing to get her a gift; the woman who said she couldn't wear her seat belt because she wanted to pet her lapdog; the truck driver who stepped out of his rig waving a bottle of vodka and wearing nothing but his underwear; and the Volkswagen Golf with the sign that read, "For sale, needs brakes." That one prompted the sergeant to quip, "Well, there's truth in advertising. Needed brakes. Needs a tow truck now."

The tale he finds most staggering may be the time a couple of detectives in an unmarked car saw a Volkswagen Jetta swerving all over the southbound lanes of Highway 400. They assumed the driver was drunk, but when they caught up to him, he was furiously playing a violin. The musician, who was in his fifties, had a concert in Toronto that night and wanted to practise along the way. "If I knew classical music," one of the detectives said, "I could have guessed what he was playing just by the way the car was moving."

Woolley thinks people are so pressed for time, especially as commutes get longer and longer, that some drivers try to multi-task. "We're seeing a lot of folks who want to own the house of their dreams and are willing to commute from farther and farther away and they're forgetting about the drive, so the time has to come from somewhere."

Lately, the most common distraction for drivers has been the cell phone. Three researchers at the University of Utah found that yakkers were as impaired as drunks on the road. Their study showed that the cell phone users were 9 percent slower to hit the brakes while also showing 24 percent greater variance in how closely they followed the car in front of them because their attention shifted between the road and their conversation.

Some jurisdictions—including much of Europe, a few states and Newfoundland and Labrador—have made it illegal to use a hand-held phone while driving. In other places, it's standard operating procedure for many drivers (even, bizarrely, in manual transmission cars). Several studies, including the University of Utah one, have suggested that hands-free units aren't really any safer because the real distraction is the driver's concentration on the conversation. But just let me say this about that: if I'm on the road and another driver has to react quickly, I'd really prefer that he or she had two hands available to put on the wheel.

Talking on the phone is dangerous enough, but OPP officers have also seen drivers preparing their lunch, doing their makeup, shaving, reading, checking their email, watching television and countless other activities that mean they aren't focused on the task of driving a vehicle. Still, while Woolley's chronicles make great copy, what causes most crashes is far more mundane. "Just being stressed out at work or home, or just daydreaming can do it, plus the actual fatigue," he said. "The highways aren't very forgiving."

AT 6 A.M., the temperature was still a crisp seven degrees Celsius and the morning sun hadn't quite burned off all the mist on the surrounding fields, but Woolley didn't seem to mind at all. Dressed in his dark blue uniform, complete with jacket and wide-brimmed hat, he was clearly enjoying himself as he bounded around, greeting shivering reporters by name and joking with fellow officers.

Minutes before, while driving north on Highway 400, I'd passed two cars that had been pulled over by cruisers. The first, I later learned from Woolley, received a $150 ticket for speeding; the second didn't slow down and move out of the right-hand lane before passing an emergency vehicle with flashing lights at the side of the road—a lapse in both consideration and the rules of the road that cost him $490. And at the service centre, officers dressed in mechanics' overalls were soon checking the roadworthiness of rusted-out vans and pickups. One of the first to come in was a red Ram 350 van with bad brakes, a blown exhaust, no signals and holes in its floor. After another officer removed its licence plates, Woolley—who expected to see about fifty such vehicles over the weekend—did a live hit with a local television crew using the van as an example.

By 7:30, the OPP had given the first Breathalyzer of the day; the driver failed. By mid-morning, Dave Potwin had stopped a woman in a black Taurus station wagon after he noticed her badly smashed windshield. She handed him a handwritten insurance card. It didn't take long for the constable to prove it was fake, give her a ten-thousand-dollar fine and take the plates off her car.

I joined the thirty-six-year-old Potwin in his cruiser just after that. A slim, fit man with light brown hair shorn short on the sides and chiselled good looks that make him appear younger than he is, he wore five-hundred-dollar Oakley sunglasses. Seven years earlier, while working as an insurance adjuster, he'd realized he wasn't cut out for a desk job and decided to become a cop. Now, he spends most of his time on the road—but doesn't consider himself a car guy. Like any red-blooded male, he'll drool over a sleek Ferrari, but he drives a fire-engine-red Toyota Tercel and worries about the environment. Potwin, who maintains a letter-writing correspondence with Canadian author and conservationist Farley Mowat, shakes his head when he sees how many people drive up to the cottage alone in their Escalades. "Future generations are going to judge us harshly for our overuse of resources," he said. "The environmental costs are staggering."

Initially, we headed north on Highway 400 as he kept his eyes out for anything out of the ordinary. "So many things stem from an expired licence sticker," he explained. "The devil is in the details." Sure enough, he pulled over a brown Chevrolet Celebrity with a licence sticker that was still valid but in the wrong corner of the plate. Potwin got out of his Ford Police Interceptor, a law enforcement version of the Crown Victoria, and walked to the passenger side and knocked on the window, clearly surprising the long-haired driver. Potwin always goes to the passenger side because that element of surprise means he often can spot any trouble—in this case, there was a large dog in the back seat but nothing else to worry about—but also because it's safer. "I've already been hit once out here," he told me, "and it will never happen again." He'd been investigating a collision when a young woman in a Honda Civic hit his cruiser at a hundred kilometres per hour. The car was totalled and he was off work for six weeks recovering. (Such collisions aren't uncommon; in fact, target fixation—or the "moth effect"—is the tendency for some drivers to involuntarily steer, like moths to a flame, into a vehicle on the side of the road because they're looking at it instead of where they're driving.)

After getting the driver's licence, registration and insurance from the man in the Celebrity, Potwin used his radio to call in the details. Everything checked out, so instead of issuing a ninety-dollar fine, he let the man off with a warning. He issued another warning to a driver in a black Chevrolet Silverado pickup with a cracked windshield. As he pulled back onto the highway, Potwin floored it and moved over to the far-left lane. He'd spotted a dark grey Hyundai Accent that was speeding and following too closely behind a Jeep: "That's aggressive driving and needs an intervention."

The twenty-two-year-old driver, who was in his father's car, shook as he spoke to Potwin and admitted that the police had never stopped him before. Figuring the young man would have learned a lot just from the experience, the constable let him off with a warning. The kid was so relieved that he started breathing again, though that didn't seem to be the source of any great amusement for Potwin.

Riding in a police cruiser offered me a different perspective on the highway. I wasn't surprised by the deference other drivers showed the marked car—at one point, a line of vehicles in all three lanes followed at a more-than-respectful distance behind us, everyone afraid to accelerate in plain view of the OPP. But I was intrigued by Potwin's approach: rather than simply enforcing the law by handing out tickets at every opportunity, he aimed to improve road safety by managing behaviour. Sometimes that meant pulling someone over and having a chat; other times he would drive up beside a speeding driver and with a look get her to slow down. "As a rookie, I was constantly surprised at what I saw," he admitted, adding that it came as a total shock to him that people would get drunk on a Sunday morning and then go for a drive. "My eyes have been opened and I've learned to expect the unexpected."

BY THE END of the weekend, Woolley had put in sixty hours over four days and done countless interviews, while the close to two hundred officers who'd taken part in the blitz across the province had a staggering ticket tally: 6,316 for speeding, 633 for failing to wear seat belts, 177 for failing to stop at a red light or a stop sign. In addition, they'd charged 133 motorists with drunk driving and another 80 with careless driving. And still, 4 people had died on the roads.

Those numbers frustrate Woolley, but he was confident that some people were getting the message. "The whole idea is to make traffic safety marketable or interesting to the public," he said. "If it's just some traffic cop telling you to obey the law it's not very newsworthy and it's not very credible, so I try to use a bit of humour and a bit of newsworthy stuff. Sometimes the silly stuff people do is kind of funny even though it was potentially dangerous. But that gets people talking and thinking about safety." (In January of 2007, the new commissioner of the OPP, Julian Fantino, put an end to the highway blitzes. His announcement seemed to suggest that Woolley's use of humour undermined the seriousness of the carnage on the roads. More than a few people speculated that what the commissioner really didn't like was the idea of anyone else being the face of the force—especially not some lowly traffic cop.)

In movies and television, a common punishment for cops who get in trouble is to be busted down to traffic, but it's actually becoming a more prestigious assignment, in part because police forces are putting more resources into traffic than ever before. Also, far more people die in cars than in murders, and for all the glory the homicide squad garners, most cases are straightforward, not the complex whodunits of television and novels. But the accident reconstruction team often investigates difficult how-did-it-happen cases.

Woolley is passionate about safety and has been able to make a difference. In fact, the OPP's officer of the year in 2005 has had high-profile success in pushing for legislation, including laws to hold truckers accountable for flying wheels and detached parts. Even people he's stopped for an infraction ask for his autograph: as he writes out the ticket, he tells them, "You're gonna get an autograph."

During his years on the force, Woolley has seen a huge shift in attitudes toward driving. "When I joined the OPP, collisions were considered inconvenient and accidents were accidents," he said. "You didn't wear seat belts, drinking and driving was kind of funny and when you're number was up, it was up. That's the way it was." Today, drinking and driving is no longer socially acceptable, while accidents are now called collisions and they are predictable and preventable—and people won't stand for them.

"If a loved one is injured, people don't have the attitude that it was an accident. They want somebody held accountable."

That doesn't mean he doesn't think some attitudes still have to change, as all the tickets handed out during the highway blitz attest. In addition, street racing remains a huge and deadly problem. And despite his otherwise conservative views, Woolley sounds like a lefty when he talks about auto advertising. "Driving is still marketed as carefree and exciting, and I think that's a mistake." He cited SUV ads as some of the worst offenders. "We see guys wiping out all the time in SUVs. They're going too fast because the TV ad said they could go up and down mountains. But you can't go the speed limit on Highway 401 in a snowstorm or you're going to find the nearest guardrail. I've had SUVs since 1976, and in the words of the great police philosopher Clint Eastwood, 'A man's got to know his limitations.'"

12 Colorado Springs "More Than I Need, Less Than I Want"

"SO ANYWAY, the garage day is typically a tour to three or four club members' homes where everyone who is interested in attending hopefully drives their Mustang if the weather cooperates," Neil Case explained to me in an email. "We include a progressive lunch during the tour, where at the first stop the host provides an appetizer, and most everybody congregates in the garage to discuss any Mustang project that may be going on. After about an hour, we all jump in our ponies and head to the next stop, where we typically have a salad and most everybody congregates in the garage to discuss any Mustang project that may be going on. After about an hour we all jump in our ponies and head to the next stop, where we typically have the main course and most everybody congregates in the garage to discuss any Mustang project that may be going on. After about an hour we all jump in our ponies and head to the next stop, where we typically have dessert and most everybody congregates in the garage to discuss any Mustang project that may be going on. We will have our club meeting during that time as well, during one of the stops. Sometimes we may skip the appetizer so the day does not get long for everybody."

Though Case was the one who responded to my request to ride along on garage day, his wife Jamie was actually the president of the Rocky Mountain Mustangers, a car club in Colorado Springs. The members take part in car shows, go on cruises, hold a swap meet and attend a monthly meeting. They also share restoration and maintenance tips with each other.

Most car clubs are social organizations as much as anything else, but all of them bring together people who share an interest in automobiles. Many clubs, such as the Mustangers, are devoted to one marque, but others welcome anyone who's interested. (Variations on the theme include the Car Club for Men, a humorous website for those with an automobile that's at least ten years old and has at least 160,000 kilometres on the odometer. My Maxima became eligible shortly after I left Toronto.) For most members, this hobby is a healthy, if expensive, passion. But some people cross the line into obsession. My friend Mike Harper, a Toronto advertising consultant, owns two Porsches and races his 911 with other members of the Porsche Club of America (Upper Canada Region). He's seen marriages break up and people spend their way into bankruptcy. "Cars," he said, "are like crack cocaine for some of these guys."

The garage day in Colorado Springs was one of the few events I'd planned before I started my road trip; after all, it combined Mustangs—not just an iconic car but my favourite (along with the Galaxie 500) when I was a kid—and the Rocky Mountains. It had to be done. Beyond following my own whims, I hoped to glean a better understanding of at least one side of our love–hate relationship with the car.

Ask serious car aficionados what they hate about automobiles and they're not going to start whining about sprawl or fretting about the environment. Instead, they'll complain about the hassle of gas prices and speeding tickets and traffic jams—and about the headaches and heartaches that go with fixing, restoring and customizing their beloved cars. As for the love, I'm not sure it's much more complicated than a kid's love for a puppy: it's wide-eyed and unconditional.

LESS THAN AN HOUR south of Denver, Colorado Springs is home to the Garden of the Gods, a park full of stunning red sandstone formations in the shadow of Pikes Peak, one of the best-known mountains in the country. Originally a resort community, it has since become home to several military bases, including the United

States Air Force Academy, as well as defence contractors and high-tech firms. Now the second-largest city in the state, with a population of about 370,000, the growth has been rapid, much of it taking place in the last couple of decades, and some of the people who moved here are now complaining about big-city problems such as crime, homelessness, high house prices, traffic and even overcrowding (although the density is under 2,000 people per square mile).

Colorado Springs also has a reputation for being extremely conservative. The population is 80 percent white, and evangelical Christians abound; Focus on the Family is just one of the many religious organizations based here. So I didn't expect to see a Jeep with a bumper sticker that read, "If you aren't a race fan, blow me (kneepads optional)." I got over my shock—and my giggles—and found my hotel just before Jamie and Neil Case showed up in their 2005 Mustang GT.

Four decades before that car rolled off the line, the original Mustang was as much a cultural phenomenon as it was an auto industry sensation. In 1960, Lee Iacocca became the vice-president and general manager of the Ford Motor Company's Ford Division. While the colossal failure of the Edsel in the late 1950s was the case of a car in search of a market, he saw an emerging market in search of a car. Not only would the number of people aged twenty to twenty-four increase by 50 percent during the 1960s, but a larger percentage of this generation would go to college than any other—and college grads bought more cars than those without higher education. The company's research also suggested that older consumers' tastes were shifting from practical economy cars to sporty and luxury models, more and more families were buying second automobiles, and women, who liked small, easy-handling vehicles, were buying more cars. Iacocca was particularly interested in the blossoming youth market and figured he could capture it with a product that combined style, performance and price. But it had to be more than a sports car. In

Iacocca: An Autobiography, the father of the Mustang wrote, "We wanted to develop a car that you could drive to the country club on Friday, to the drag strip on Saturday, and to church on Sunday."

At the same time, he was surprised to learn how many people who bought the Ford Falcon—which had been a huge success for the company—were paying to add white-wall tires, automatic transmissions and more powerful engines to what was supposed to be a low-priced economy car. "The American car buyer," he realized, "wants economy so badly he'll pay almost anything to get it!" So instead of offering several different models, Ford made one base Mustang and let buyers customize from an array of options, including eight-cylinder engines, automatic transmission and radios. That flexibility kept the base car affordable—it originally sold for $2,368, though buyers spent an average of $1,000 on options—and helped ensure the Mustang's enduring popularity.

And popular it was. Although the Big Three traditionally introduced new models in the fall, Ford unveiled the Mustang in April at the 1964 New York World's Fair. On the day of the launch, people swarmed dealerships. After fifteen people in Garland, Texas, vied for the lone Mustang in a display window, the highest bidder—fearing someone else would snap it up—slept in it until his cheque cleared. Ford sold more than 417,000 Mustangs in the first year.

The Rocky Mountain Mustangers started two years later. Today, the club counts sixty-two families, including the Cases, as members. When Neil, who is a mechanical engineer with the school district, was in high school he worked on a friend's Camaro, but he's a Mustang guy now. He and Jamie joined the club in 1992, before they even owned a pony. Neil soon bought a 1968 Coupe for seven hundred dollars, which was his daily driver for six months before he got around to restoring it. The couple now owns four Mustangs, including a 1966 Coupe, which he put a 302 engine in so he could enter Autocross races; a 1967 Coupe;

and a 1968 High Country Special, one of only 251 made, that sits outside waiting to be restored.

We had some time, so Neil, who wore jeans on his long, thin legs and a jean jacket, took me on a quick tour of town and a drive-through of the Garden of the Gods. Jamie, a physician assistant who specializes in chronic pain management, sat in the back seat and admitted wearily, "I kind of adopted Neil's interest." She's now a convert and especially loves racing. They both do Autocross, which is safer than traditional racing because the drivers go through the course one at a time. Though the clock ticks away, car-handling skills and the ability to come up with the best strategy for getting through the traffic-cone course matter as much as sheer speed.

The first house on the garage day itinerary was in Peregrine, an upscale neighbourhood on the western edge of town between the Garden of the Gods and the Air Force Academy. Despite the cold and the occasional snow flurries when the sun would disappear, most people milled about on the driveway. There were three cars in Dave Gardner's garage—a 2005 Corvette, a red 1969 Mach 1 Mustang and a black 1967 Fairlane—but he owns a total of twelve vehicles, including a 1967 Mustang convertible, a Volvo and three school buses for the three daycare centres he owns. He introduced himself by saying, "Car people are different."

Tall, thin and balding, Gardner wore a suede jacket, a plaid shirt and wire-frame sunglasses. He was in the military for many years, including stints as a chopper pilot in Vietnam, a rescue pilot and an air traffic controller, but says none of that was as stressful as running three businesses, so his car collection was his great joy. While he admitted many Vette owners are snobbish about their wheels, he declared, "I just love cars."

Gardner's special project was the Fairlane. A couple of years ago, his son Brent was diagnosed with ALS and Gardner wanted to get the Fairlane restored before his son could no longer drive. Already his son was unable to help but still likes to be there when

Gardner and other club members do the work. "It's the only thing that makes him happy," Gardner said sadly. He has put many, many hours and about thirty thousand dollars into it so far. Before we moved on, he started the Fairlane and let it roar, much to everyone's delight.

The next stop was Stew Harding's place, a split-level with a two-door garage in Village Seven, an eastern neighbourhood that wasn't as posh as the one Gardner lives in. The turnout was growing: ten or twelve members, at least as many women as men, had dropped by the first house, but an additional half-dozen showed up to the second. A black 1969 Mach 1 Mustang sat in one garage bay, but Harding was storing his other Mustang, a 1965 Fastback, in a friend's barn, so several people hovered around the food table in the other bay. He has reddish hair and a goatee and was wearing a red sweatshirt and blue workout pants. As a boy in Wyoming, he was thrilled when his parents bought a pony in 1967. "I grew up in the back of that old car. So I've just loved Mustangs since I was just a kid."

His first car was a Chevy II Nova, but he soon traded up to a 1966 Mustang. And he hasn't looked back; although he sells auto parts at a GM dealership, he admitted, "I've been a died-in-the-wool Ford guy my whole life." For him, part of the allure of the Mustang is that it was a blue-collar performance car that a buyer could personalize. A row of photos on his garage wall shows the eight Mustangs he's owned over the years. One of the pictures shows him drag racing at Bandimere Speedway in Denver. "Never was very successful, but I sure tried hard," he said. "It was a blast. There ain't nothing like doing a big old hairy burnout to get the slicks hot and then a couple of dry hops and then the light comes down. I'm getting goosebumps even thinking about it now. Just a blast."

For about five years in the mid-1980s, he didn't own a Mustang because he was buying and fixing up his house. After all, it's easy to spend four to five hundred dollars a month on a couple of old cars, and he estimated that it would take at least thirty thousand dollars to fix up an average unrestored mid-1960s Mustang. He bought his Mach 1 six years ago for twelve thousand and has put another five thousand into it and could probably sell it for about thirty thousand; on the other hand, he's sunk a lot more into the 1965 Fastback than he could ever hope to get out. "It's extremely expensive and if I had to hire out a lot of the work, it would be worse yet."

The third house of the day belonged to Mike Taylor. There were Mustang posters on his garage walls and a food table in the middle of one bay. In the other, there was a 1993 GT under a fitted tarp and an engine from a 1965 Fastback on a stand in the corner. A maintenance technician for Schlage locks, he bought the Fastback for just $275—much to his wife's displeasure—and for the amount he's spent on the car, he could have picked up a brand new Shelby Mustang. He's been working on it for more than twenty years, including as much as ten to fifteen hours a week in the past year, and still doesn't know when he'll be finished except to say, "I think my grandkids are going to get a nice car."

Next, I rode with Kathryn Blacharski. Since she lives up in the mountains and the weather was iffy, she'd left her 2004 Mystichrome convertible Cobra at home and drove a black Ford 150 XLT pickup with a licence plate that read "Tall 1." Country music played softly on the radio. A tall woman with long blond hair, she works as a systems administrator. Her father was a mechanic, and as a girl she liked to hang out with him at his garage. She says she fell in love with the Mustang in "1964 and a half." (Because Ford launched the car in April instead of the fall, the model year of the original Mustang is 1964 $^1/_2$.) But she didn't buy her first one—a 2003 six-cylinder yellow convertible—until two years ago because as a single mother she had to wait to raise her two kids before she could splurge. "I loved her to death," she said. "And there was absolutely nothing wrong with her and I'm not exactly sure why, but I went looking for a Cobra." When she had a chance to buy the Mystichrome convertible, she scraped together every penny she could find. A limited edition option in 2004 only, Mystichrome is paint that appears to change colour, depending on the angle and the light, from green to blue to purple to black. "It's pretty nifty." She drives it to work once a week when the weather is good, takes it to car shows and runs it in Autocross races. She got into racing after riding with Jamie Case. "It was just so exciting. All it took was one ride-along and I got hooked," she said. "It's a whole lot of fun and it's legal." Even better, she does it in a car she loves so much she'll never sell it. "I'll eat pork and beans before I get rid of my car."

The fourth house was out in the country and belongs to Terry Myers. The general manager of a wholesale distribution company, he wore bib overalls and a black racing shirt. He looks a bit like John Denver, but wound tighter. Judging from the way he keeps his three-door garage, he's also a bit of a neat freak. On the wall, he'd put up Mustang posters, a Ford racing flag and a sign that read "Ford Parking Only All Others Will Be Towed." He does own a Chevy pickup, but insisted, "I hate it." His first car was a Ford Torino at the insistence of his father. Then he had a 1964 Fairlane, the first of three Fairlanes he owned. "I was working up to a Mustang," he said. The grandson of a car dealer, he's owned about thirty cars in his life, but one year he bought and sold seventeen. Today, he owns a 2001 Cobra and a 1965 Coupe, which was up on blocks, and spends five to six hours a week on them. Several club members crowded around to inspect the work he'd been doing on the Coupe's engine. Myers, who Autocrosses it, explained that racers actually make up only 10 percent of the club; it just seems like more because they talk about it all the time. His appetite for Mustangs will never be satisfied. "There will always be another one," he said. "My wife concedes that. There will always be another one I want."

Upstairs, the second floor of the garage was his parts department. It was all chipboard and exposed rafters; the insulation that would someday go up was still in bags. Myers held court, regaling half a dozen other male club members—the women all stayed downstairs—with the trials and tribulations of fixing the 2001 Ford Focus he'd given his son. It was supposed to be a reliable car to get to and from college, but they also put a supercharger in it for Autocross races. Then the engine blew and it was one frustration after another to get it working again—and suddenly two days to fix it became seven. The people listening had obviously heard this tale before, perhaps many times, but that didn't matter—they clearly enjoyed hearing it again.

The final stop of the day was Bambino's, a restaurant with unremarkable Italian food in a sketchy section of town. While the club executive put up a yellow club banner, other members chatted about cars mostly, though occasionally real estate crept into the conversation. A few people ordered beer. It was a mostly middle-aged crowd, fortyish and up (there is another, less-formal club in town called the Mustang Mafia, which attracts younger enthusiasts). Everyone in the room was white, but there was diversity of professions—from an engineer to a postman—and socioeconomic class. Jamie Case, who wore a sweatshirt with "Colorado" on it and kept her light brown hair in a ponytail, chaired the meeting, and though she had a casual, occasionally giggly attitude toward *Robert's Rules of Order*, she was good at it, moving through the agenda efficiently and good-naturedly. One item was the gift exchange at the upcoming Christmas party, and Case, apparently speaking from past experience, asked that everyone spend about fifteen dollars, resist the temptation to give gag gifts such as blow-up dolls and refrain from giving alcohol— even if it came in a "really cool Mustang decanter"—because some of the people getting the presents might be under twenty-one.

Case introduced a former member, Jack Howard, who had a Mustang to sell, and three new members. One was a young guy who was there with his wife. He stood up and described himself as recently married—and recently married to a 1967 Mustang, which he'd just bought for eight hundred dollars and was "all primer," meaning it was painted with primer. Case welcomed him and suggested that as he got to know the other members, he'd find there were several who had experience restoring Mustangs. "They'll be able to tell you what not to do."

That prompted several mock cries of "Don't start!"

TWO WEEKS BEFORE I met the Rocky Mountain Mustangers, I'd spent the day with the Gateway Camaro Club. By 8:30 on Sunday morning—half an hour before the official start of the annual Fall Colors Tour—a few Camaro lovers had already gathered in the parking lot of the Drury Inn in Fenton, Missouri, about twenty miles from downtown St. Louis. Since the Chevrolet Camaro, launched in the fall of 1966, was GM's response to the Mustang, I wasn't surprised to hear some of the Gateway guys cracking wise about ponies and their owners, though when pressed they admitted it was really just a friendly rivalry. Said one: "At least their cars are American."

Marv Hoefel, a potbellied guy with a red face dressed in a purple shirt, black suspenders and a baseball cap with the club logo on it, had organized the event and even did a dry run to make sure everything would go smoothly. The last thing he wanted to hear was the razzing he'd get if it didn't. His wife, Briann, handed out maps of the route while club president Mike Steitz made sure every car had a two-way radio in case anyone got lost or broke down or ran out of gas. Shortly after nine o'clock, we got in the Camaros and took off.

Most members were riding with someone else—a wife, a son, a friend—but Steve Blumfelder was alone, so I started the day in his 1997 Z28 SS 30th Anniversary Edition, a pre-production West Coast auto show model that's white with orange stripes. As we all filed out of the parking lot, a driver at a stop sign just let everyone go instead of taking his turn, and along the route, a lot of people turned and stared. Twenty Camaros in a row was something worth watching.

"I don't know if you inherit the car disease from somebody," said Blumfelder, whose uncle was a driver at GM's Desert Proving Grounds in Arizona. For some reason in 1987, as a fifteen-year-old in Florissant, another St. Louis suburb, he fell in love with a Hugger Orange 1969 Camaro Rally Sport SS that was available for three thousand dollars. It was mostly primer and he spent all his savings on it. "My dad had a fit," he remembered. "He didn't understand, but I always liked the way Camaros looked. I needed one of those cars." Despite his misgivings, Blumfelder's father drove the car home for his underage son and now sometimes joins him at car shows.

A thirty-five-year-old auto-damage appraiser for an insurance company who spends six to ten hours a week on his three Camaros, Blumfelder wore a white golf shirt with chequered trim and the club logo (an arch and a blue Chevrolet cross with "Camaro" written in it). His 2002 Camaro ZL1 has just eighteen miles on the odometer—it is, in car-guy jargon, a "trailer queen." He'd bought the fourth-generation Camaro as a collector's item, figuring that as one of the last ones ever made, it would only become more valuable. (GM's decision to relaunch the old classic with a fifth generation that will go on sale in 2009 may threaten the value of Blumfelder's investment, but he's excited about the car's return.) As he was listing his vehicles, including a Chevy 454 pickup, he sheepishly warned me that one of them was from a different manufacturer. Here it is, I thought, a Japanese car. But no, his idea of stepping out was to buy a diesel truck from Dodge.

Many people assume that the current fascination with Camaros, Mustangs and other popular cars from the 1960s is little more than a bunch of aging baby boomers wanting to relive their youth and finally having enough money to do something about it. But Blumfelder's affection for Camaros has nothing to do with nostalgia; after all, his first one was built before he was born. And he believes the car's appeal cuts across all generations: "The other day I was at the gas station with my '69 and a kid—maybe thirteen, fourteen—rode up on his skateboard. He had a camera phone and he was snapping pictures. That was pretty cool and it was good to see that from someone younger."

Blumfelder joined the club a few months after it started in 1989 and later did a five-year stint as president. The spring and fall cruises are the events he enjoys the most. "It's not so much the drive," he told me, though he loves the drive, "it's more the camaraderie because the car brought us all together."

THAT CAMARADERIE is fitting given that *camaro* is an old French slang term for friend, pal or comrade. (There's also a story, perhaps apocryphal, that some Chevrolet executives initially tried to convince people that a Camaro was a "small, vicious animal that eats Mustangs.") Scott Settlemire, a thirty-year GM veteran, is now manager of shows and exhibits for Chevrolet, but he was the product manager and assistant brand manager for the Camaro before the company stopped production. The decision was so unpopular that Settlemire received obscene phone calls as well as threatening letters and emails. "People were really up in arms," he said. "But they were preaching to the choir with me." Indeed, the Camaro has been a passion of his since he first saw one. His father and uncle owned Chevy dealerships in the Pittsburgh area, so the twelve-year-old got a sneak peak at a bolero-red convertible Rally Sport nearly three weeks before the official launch. "I thought that was the most beautiful car I'd ever seen." Since then, he's bought a dozen of them and still owns two. "I've just always been crazy about the car. It's performance American-style. On a really bad day at work you go out there at nine o'clock at night and you feel really bad and you crank over that V8 engine and you hear that sound and you take off down that street and it can't help but put a smile on your face."

Despite his new job, he keeps in touch with enthusiasts of the Camaro and its F-body cousin, the Pontiac Firebird. Also produced from 1967 until 2002, the Firebird still has its fans—many of whom are bummed their car isn't also returning. While it may not be as iconic as the Camaro, the Firebird has its own place in popular culture. In *American Beauty*, Lester Burnham, played by Kevin Spacey, is a middle-aged guy stuck in a soulless marriage to an unpleasant wife. He quits his job and embraces his mid-life crisis. After he sells his Toyota, his wife comes home and asks: "Uh, whose car is that out front?"

"Mine," he says. "1970 Pontiac Firebird. The car I've always wanted and now I have it. I rule!"

Settlemire keeps about a thousand names on an email list so he can send updates to club presidents and webmasters—including some in Sweden, Germany and Australia—who forward the messages or post them on their websites. Settlemire believes club members are the company's best ambassadors: "And, frankly, I think the letters we got from them over the years are one of the reasons the Camaro is coming back off hiatus." When he visits a city, he'll invite local clubs to meet him in a hotel lobby for a drink and some car talk; sometimes three people show up, sometimes fifty do. He also arranged for 250 club members and other enthusiasts to attend the unveiling of the fifth-generation Camaro in January 2006. Some people within the company worried the move might backfire if the response was underwhelming, but his confidence proved well founded. "We had full-grown men in tears," he said. "People get emotional over this car."

THOUGH IT WAS a little too early for much colour in the trees, the drive through the country outside St. Louis featured enough hills and curves to make it fun for the drivers, who cruised at a leisurely pace. I was surprised at how slowly the procession moved until I learned that the club's unofficial motto is, "Drive slow, stop often and eat a lot." Judging by the girth of many of the club members, it's appropriate. Jim Hairston drove a white 1996 Brickyard pace car and joked about his "porn-sized clothes—triple XL." But it's also an indication that while the members are serious about their cars, they don't take themselves too seriously. "If you can't take a joke," Bill Robison warned me, "you don't need to be in this club. I'll tell you that right now."

The first stop was a parking lot at Meramec State Park. According to Hoefel's route map, they had an hour to "explore the park," but everyone just got out of their cars to gab and tease each other. After a while, we drove up to another parking lot that was empty, and the drivers lined their cars up in four rows of five for a picture-taking session. I rode with Robison in a Z28 pace car that was black and white with a T-top and automatic transmission. (Auto races use a pace car to limit speed after a collision or because of an obstruction on the track. The Indianapolis 500 has selected the Camaro as the pace car four times, giving Chevrolet an opportunity to produce a limited run of highly prized replicas.)

A fifty-two-year-old maintenance mechanic and truck driver for an asphalt construction company, Robison had dirt under his fingernails and a bushy moustache and goatee (having only recently shaved a beard that made him look like Uncle Jesse on *The Dukes of Hazzard*).

"How many Camaros do you own?" I asked.

"More than I need, less than I want."

In the past, to make some extra dough, he would buy one, drive it for six months while fixing it up, then sell it and buy another one. Today, he owns a 1993 pace car; a 1969 pace car that he bought in 1974 and still drives; an original, unrestored 1967 Coupe that he hasn't driven in about ten years; and a 1967 pace car he just acquired that also needs restoring. Another past president of the Gateway club and a member since 1989, he spends ten to fifteen hours a week on his cars, often with his thirty-year-old son, Derrick, who owns three Camaros of his own.

Robison is also a Corvair collector, though he's now down to just one, a 1964 Monza Coupe that still needs a lot of work. The Chevrolet Corvair became one of the most controversial cars in automobile history after Ralph Nader wrote *Unsafe at Any Speed*, his attack on automakers for selling deathtraps. The 1965 book, which uses the Corvair as Exhibit A, made Nader a household name and began a long march of safety improvements. But Robison believes the Corvair was unfairly maligned. While he conceded that they leaked oil and some of the materials weren't the best quality, a lot of owners didn't follow the owner's manual; many people, for example, over-inflated the tires. As for Nader's campaign, Robison believes the consumer advocate used film that Ford had cooked up to misrepresent the competition. "People have taken the film footage that Ralph Nader used to show the poor handling of the Corvair and slowed it down and you can see that the rear shocks were removed," he contended, making me imagine Monza lovers scrutinizing the footage the way conspiracy theorists obsess over the Zapruder film. "The Ford Motor Company wanted to show how much better their Mustang handled compared to the Corvair, and Nader took the film without researching it." Robison doesn't hold a grudge against Mustangs, but he doesn't own any. "I actually think they're cheaper-built, but they're all cars," he said. "They're just like people—they're all different, you know."

We stopped for lunch at Buffalo's Southwest Cafe, a chain restaurant located beside a Wal-Mart in Sullivan, Missouri. There were forty of us sitting at the tables arranged in a big U in a private room. The club has sixty-nine members, and the core group plus a few others showed up at the Fall Colors Tour. The oldest was seventy-eight-year-old Charlie Rothweiler; the youngest was a baby that a young couple had brought along. Bob Lance, a tugboat captain with a red 2000 convertible hails from Scott City, 120 miles away in the southeastern part of the state, but he tried a

Camaro club closer to home and after one year, didn't renew his membership.

As president, Steitz made sure to go around the table at lunch and say a few words to everyone. A mechanic with Saturn, he wore a white golf shirt with the club logo, a club cap and a name tag. He has four Camaros—all from 1970, the first year of the second generation—including one he's restoring and a brown Z28 trailer queen.

The lunchtime conversation was dominated by talk about engines, paint jobs and bodywork—and lots of ribbing. Blumfelder took good-natured grief over his trailer queen, his model Camaros that are still in their original boxes and when he was going to get married. As Hairston and Al Rothweiler mugged for a camera, Hairston rammed a finger into one of his nostrils. By the end of lunch, at least one bun had been tossed and several more had been stashed away for later use.

While there was no alcohol on the table, there was a lot of fried food. At least one person ordered and ate twenty-four chicken wings and some people had dessert. Briann Hoefel, who drives a Honda and teaches dietetics at a local junior collage, sat across from me. In a departure from all the car chatter, we discussed the obesity epidemic in America, but she didn't mention anything about the role our addiction to the automobile plays in that problem.

After lunch, I rode with Al Rothweiler, while his friend Mark Campbell moved to the back seat. A club member even though he doesn't own a Camaro, Campbell owns a Gremlin, which is a source of great mirth for Rothweiler. An American Motors subcompact introduced in 1970, the Gremlin sold well but developed a reputation for being poorly made and eventually became ironic shorthand for the wacky futility of the 1970s. The Camaro, in contrast, reeked of cool back then.

We were riding in a 1969 Camaro SS-427 that belongs to Rothweiler's dad. Restored in 1983, the car is Daytona Yellow, which makes it stand out even in a group of Camaros. "I get a lot of thumbs up from people," said Rothweiler, who wore his club name tag—he was, after all, the one who'd suggested members get them in the first place—and has close-cropped, thinning hair, oversized aviator glasses and a big gut. I'd been told he came up with the club motto, though when I asked him about it, he assured me it was a group effort. Just then, Steve Blumfelder drove up beside us and we saw three buns from the restaurant stuck on his antenna.

Like a lot of car lovers, Rothweiler has trouble explaining what it is about the Camaro that appeals to him so much. He's always been around specialty cars because his father has owned a 1930 Auburn since 1952. "And when I was in high school, a friend had a '69 Camaro and I kinda lusted for one," he explained. "I guess I was young and at that impressionable point that that's what I noticed." A car crush, it seems, just isn't that complex.

The next, and final, stop was just a few minutes away at the Antique Toy Museum on Route 66 in Stanton. The collection included many toy cars and trucks, some dating from the 1920s. I remembered owning a few, including Dinky Toys, Matchbox cars, Tonka trucks and, especially, Hot Wheels. Mattel released the toy cars in 1968 and I spent hours and hours racing them on the loops, jumps and curves of the set's plastic orange track. Among the first sixteen models, all made of die-cast metal, were the Camaro, the Mustang and the Corvette.

Outside the museum, I chatted with Charlie Connoyer, the club's secretary, treasurer and newsletter editor. The former Anheuser-Busch project engineer took early retirement thirteen years ago, which means that unlike the others, he has time for golf as well as cars. He joined the club in 2000 after Steitz, his son-in-law, convinced him to buy a Camaro. He now owns three: his original 1972 Rally Sport; a 1973 Z28, which he bought in 2004; and a Z28 30th Anniversary Edition, which he bought last year. "It's like an addiction," he admitted. "One's not enough."

He has a basement full of trophies from car shows, but the hardware offers just a few seconds of ego gratification. "I go to shows to BS with other club members and to watch people come up and ogle my car." He particularly enjoys it when an ogler says, "I had one like that," or "My dad had one." He's been to shows that have forty cars in a class and others that have three (and if there's first-, second- and third-place trophies, everybody wins one). "If you're going for a trophy, you're going for the wrong reason," he told me the next day when I called him to continue our chat. "I've got a basement full of trophies that my wife says I've got to give to the Boy Scouts." The shows are often charity fundraisers and many have good food, which he admits is part of the attraction. He has another son-in-law who is a Mustang guy. "We don't hold it against him and we let him come with us."

For Connoyer, the Camaro club is all about the people: "Without the folks, you don't have a club." Still, getting members out to events is one thing; convincing them to become officers is another. The treasurer position isn't onerous (he writes about a dozen cheques a year) and as secretary he checks the post office box occasionally, but as editor of the monthly newsletter, he finds filling six pages in the winter tough (summer's not so bad because there are so many shows and other events). Though an email newsletter would be less time-consuming, he thinks hard copy is better because then the whole family reads it. When he joined, no wives ever showed up at events, but at the Fall Colours Tour, several wives, including Mary Connoyer, showed up. So did several sons, including Tim Steitz, who'd just turned sixteen and is into cars in general and Camaros in particular, though he's not likely to get his hands on his dad's treasures any time soon. "Unfortunately, he's going to end up driving a Saturn for a while," Connoyer said. "He has a better chance of driving one of his granddad's Camaros."

THE IDEA that people's social lives could revolve around a car seems so American to me—right up there with high-school football on Friday evenings and Sunday mornings at church. But as I discovered in Argentina, the car club is an international phenomenon, and though the nature of the relationship with the car may vary in other countries, the passion is just as strong.

At 7:30 in the evening, the traffic was still heavy in Buenos Aires and on the highway, so the travel time to the old suburb of Monte Grande was about an hour, double the return drive. Our destination was a massive old building that was once a linen factory but is now home to about two hundred cars owned by the 350-member Club de Automóviles Clásicos de Esteban Echeverría. Ruben Ferro, the vice-president, showed Carmen Merrifield—my wife and translator—and me around the chilly site, which had large ads for local businesses on the walls.

A tall, leonine man with a grey goatee and a twinkle in his eye, Ferro's two loves are women and cars. And, as if to prove it, he shamelessly flirted with Carmen while he enthusiastically showed us the cars. Four Model Ts, a Ford V8, a Second World War Jeep, a beautiful blue 1958 Impala and a 1973 Dodge racing car were among the vehicles in the large rooms at the front of the club. We moved along and Ferro pointed across a cavernous room to the *parilla*. He explained that it was the most important part of the club: the place where they eat and drink. Then he hailed a man named Alberto and asked him to get a key.

As we waited, our tour guide explained that we were about to enter a private room with a special collection. Once Alberto appeared and unlocked the door, we saw a row of cars draped with sheets and tarps. Ferro removed the covers slowly and dramatically, revealing one immaculate car after another: a yellow 1976 Mini Cooper; a silver 1985 Porsche; three Fiats, including a limited edition 1972 Sorpasso 1300 Series; a mustard Peugeot 404; and two Alfa Romeos. As he and Carmen replaced the sheet on one of them, he joked that he makes the bed at the club more than he does at home.

Actually, he probably wasn't joking. His charm had more than a dash of machismo in it. "The bigger the car, the more powerful the engine, the more manly the man is," he assured us. "It's the man's personality." But he added that as a man ages, his attraction to cars grows more sophisticated: "What do young people want? To feel the speed and power. And so they fall in love with cars. When the years go by they look for a more classic one, more sumptuous, with a softer line."

Just before we reached the final car in the room, club secretary Norberto Coelho joined us. His reading glasses dangled on a cord around his neck and he wore white running shoes and a tan flat cap with car pins on it. He was less refined and courtly than Ferro, but just as passionate. An expectant hush fell over all of us as they unveiled the highlight of the collection: a brick-coloured Torino 380, a legendary racing car made by Industrias Kaiser Argentina. Some people consider it the country's national car, noted Coelho, adding proudly, "It represents us."

As we left the collection, three younger men joined us and we all walked through a room with several BMW micro coupes on our way to a big room in the back that housed dozens of covered cars, including some of Ferro's own collection. He acquired his first set of wheels, a 1959 Chevrolet Impala, when he was fifteen. Since then he's owned, at one time or another, about a hundred cars and trucks, as well as company vehicles at his crane manufacturing business. He can't pick a favourite because he loved them all like they were his children. As I wondered if I should read anything into the fact that he has three daughters and seven cars, he admitted that he takes some grief at home. "My daughters tell me that I have too many cars," he said. "They question me as a father."

Among the cars he kept at the club were a red 1996 Camaro, a brown 1996 BMW 320 and a 1980 dark green Ford Falcon. The Falcon was Ford's answer to the small imports that had somehow snatched nearly 10 percent of the U.S. market. To Americans, it was an inexpensive compact, but since it could seat six it was big enough to be a family car. Introduced in the fall of 1959, the Falcon was such a hit—the company sold 417,000 in the first year—that Robert McNamara, the man behind the project, earned a promotion. In 1960, he became the first president of the company who wasn't a member of the Ford family. His stay at the top was brief, though, because before long President John F. Kennedy appointed him Secretary of Defense.

Ford made and sold the Falcon in the United States until 1970, but the car had an even longer and more successful life in other parts of the world, where many saw it as a mid-size model. In Australia, it remains the company's best-seller. And in Argentina, the Falcon was not just the most-produced car, with half a million built between 1962 and 1991, but also a hugely important one culturally. The Falcon was a racing car, a family car, a taxi, a police car—and, from 1976 to 1983, a sinister symbol of the country's military dictatorship and the "Dirty War" that the generals who ruled after the *coup d'état* waged against their own people. Death squads used dark green Falcons to "disappear" trade unionists, artists, students and anyone else who might oppose or question the junta. Since the squads illegally arrested, tortured or killed an estimated thirty thousand people, the car now stirs bitter emotions for many Argentines. (Lawrence Thornton's 1988 novel, *Imagining Argentina*, does a hauntingly good job of capturing the ominous mood those dark green birds of prey created.) Even today, some people in Buenos Aires won't get into a taxi if it's a Falcon, and a tour operator in the northern city of Salta, who would have been just four or five when the dictatorship crumbled, told me, "I don't like it when I see a Ford Falcon. I get bad memories."

But not everyone feels that way. "It's a car that always works. It is faithful, noble and safe," said Coelho. "The mechanics are simple. It always runs and it doesn't leave you on the road." And, as it turned out, the three men who had joined us were from the Club Amigos del Ford Falcon. One of them was Oscar Mota, an organizer of that 350-member organization, whom I'd arranged to meet. He'd brought along two younger members, Adrian Alejandro and Daniel Dominquez.

Just as we were introducing ourselves, another man appeared and announced, "Food is ready!"

"Will you have your meeting while you eat?" Carmen asked.

"No, we're done," replied Coelho. "Otherwise we'll fight. Now we'll continue talking about cars."

We walked back to the *parilla* and into a festive scene. The room wasn't much—the white walls were covered with framed drawings of old cars, club photos and a large flag of the club logo—but about thirty boisterous men, all talking at once, sat at a long, thin table covered in a white tablecloth and filled with white plates, bottles of wine and big plastic containers of Coke. As we walked in, the men abruptly fell silent, swivelled their heads and stared at the woman entering the room.

We joined Dominquez, Alejandro and Mota at a small, round table at the end of the long, thin one. The dinner was sausage, seriously well-done beef and salad; the conversation was cars. The son of a Falcon owner, Dominquez, a curly-headed man who works for a doors and windows business, first fell in love with the car when he went to races as a boy. After selling one four years ago so he could get married and buy a house, he bought a 1979 Falcon Sprint a year ago. The clean-cut Alejandro, who was dressed in a white sweater and works in foreign investment for an oil company, bought a 1978 Falcon two years ago for ten thousand dollars. His father has owned a Falcon for thirty years. Their club's only requirement is that members must keep their cars in good condition, meaning that the owners of the many beat-up ones on the streets of Buenos Aires need not apply. Alejandro admitted that most wives, including his, aren't that supportive. "They don't understand what we feel," he said. "We polish our cars. We pet them. So they don't get it. They don't understand the way we take better care of our cars than of our wives."

A burly guy in his forties with curly dark hair and large wire-frame glasses, Mota looked a bit like hockey great Phil Esposito and had the hands of a working man: thick, rough and lined with grease. All of the men on Mota's father's side of the family were car lovers and he now owns three Falcons: a 1962 model built in the United States, a 1969 Futura and a 1979 Sprint. When Carmen wondered why he needed three, he said, "They are different."

I suspected that the mechanic was taciturn at the best of times, but he was clearly skeptical about us, and his apprehension grew as we inched toward the topic of the Falcon's controversial history. His answers were short and curt, with none of the flamboyant pride we'd seen in Ferro. In fact, I figured he'd brought Alejandro and Dominquez along as backup.

Sure enough, Dominquez, who would have been a small boy during the Dirty War, was the one who spoke to the controversy. That government, he pointed out, also had Torinos and Chevrolets, but drove Falcons the most for the same reason everyone else did: they were the most reliable. And that part of the car's history doesn't disturb him any more than a Jeep lover would mind that armies use Jeeps. "The government gave it a bad reputation, but the car isn't to blame for those acts," he said. "The people who blame the car rather than the military are just looking for something to blame."

Once we moved past that subject, Mota relaxed a bit and told us that he spends about six hours a week on his cars and that his wife shares his passion. He would love to own a Ferrari but can't afford one. Eventually, without saying a word, he left the table, walked over to where the photos hung on the wall and took something down as the men at the long table razzed him loudly. He brought it back and handed it to us. Under the glass were a photo of Mota's gleaming turquoise 1962 Falcon, a Ford logo and some text that began, "I have a heart that's blue and oval," and went on to explain what each of the letters in Ford stands for: F is for strength; O is for pride; R is for racing hard and reliability; D is for the destiny that put the Falcon at his side to be his companion, his loyal friend, more than something that just transports him, his guide, his Ford for life. "If I die of old age," it ended, "you will keep on running." This quiet man, for whom expressing emotion did not appear easy, had written a love letter to his car.

13 Glendale
"The Biggest Wins"

THREE WEEKS into my road trip, I'd travelled over 3,200 miles and it was time for some automotive and personal maintenance. The car needed an oil change and a good cleaning, and I needed to do a load of laundry and get in a workout. So I dropped my machine off at a nearby Grease Monkey franchise and then walked a few blocks to a Bally's for some overdue exercise.

My hotel was in Glendale through chance more than anything else. I'd checked in there on Friday evening because it was close to Denver University, where Scott and I went to see a hockey game. I spent Saturday night in Colorado Springs and, after hiking in the Garden of the Gods on Sunday, returned to the hotel because it was the most luxurious place I'd stayed so far on my trip and the early-week room rates were more appealing than what I could get downtown.

Bisected by Cherry Creek, Glendale is an inner suburb of Denver dominated by offices, shopping malls and apartment buildings. The small enclave's density of more than five thousand people per square mile is not particularly high, but it's not an inviting environment, so it's the sort of place that gives succor to those who say a dense existence is an unpleasant one. Of course, the real problem is not the density but the urban design. The streets are too wide and the traffic lights are timed for drivers rather than pedestrians. What really surprised me, though, was the impatience some drivers had for those of us on foot.

Fortunately, no one ran me over and I made it to the gym and back in one piece. So I took my tuned-up vehicle to a nearby car wash. It cost $16.95, about what I pay at home, and I was surprised to see everyone in front of me tipping. Americans do tend to be more generous tippers than Canadians, but I couldn't remember ever seeing anyone tip at a car wash. Then I saw how long the employees spent on the car after it had gone through the wash— they polished and buffed everything. One man with two bottles went to work on the wheels, and the boss made another guy go back at the dash and the inside of the windshield twice. I was so impressed that I pulled a few bucks out of my pocket. My car hadn't looked that good in years.

THE ANNOYED LOOKS on the faces of drivers forced to wait as I crossed the street—with the lights—in Glendale was at least better than the complete contempt drivers have for pedestrians in Argentina. Buenos Aires is, like many European cities, a great walking town, but pedestrians have to worry about two things. First, everyone, it seems, owns a dog and yet no one poops and scoops. This presents a dilemma: enjoy the beautiful architecture or play it safe and watch underfoot. Second, when it comes to crossing the street, even at a light, it's definitely a case of pedestrian beware.

My wife and I arrived in Buenos Aires on a Sunday afternoon and, despite having heard stories about the traffic problems, zoomed into town. The streets were still damp, but the rain had stopped and there were hardly any cars on the highway or near our hotel in San Telmo, one of the oldest barrios in the city. After checking in, we walked among the antique stalls along Defensa, which becomes a pedestrian mall on Sundays for the market. But even at the cross streets, and when we got to Plaza de Mayo, we saw few cars.

Though it's in South America, Buenos Aires has a European feel to its cityscape, cuisine and culture because of waves of immigration from countries such as Italy, Spain and Germany. Almost 2.8 million people live in the city, which has a density of more than 35,000 per square mile, but the population isn't growing because so many residents are leaving town. The metropolitan area has a population of more than 12 million. Ruben Ferro, the car club vice-president, told us many people have tired of the congestion and crime in the city and are moving to the suburbs and even into gated communities. "So they need to have two or three cars," he said. "We are getting more American."

Sure enough, at 5:30 Monday morning, the roar of cars woke me up. Although ownership rates are much lower than in the United States, they are rising; in fact, the city is adding between three and four hundred thousand cars a year and, as the number of old clunkers on the road suggest, retiring few. Almost everyone drives stick, and small cars predominate: Volkswagens, Renaults, Peugeots, Fiats, Hondas, small Chevrolets, Ford Fiestas and some old Falcons. Minivans, SUVs and pickups are rare and tend to be driven by people who need them for work. With so many old cars on the road, toxin-spewing tailpipes are common. Unlike Mexico City, though, Buenos Aires is on the plains and the good winds blow most of the pollution away.

Rather than orderly congestion, the traffic is a (mostly) fluid chaos with much bobbing and weaving. The lane lines appear to be mere suggestions as *Porteños*, as the residents call themselves, prefer to squeeze more cars across a road than it's designed for. Meanwhile, signalling lane changes is evidently optional—and probably even a sign of weakness. Everyone goes in every direction at once and stop signs are rare, so if there's no traffic light, cars slow, look and go. Once, Carmen and I took a taxi to meet a friend who lived outside the downtown core. At one point, our taxi had to go through a busy street and there was no signal or stop sign; it slowed and then began to creep across. A couple of cars flashed their lights and kept going. Finally, our cabbie just bulled his way to the other side. More than once during my stay, I was sure we'd be T-boned. Yet no one ever hit us and I never even saw any fender-benders, though dented cars were everywhere.

The best place to see Buenos Aires traffic is on the Avenida 9 de Julio, a north–south boulevard that is 140 metres wide and is actually made up of three parallel roads. All that open space in a dense city is an impressive sight, but nineteen lanes of thick traffic create too much noise and pollution to make outdoor patios appealing. They also suggest the planners favoured cars too heavily—at the expense of pedestrian safety. And with the completion of connecting motorways in the mid-1990s, traffic on the boulevard tripled. "You could say it's three streets," observed Andres Borthagaray, the former undersecretary for traffic and transportation for the city, "or it's a motorway."

I met Borthagaray for an espresso in the lobby bar of the Panamericano Hotel on Avenida 9 de Julio. Now the director of the city's strategic planning council and a member of the steering committee at the Institut pour la Ville en Mouvement, an urban think tank sponsored by Peugeot Citroën, he has thick, dark hair parted on the side and showed up carrying a trench coat and a black briefcase and wearing a blue jacket over a salmon-coloured shirt and a blue V-neck sweater. He looked like a twelve-year-old dressed up for his school photo. A bow tie would have been the perfect final touch. An architect with training and experience in urban planning as well public policy and government, he said, "Political skills are the most important to get things done."

Borthagaray drives his Renault Megan mostly on weekends, preferring to take the subway or a taxi to work. "I like to drive. I feel the difference between a good car and a standard car. But it's not my number one priority," he said. "For me, the question is not whether one should have a car, if one can, but whether the car is the best way to go for everyday trips downtown."

Given the good walking and the cheap and plentiful taxis—there are thirty-eight thousand licensed cabs in the city and a lot of unlicensed ones—my wife and I hadn't been in a rush to ride the subway (called *el subte*). Frankly, she was reluctant because of her experiences on the Mexico City metro. But I convinced her to take it with me to the Panamericano and she was pleasantly surprised. While it was old—the first station opened in 1913—it was clean and safe and the riders appeared to be from a mix of socioeconomic classes. It was also, at three o'clock in the afternoon, packed.

Still, not even 10 percent of *Porteños* take the subway, and the percentage of people commuting by all forms of public transportation is actually shrinking as more and more people drive. The government has neglected the commuter rail infrastructure, and the system has become less reliable with the shift in focus to building motorways in the last couple of decades. Today, more people drive their cars than ride the bus, which had been the most popular form of transportation in the city. And while the subway system is expanding at about a kilometre a year, Borthagaray thinks it should be expanding even faster. He'd also like to see the speed, comfort and condition of the buses improve. On the roads, he suggests higher parking fees and HOV lanes for carpoolers and buses. He respects people's freedom to travel the way they want, but if their choices hurt society as a whole, "The ones who decide to do that should assume part of the responsibility."

Argentina is among the most dangerous places in the world for car crashes, especially for pedestrians. Driver fatigue, alcohol and dangerous passing are the major causes of highway deaths. As for the pedestrian slaughter, Borthagaray attributes it to three factors. One, many intersections are uncontrolled. Two, inattention to car safety means that many vehicles are in such bad shape that the brakes don't work. Three, driver education is poor, drunk driving is too common and there's a general indifference to the rules of the road and the vulnerability of pedestrians.

"I don't get the impression there's much enforcement here," I suggested.

"You have the right impression," he replied with a little laugh. "That's one of the big problems."

Indeed, although there's a heavy police presence in this country, traffic infractions seem to be the last thing on the minds of the cops. Part of the problem is that the police are federal, with little interest in municipal matters, so driving infractions are a low priority (this doesn't have to be the case—the police in Paris are federal and they enforce rules better than they do in Buenos Aires). "We are cynical," he admitted. "On the one hand, we want more enforcement. On the other, we don't respect the law." He thinks education campaigns about the high death rate could make it possible for Argentines to accept more enforcement, but so far all the government has tried are two-day blitzes that no one takes seriously.

Until enforcement improves, pedestrians will have to be ever vigilant—and not just in Buenos Aires. "It's the law of the jungle," one car lover in the northern city of Salta told me. "The biggest wins."

WAYNE CHERRY, GM's retired vice-president of design, spent twenty-six years in Britain and Germany with the company, so he's familiar with driving habits on both sides of the Atlantic. "In Europe, people have a lot of discipline in the way they drive," he told me, noting that over there, drivers communicate with their lights, use their turn signals and respect lanes. "And in America, they ... kind of ... don't. I think that's part of the pioneering spirit."

He then told a story about finding himself in a discussion about turn signals after he returned to the States. At one point he asked, "Why do we need them? Nobody uses them here."

If he thought the United States was bad, I replied, he should go to Argentina. Without missing a beat, he said, "Well, see, there are no pedestrians in North America, so that helps. There are no sidewalks and nobody walks."

His tone was jocular, but I wondered if it was a case of true words spoken in jest. He was, after all, a former auto exec. But while there certainly are places where no one gets around by foot, a few American cities are ideal for walking. And others are making an effort to encourage pedestrians, as I discovered when I left Glendale and moved into a hotel in downtown Denver.

14 Denver
Pedestrians Wanted

IN 1978, having just finished high school, James van Hemert and two friends rode their bicycles across Canada. First, they dipped their tires in the Pacific Ocean at Tofino, on the west coast of Vancouver Island; three months later, they dunked their wheels in the Atlantic Ocean at Halifax, Nova Scotia. Along with being a lot of fun, the adventure taught him that there's more than one way to travel from place to place. "It opened things up for me in many ways," said van Hemert, who grew up in a car-filled suburb of Vancouver, British Columbia. "And I realized for the very first time in my life that I can use a bicycle to get around."

Today, the urban planner lives about a mile from his office at Denver University and commutes by walking or biking. Ever since his sixteen-year-old Toyota Camry died in 2005 after lasting 215,000 miles, his family has happily lived with one car. His wife commutes to work in their Plymouth Voyager, and if he needs a car, he rents one. Most people equate automobiles with freedom, and the more they have, the greater the independence, but the executive director of DU's Rocky Mountain Land Use Institute doesn't see it that way. "Owning three cars is enslavement," he told me, citing all the time and money needed to maintain vehicles. "If we walk or bike, we can be free. That, in fact, is more freedom than being forced to buy three cars."

I met with van Hemert at Kaladi Brothers Coffee, a small but comfortable café and roaster of organic and fair trade coffee near the university. The place had a bohemian charm—and Steve McQueen posters in the restroom. At 7:30 a.m., van Hemert was in his usual haunt on the right side of the café at a table beside a bookshelf. A large, round insignia with the words "Kaladi Coffee Academy" on the top and "Intellectualize, Socialize, Revolutionize" on the bottom adorned one of the red clay–coloured walls. The half-dozen or so other men at the table were middle-aged or older, except for one slightly younger man with a shaved head and a young daughter. They weren't all professors, just an eclectic and politically diverse bunch that gathers for some lively discussion over their morning jolts of caffeine.

When I arrived, the topic inevitably turned to cars. One member of the round-table gang, Gerry Edelstein, kept on reading his paper, but every once in a while, he would lift his head and offer his iconoclastic point of view. First, he pointed out that the car was originally an environmental solution and argued that we'd never have had our highly developed society if we were still travelling by horse, to which someone else chimed in: "But we'd never be short of fertilizer." A few minutes later, the contrarian physicist took his eyes off *The New York Times* long enough to suggest that we should deplete all fossil fuels as fast as possible in order to ensure the development of alternatives: "I'd like to see a tax on all vehicles that get more than ten miles to the gallon."

As we moved to another table, van Hemert confided, "We're never sure if he's joking or not."

In the mid-1990s, van Hemert served as a planning director in Mississippi. He was already convinced of the wisdom of public transit, high-density development and mixed-use zoning. "But I kept my mouth shut. There was no hope. Southaven, Mississippi, is one hundred percent car culture. The only people who take a bus in that part of the country are the poor, and the bus service is rotten," he admitted, adding that even he drove a car everywhere. "The best I could do was to ask for sidewalks. People said, 'Why put sidewalks there? Nobody walks there.' I'm serious, that's what I was told. I could get sidewalks in residential areas, but not on major arterials."

Later, he moved to the planning department in Douglas County, Colorado, which includes Highlands Ranch, a community that became the poster child for sprawl when it made the cover of *National Geographic* in 1996. After he became chief planner for the county, his department had a chance to recraft some of the land use patterns. The 1979 plan for Highlands Ranch included two town centres. The first one was a dismal effort, and city hall ended up in a strip mall. When it came time to build the second one, van Hemert was determined to win a greater mix of uses, better design standards and pedestrian-oriented streets. A requirement for a minimum average height of twenty-eight feet produced a sense of enclosure and fostered more vitality; and, though it took a while, the engineering department agreed to slightly narrower streets. The town centre is not as dense as he would have liked because the developer couldn't afford to wait until enough demand for that kind of housing emerged, but some brownstone-style townhouses went up. And the developer built a parking garage rather than relying on surface lots. "As long as you still have surface parking, you can't create a very vibrant, immersive urban environment," explained van Hemert. His department also attracted a library branch. Allowing a big-box Home Depot to move in was a sacrifice, but it did drive business to the other retailers, 80 percent of which aren't chain stores.

Despite that success, qualified as it may have been, he jumped to the Land Use Institute, an interdisciplinary forum for planning and environmental issues, in 2004. He was tired of his daily fifty-mile commute and fed up with all the shortsighted and selfish opposition that too many good ideas face from residents—or, as he calls them, the "incumbent club"—who are determined to fight anything in their backyard. "Quite frankly," he confessed when I asked why he'd switched into academia, "I was sick of NIMBYs."

Dressed in a tweed sport coat over an indigo shirt, van Hemert has a long, slender face and a beard. Although calm and mild mannered, he was clearly passionate about the subject of sprawl and our need to get over the car. As he talked, he often bounced around in his seat or leaned forward with excitement. The smell of the fresh coffee beans inside the café was intoxicating and stayed with me—perhaps in my clothes and hair—for hours after I left. Many of van Hemert's ideas stayed with me even longer.

MY HALF-HOUR JAUNT to Kaladi had been a great way to start the day. If the old sailors' adage held, the red sky suggested that the forecasts for a coming snowstorm would prove true, but Denver is just fifteen miles east of the foothills and I enjoyed the morning light on the Rocky Mountains as I strode west along Evans Avenue. The people of Colorado are proud that they live in the thinnest state in the nation, but self-selection has a lot to do with it since skiers, mountain bikers and other active people move here for the recreational opportunities. That's one reason the metropolitan area now has a population of more than 2.3 million.

But the geography has its downside: even the city government's website admits, "To tackle long distances and tough terrain, Coloradoans have become auto-dependent." With one car for every man, woman and child, Denver's ownership rate is one of the highest in the country. In the 1990s, an outer ring of new freeways immediately became clogged, and even after the Regional Transportation District (RTD) started building a light rail system, highway congestion remained the top complaint for many residents. So while the region is booming, most of the growth has been of the car-fuelled variety; even Denver proper—population: 575,000—has a density under 3,700 people per square mile.

It's a problem van Hemert spends a lot of time thinking about. During the summer, he and two law professors co-wrote an op-ed piece for the *Denver Post* that questioned whether Mayor John Hickenlooper's "Greenprint Denver" plan—which aims to cut greenhouse gas emissions, increase tree cover and promote recycling—was green enough. Instead of advocating feel-good measures, the authors argued, the mayor needed to get serious: "A city in which more people live closer to where they work and shop is a cleaner city (less air pollution from vehicles), a more efficient city (less fuel consumption), and a healthier city (more people bike or walk). If you commute 50 miles every day by car (even with a hybrid), no quantity of reusable shopping bags is going to balance out the pollution you emit and the fuel you consume."

The piece didn't get much of a reaction from the round-table gang—which disappointed van Hemert—but a few days later, Vincent Carroll, the editorial page editor at the rival *Rocky Mountain News*, responded with a column that took particular umbrage at this line: "We will be happier, healthier, richer, more efficient and more environmentally friendly if there are more of us per square mile." He blustered that "a more dubious claim can hardly be imagined," but his rebuttal was unconvincing. In response to the suggestion that a denser city is a more efficient one, Carroll wrote, "The claim that low-density housing wastes resources on roads, utilities and public services such as trash pickup has been around since at least 1973 when the Council on Environmental Quality released a report titled 'The Costs of Sprawl.' But this conclusion remains a matter of debate, and many serious scholars have taken issue with it over the years." This is a classic tactic for conservatives: dismiss as junk science any research that challenges their reactionary ideology. But the most depressing aspect of Carroll's libertarian argument was that it reinforced the misconception—far too common in far too many places—that living "cheek-by-jowl with our neighbours" is unpleasant.

High density doesn't have to mean run-down tenements or living on the twenty-fifth floor in a city that never sleeps. True, New York City isn't for everyone; indeed, while some people wish they lived in SoHo or the Upper East Side, many more couldn't imagine a worse fate. And plenty of long-time Manhattan residents eventually make the move to New Jersey or Connecticut after tiring of the noise, the traffic and the yardless lifestyle. Still, van Hemert calls Manhattan the greenest place in America. "If you live in the bucolic countryside on five acres, you need three cars to survive. You have a huge house so you're burning up a lot more fossil fuel and you acquire more stuff," he argued. "There's nothing very green about it when you look at your ecological footprint and the amount you're contributing to climate change."

Mid-rise buildings as low as five stories offer an effective and comforting alternative to intimidating towers, and even neighbourhoods filled with single-family houses don't have to take up so much land. "We love single-family homes in America," said van Hemert. "But if we narrow our streets a little bit and are more clever about how we arrange things, we can still have high density." Along with a greater concentration of units—in California, for example, some developers are building ten to twelve homes to the acre—he'd like to see more basement suites, granny flats, coach houses and apartments over garages. They provide affordable housing for those who need it and income for homeowners. By discouraging these dwellings, cities such as Denver are encouraging sprawl; fortunately, more and more residents are adding units anyway.

Even bigger change is likely to come with Denver's aggressive transit expansion. Americans don't often vote for more taxes and, true to form, the residents of the region defeated a 1997 proposal to pay for expanded public transit by boosting the sales tax. But advocacy groups, the business community, governments and some citizens worked tirelessly toward a second vote, and in 2004 the idea passed. Funded by the 0.4 percent increase in the sales tax as well as federal and other money, FasTracks is a twelve-year, $4.7-billion plan that will give the region 119 miles of new light rail and commuter train service and 18 miles of bus rapid transit. Knowing that the existing light rail service, though limited, had exceeded ridership expectations from the first day, cities in the region quickly fought for stations and to get their line built first.

A few weeks after I met with van Hemert, the new nineteen-mile Southeast Corridor light rail line opened as part of project called T-REX (from Transportation Expansion), which included additional lanes and other improvements to Interstate 25. The infrastructure investment was one reason van Hemert, who knows people who have sold their homes and bought places within walking distance of new stations, thinks sprawl can be conquered in Denver. "There's a strong link between transportation and land use. If all you build are freeways and six-lane arterials, all you get are single-family homes spread all the way to Kansas," he argued, adding that the new line will make a huge difference. "Around the stations, you're already seeing changes in the land use pattern and you're seeing changes in the way properties are marketed."

Not that he didn't have some reservations. For one thing, density follows transit only if zoning allows it. But around some stations, the rules have stayed the same because either the planners couldn't decide what to do or neighbours opposed any changes. "It's a huge waste to have a station that serves single-family residential and a few strip centres," he said. "But as you go farther south, where there was more opportunity, you're seeing some very high-density development that has already been constructed in anticipation of the light rail lines." The planning community tends to prefer higher densities, more mixed use and a richer array of amenities, but neighbourhoods don't want change, so battles between progressive planners and reactionary residents are hard to avoid. It's not just that people in single-family homes oppose out-of-scale apartment towers going up right next door—that might be understandable—but those in three-hundred-thousand-dollar houses fight proposals for two-hundred-thousand-dollar houses. That's making developers and planners strange bed-fellows. "The market will generally want more density and mixed use," noted van Hemert, "so actually I often feel more comfortable speaking with developers and real estate professionals than the incumbent club."

Parking never fails to rile up the incumbents. Because it's a problem at some existing stations, the FasTrack plan calls for twenty-one thousand new spots, and all but one of thirteen stations on the new line offer free parking. "Even though we're building all this light rail, it's completely car dominated," he said. "We want more people to walk, but people are not getting out of their cars, they're driving to the stations, and light rail is just a convenient way to save on the hassle of parking downtown." When people living near the stations complain that they don't want other people's cars on their streets, the local politicians listen. "We shouldn't be counting on parking garages," argued van Hemert. "We should be counting on people coming by bike, by foot and by bus."

Enticing people onto buses, which bear the stigma of second-class transportation, is a challenge throughout North America, especially in the West. People who'll happily ride subways or streetcars shy away from buses even though they're cheaper to put on the road and more flexible because one breakdown doesn't snarl the whole system. Van Hemert's wife, who is originally from Montana, has never taken a bus in Denver. "She's a Western girl who loves her car," he said. But the city doesn't have the density—or the money—to build light rail for everyone, so people will have to learn to love, or at least not hate, the bus. Dedicated lanes will help drivers see the advantages of the bus; so will better stops. Too many are now in uninviting spots without shelters or benches—or even, in some cases, sidewalks. "That's the next step to making transit work in this city—making the bus-riding experience more acceptable to get people out of their cars."

Looking even farther into the future, van Hemert believes Denver will be the centre of an emerging Front Range megalopolis. Running from Cheyenne, Wyoming, down to Albuquerque, New Mexico, it could be home to more than 8.3 million people by 2035, an increase of more than 50 percent from the current population. "If that's going to be a sustainable, dynamic, economically competitive region—like a Los Angeles or a Boston to Washington corridor—we need to be linked by rail," argued van Hemert, who is the co-author of *True West: Authentic Development Patterns for Small Towns and Rural Areas*, a 2003 book that among other topics looks at car dependency in the West. In the short term, high-speed inter-city rail is a more expensive solution than highway expansion, but it's better for the environment, more likely to foster compact, mixed-use communities and be cheaper in the long run.

The region must also contend with a limited water supply. Since it's west of the hundredth meridian, Denver averages less than sixteen inches of precipitation a year, and some of the surrounding area doesn't receive even that much. Already large lots are becoming increasingly scarce as suburbs balk at the cost of delivering water to far-flung residents while developers are finding it cheaper and less hassle to build in the city, which already has the infrastructure in place.

Beyond the desire to conserve water, remain economically competitive and create more livable, healthier and ecological communities, van Hemert sees sprawl as a social justice issue. Since the country has more cars than drivers, it's easy to forget that nearly a third of Americans—including anyone too old or too young to drive, the handicapped and those who can't afford a car—don't drive. The Joad family in *The Grapes of Wrath* owned a truck during the Depression, but gas was cheap, parking was free and they didn't have to pay for insurance. A car is a much more expensive proposition today. Most of the people trapped in New Orleans during Hurricane Katrina didn't have a way to get out of town; they didn't have a car. And with our aging population, more and more people won't be able to drive because of failing eyesight, senility or other medical problems. "I don't think it's appropriate for us to be building communities where the only way to live an active, successful lifestyle is by owning two or three cars."

After some prodding, van Hemert gave Denver an average

grade on coping with the car. Like most other cities, it's still planning and building for the automobile, but attitudes are changing. When he and his family arrived a decade ago, there were only a few miles of light rail and people said, "This city will never go on the train. We are in the West, we love our cars and we have lots of space." That wasn't true. Even though he knows some drivers voted to fund transit with a tax increase only because they hoped others would use the train, leaving more room on the roads, light rail ridership has exceeded all projections. And he's heartened to see condos going up downtown and even around his university. The battle isn't over, but he likes the trends. "We have to make it a little bit more difficult to use the car, we have to make the place attractive and we have to make walking and biking the obvious ways to get around," he told me. "Really, what we're looking at is a paradigm shift in society, and it's happening here in Denver, but it's going to take time."

AFTER MY MEETING with van Hemert, I moved downtown. Although the Mile High City is polycentric, it has one of the stronger cores in the West. Established by gold prospectors in 1858, the place grew chaotically and not too beautifully. By 1890, Denver was the second-largest city in the West after San Francisco, with more than 106,000 people, but the downtown did not include a single park or public square. That changed dramatically once Robert W. Speer became mayor in 1904. "Denver can be made one of the ordinary cities of the country," he proclaimed, "or she can be made the Paris of America." He planted trees; built parks, playgrounds and parkways; preserved Cherry Creek; and erected statues. Heavily influenced by the then-popular City Beautiful movement, Speer also pushed for more attractive public buildings and created the Civic Center, a plaza just south of the central business district. Along with statues, fountains and formal gardens, the Civic Center is home to several public buildings, including the Denver Art Museum with its new addition designed by architect Daniel

Libeskind; the central branch of the Denver Public Library, built by the Andrew Carnegie Foundation; and the Colorado State Capitol.

The first thing I did was walk down the pedestrian mall on 16th Street. A lot of cities have experimented with car-free zones, with mixed results. People with money to spend soon tire of the clots of teenagers, the panhandlers and the ne'er-do-wells. Though the 16th Street Mall, which opened in 1982 along one of the city's major spines, had some of those less-desirables, it seemed reasonably healthy and I wondered if it helped that a free shuttle bus ran up and down the street.

Given that pedestrian malls are for tourists and shoppers, I wouldn't want to live on one. But that doesn't mean there aren't a lot of other places in central Denver that would be appealing. On Thursday, I woke up to the aftermath of the predicted blizzard and stayed put for a while. By the afternoon, though, I was keen for a walkabout. There was slush on the sidewalks and snow on awnings and cars, but while as much as a foot of snow had fallen in some nearby towns, downtown got a mix of rain and snow, and much of the snow was already beginning to melt. Still, it was cold and windy and, at first, a light rain fell. I headed over to the Civic Center and an up-and-coming neighbourhood known as the Golden Triangle. Then I walked down to LoDo. Denver's historic Lower Downtown is a gentrified neighbourhood that includes nightclubs, bars, restaurants, shops and galleries in the area between Coors Field, where the Rockies play baseball, and the Pepsi Center, where the Avalanche play hockey. Denver's Union Station is also here; like so many old train stations, it's grown tired—and, when I visited, was all but deserted. Not surprisingly, most people think the Beaux Arts–style building could be so much more, and the RTD, which owns it, has plans to turn the station into a transportation hub for the FasTracks expansion and make it the heart of a redevelopment project that will include residential, office and retail space.

As I walked around, Denver's potential was obvious. It has many good buildings with plenty of character—and a good number of cabs. All the downtown needed was more people. They are coming, though. Four residential buildings of forty storeys or more were going up while I was there, and the developers weren't investing in these condo projects as an altruistic experiment. They were doing it because they're convinced that, as in many cities across America, Denverites—especially empty-nester baby boomers and young first-time homebuyers—want to live downtown.

THAT NIGHT, I returned to LoDo to see Pulitzer Prize–winning author Richard Ford read at the Tattered Cover Book Store. Tucked away at the back of the second floor was a room full of people sitting on folding chairs. Ford is a guy about whom his friend Raymond Carver, the late, great American short story writer, once wrote, "There was an elegance about his bearing, his clothes, even his speech—which was poised and courtly and southern." The book he was promoting was *The Lay of the Land*, the third of a trilogy of novels about Frank Bascombe (who, while in his Chevy Suburban, thinks, "Why do so many things happen in cars? Are they the only interior life left?").

Someone from the audience asked why he'd made the Bascombe character a real estate agent. All Americans, Ford figured, were experts in real estate. It's true, home ownership is an obsession—and not a bad one—and where we live remains crucial to us. For decades, the settlement pattern of immigrants to North America followed a path from inner-city ethnic ghettos to better neighbourhoods often filled with the same people (in fact, that was part of the attraction). Moving meant a bigger house on a bigger lot on a more prestigious street. And for both immigrants and people who have been here for generations, the dream of a big yard and a white picket fence in the suburbs was a powerful motivator. In the last few decades, some people have even hankered for homes in gated communities.

Something different may be happening, if Rich McClintock is right. An advocate for smart growth in the Denver region for fifteen years, he believes a desirable location now has more to do with being close to our frequent destinations—where we work, shop and play—than the size of our yard or the reputation of the community. For young people, that means living close to bars and restaurants and galleries; for older people, it's being able to walk to a movie or the doctor's office or a quiet place to have coffee with friends. Even parents want to live where commute times are shorter and every member of the family has the option of walking or biking. "Change the place, change the land uses, change the destinations and you'll see changes in how people get around," said the native of Boston who moved out West twenty years ago. "Denver is a place where that is playing out. It has grown up around the car, but it's still growing quite significantly and there's much more of a sense now of it being a balanced place."

I met McClintock just a few hours before I left town. A consultant who does most of his work with public interest groups, he was also the founding program director of the Livable Communities Support Center, an organization dedicated to smart growth and policies that promote healthy living, and someone who worked on both campaigns to fund transit expansion through a sales tax increase. We sat in the Corner Bakery café at the south end of the 16th Street Mall. A chain operation, it had none of the charm of Kaladi Brothers Coffee, but then I wasn't there for the ambience.

As someone with kids, McClintock does have to drive every day but rarely spends more than fifteen minutes going anywhere. And a number of his trips are on foot or bike. "There are car worshippers and car haters, and for a whole bunch of us in the middle, it's a tool. I don't hate the car, I just don't want to spend time in it," he said, adding that he owns a 1992 Honda Accord and his wife drives a Toyota Highlander that seats seven so she can drive the couple's daughters and their friends to soccer. "I live in Congress Park, where I can walk to coffee, pizza, pharmacy, grocery store, yarn shop, hardware store, twelve restaurants—all within a fifteen-minute walk."

Convinced there's a backlash brewing against spending too much time in the car, he believes denser development offers the solution. "Time is the currency of families and people all over the world," said McClintock, who is greying and balding with a bushy moustache and glasses. "And there are benefits to arranging your life so you can spend more time with your family—playing a game in the living room or going for a bike ride or a walk because you have the time now given the way you've chosen to place where you work and live."

Like van Hemert, McClintock ranks his city in the middle of the pack as far as livable, walkable and bikable communities go. But, as a third-wave American city, Denver has an opportunity to not just get things right for its own citizens but be a model for others. First-wave cities, such as Boston, Chicago and New York were important centres long before the automobile. Though inner-city expressways and the flight to the suburbs did do some damage, these places generally had enough history and infrastructure to withstand the car. Second-wave cities, such as Detroit and St. Louis, weren't so lucky. Their metropolitan areas boomed in the years following the Second World War, when car culture dominated land use development, but the core wasn't strong enough to survive. The third wave, including Albuquerque and Denver, are booming now and developing as clusters of communities rather than as regions where the downtown struggles to hold its own against the sprawling suburbs. Planners, architects and politicians who once thought only of the car now increasingly add transit users, cyclists and pedestrians to the mix. "We're entering a third phase where the car is certainly a major part of the overall culture," argued McClintock, "but there are now many other factors influencing land use patterns."

Our health may depend on it. Too many people live in places where they have no choice but to drive. And since one of McClintock's daughters was born in 2000, estimates from the Centers for Disease Control that one child in three born that year will develop type 2 diabetes in his or her lifetime have special meaning for him. Obesity and inactivity are two of the greatest risk factors for the disease. As for Colorado being the thinnest state, he's unimpressed. "We're the best of a bad lot," he said. Worse, with the increasing dependence on the car, second-generation Coloradoans will be more sedentary. A teenager in Highlands Ranch with few options but to get around by car is more likely to be overweight than a teenager from the same socioeconomic background living in a walkable community: "Cultures that don't completely rely on cars are healthier."

Planners once used zoning regulations to separate homes from industrial areas because living close to slaughterhouses and factories was not just unpleasant but also unhealthy. Today, so many jobs are in clean settings such as offices, restaurants and stores that living close to work is no longer dangerous—in fact, separating those activities by long car commutes is what's damaging. "Now what we're starting to see is that for health reasons we need to bring those uses closer together again," McClintock pointed out. "So, ironically, public health has played a role both times."

The civic health of our society may also be at stake. In his influential 2000 book *Bowling Alone: The Collapse and Revival of American Community*, Robert D. Putnam makes the link between sprawl and the decline in social connectedness and engagement. Developers have long promoted the suburbs as offering the benefits of small-town living, including being a place where people know their neighbours. If that was ever true, it certainly isn't anymore. "Far from seeking small-town connectedness, suburban-ites kept to themselves, asking little of their neighbors and expecting little in return," according to Putnam. He goes on to quote writer and urban thinker Lewis Mumford, who called the suburbs "a collective effort to lead a private life." Worse, the longer we spend alone in the car driving between home, work and the large, impersonal malls we shop in, the less likely we are to do volunteer work, chair a committee, attend a public meeting, sign a petition or even attend church. Putnam's research shows that "each additional ten minutes in daily commuting time cuts involvement in community affairs by ten per cent." And as the commuters drop out, participation by stay-at-home spouses also slips.

Just because McClintock and van Hemert agree on the need for denser, mixed-use walkable communities doesn't mean that they agree on what they should look like. McClintock is a fan of Stapleton: the largest infill project inside an American city is transforming the old airport five miles east of downtown into homes for 30,000 residents and office space for 35,000 workers on 4,700 acres. It's an example of New Urbanism, a planning movement based on traditional urban design, that features compact, mixed-use neighbourhoods allowing residents to live within walking distance of many daily activities; a variety of housing, both in terms of cost and style (a mix of single-family homes, townhouses and apartments, for example) to welcome a range of people, regardless of age, ethnicity or income; good access to public transit; parking at the rear of buildings, accessible by alleys; narrow streets designed to slow and disperse traffic and be inviting to pedestrians and cyclists; schools within walking or biking distance for children; parks, playgrounds and public squares; a variety of shops; and offices to provide jobs. The celebrated first example of the trend is the community of Seaside in Florida, designed by Miami architects Andrés Duany and Elizabeth Plater-Zyberk. Since 1982, the eighty-acre town has been praised and imitated; it's also been mocked as inauthentic and conformist. When director Peter Weir needed a place that looked fake to play the ersatz town of Seahaven in his 1998 film *The Truman Show*, he used the real town of Seaside instead of building his own set.

It all sounds wonderful, but don't tell that to van Hemert. "What is New Urbanism really achieving? Is it helping us reduce sprawl? No, it's not," he contended. "Maybe, at a micro level, you see more people walking in these neighbourhoods, but the whole New Urbanist movement is still almost completely car oriented." He gives the crusaders behind the trend credit for helping to popularize the idea of people living within walking distance of a mix of land uses, but lamented that planners were actually part of the problem. "We over-regulate stuff and we need to step back a little bit," he said. It doesn't help that the Congress for the New Urbanism, a San Francisco–based organization that promotes the theories, has turned them into their own orthodoxy. "They have become so doctrinaire about what New Urbanism should look like," complained van Hemert, who finds it bitterly ironic that the movement draws considerable inspiration from Jane Jacobs, particularly her ideas about mixed-use neighbourhoods. "I think she would be aghast at a lot of what the New Urbanists have done because it is very sanitized, homogenized, pasteurized and boring. They try to make it mixed use and exciting, but they over-plan every single detail. And that's not what Jane Jacobs wanted. It's the opposite."

Given those views, it's no surprise that he's not a Stapleton supporter. He's been disappointed with the number of pedestrians he's seen there and noted that though there are sidewalks around the big-box stores, they don't make for pleasant walking because the parking lots are so big. And the people who move there want to live in the city but still demand all the creature comforts—including big closets and three-car garages—they left behind in Highlands Ranch. So not only is Stapleton boring and predictable, it's not that dense despite all the press it has received. Worse, some of the residents complain when they see a bus standing on the street. "This is car culture all over again—it just looks nicer," he said. "Stapleton doesn't really take us where we need to go."

A much more successful model, to his way of thinking, can be found in Belmar, ten minutes west of downtown Denver. The project, which replaces an old mall in the city of Lakewood, features condos, lofts and rental apartments in low- to mid-rise buildings as well as row houses, plus office space, shops, restaurants and a theatre. "It's a dynamite neighbourhood," said van Hemert. He also points to Boulder, thirty-five miles northwest of Denver, as a model. Sometimes known as the People's Republic of Boulder because of its progressive politics, it created a green belt around the city to control growth. The downside is that the cost of housing has gone up so much that many people who work there have no choice but to live outside the greenbelt, which really just exports the sprawl. Less controversially, Boulder has an innovative bus system, 362 miles of bike lanes, routes and paths, and aggressively promotes walking.

Denver also has a bicycle commission and tries to make life easier for cyclists. Like walking, biking is healthy, efficient and environmentally benign, but is often a more practical option. Walking is great for Manhattan, but the Denver region isn't that compact. "We ought to really celebrate the bicycle," said McClintock, "because one of the battles we're facing is the collision between the car culture and the bike culture on the roads. Too many people are being killed."

A powerful weapon in that battle is the complete street—one designed for pedestrians, cyclists and transit users as well as drivers. By adding bike lanes, wider sidewalks and improved pedestrian crossings, streets become safer, more efficient and more inviting. Commerce City, a growing suburb north of Denver, planned for traditional six-lane arterial roads until some consultants suggested the town could manage all of its traffic for the next twenty or thirty years with four-lane roads that included parking and bike lanes as long as there was a good secondary collector-street system in place so all the traffic doesn't funnel onto the arterials. It's an approach more cities need to take, according to van Hemert: "All streets should be complete streets, except for freeways."

McClintock is also excited about some of the small changes Denver has made with foot traffic in mind. One example is the installation of countdown timers for pedestrians at intersections, as well as more all-way stops that give walkers the opportunity to cross in every direction, including diagonally. These pedestrian scrambles are sometimes called "Barnes Dances" (although he copied the idea from other cities in the 1940s, Henry Barnes, Denver's first professional traffic engineer, gets credit for promoting them). After finishing his latte and sticking his gum on the plastic lid of his takeout cup, McClintock offered to show me what he meant. We left the café, walked around the corner and down the block to 15th and Glenarm. Each direction of Glenarm has one car lane, a bike lane, parking and a fifteen-foot-wide sidewalk. On the other hand, 15th Street has five car lanes. At the intersection, McClintock used his watch to time the Barnes Dance at twenty-five seconds on every second red light. "Because it's a car-oriented street, we've made the changes to say to pedestrians, 'Okay, you're going to have your moment in the sun,'" he boasted, adding that if the all-stops are short enough, drivers don't even really notice them. "The biggest thing that's changing right now is that we're trying to make our streets complete to work for everybody."

Street light timing may seem like a rather inconsequential improvement to get excited about in the face of an overwhelming problem such as sprawl, but both McClintock and van Hemert know that people in the West love their cars, changing behaviour isn't easy and NIMBYism will always make improvements more difficult, so small victories are to be savoured. Besides, they see a lot of forces working in their favour: shifting demographics and attitudes; increased awareness of the health problems associated with car dependency; less willingness to put up with long commutes on congested roads; and the realization that owning several cars makes living in the suburbs less affordable. In addition, sprawl is becoming an environmental imperative. "People think if you label something green that it's the silver bullet, that it's enough. You recycle, that's good. You get a hybrid car, put up some solar panels, that's all good," said van Hemert. "But it's the land use pattern—the mixed use and the higher density—that is really going to get us to a point where we can seriously preserve resources."

For his part, McClintock is rooting for those developing alternative fuels and other ways to make cars less of an environmental burden, but he knows the perfect car won't solve every problem. People in the Denver region now drive sixty million miles a day, and by 2030, that number could increase to ninety million miles a day—the same distance, coincidentally, as the earth is from the sun. "Even if we find a way to be more efficient and pollute less as we drive to the sun every day, would it be progress? Yes, on one level, but not in terms of these other values of walkable communities," he said, adding that we need to reduce the amount of time we spend in the car. "If we could figure out ways to get out of our cars and have shorter distances between destinations, the benefits would include better health, greater civic engagement, more time with families and personal happiness."

I had plenty more time in my car ahead of me, but that afternoon, as I drove south from Denver in the bright sunshine, I was feeling surprisingly optimistic.

15 Las Vegas
Muscle Bound for Glory

THE COUPLE IN THE NEXT ROOM was going at it. The participants moaned and panted, the bedsprings squeaked and the headboard slapped rhythmically against the thin wall between their bed and mine. I slipped my earbuds in my ears, turned up the volume on my iPod and cursed cheap hotels as I tried to sleep.

I was in Española, New Mexico, a town of ten thousand that is the Lowrider Capital of the World in the summer but doesn't offer travellers much to do on a Friday night in the fall. I'd been on my own for a week, and the loneliness of the long-distance driver was setting in. But while moving from hotel to hotel—the morning pack-up, the evening check-in—was certainly getting on my nerves, I wasn't fed up with being in my car and I never felt lonely there because I always had good music to listen to, the driving gave me something to do and I'm always content thinking my little thoughts. As I drove toward Las Vegas on Sunday evening, the city's lights seemed to spread out forever and I had to admit that, at night, urban sprawl looked pretty cool.

A mess of traffic congestion, high crime rates and bad planning all impractically set in the middle of a desert, Vegas has grown from 65,000 residents in 1960 to more than 575,000 now. That boom has come without much intensification—there are only a little more than 4,200 people per square mile—or investment in public transit. More of a gimmick than an effective solution, the monorail runs for just 3.9 miles beside Las Vegas Boulevard—better known as The Strip—and over to the convention centre, costs a steep $5 a ride and, shortly after it opened in

2004, had to shut down for more than three months because it was shedding parts.

On Halloween, I spent a couple of hours walking along The Strip, popping into various bars and casinos (strictly for research purposes, of course). A few people were already in costume as I walked into the Stardust Resort and Casino, which was scheduled to close the next day. One of the oldest landmarks on The Strip, it was the largest hotel with the largest casino in the city when it opened in 1958. But this is a town where no one, and certainly no developer, has any interest in the middle-aged or the historical, so while the famous sign was destined for the Neon Museum downtown, the building itself was doomed to implosion so a resort and convention centre called the Echelon Place could replace it.

My hotel was on Paradise Road and I'd enjoyed a pleasant enough stroll to the Stardust along Convention Center Drive. Once I got to The Strip, it was, not surprisingly, packed with people. Later, I walked back to my hotel along Sands Avenue. Fences lined much of the road and there were few if any pedestrians; eventually I started to feel a little uncomfortable and decided to hail a taxi. I was surprised when the cabbie explained that he had taken a risk picking me up: not that I looked dangerous, just that flagging a cab is illegal in Las Vegas. Officially, the ban is a safety measure, even though millions do it in other cities every day and survive. Whatever the reason, tourists and locals must call a taxi or go to a hotel and line up. At peak periods, these lineups can easily last half an hour or more, but no doubt the hotels, and especially the doormen who pocket the tips, think this is an excellent policy.

Vegas welcomed an estimated thirty-nine million visitors in 2006. Other than what they watch on the hit television show *CSI: Crime Scene Investigation*, most tourists see little but the tacky glitz of The Strip, the smoke-filled casinos and over-priced performances by Celine Dion, Barry Manilow and other cheesy crooners. Beyond these dubious attractions—and perhaps because of them—Las Vegas hosts more than twenty-two thousand conventions and trade shows every year, and I was there for one of the big ones. The SEMA Show, put on by the Special Equipment Market Association, is an unabashed orgy of goodies, from tires to audio equipment, car-care products to high-tech gadgets, filters to concept cars. It is hardware heaven.

Held every fall, it runs the same week as the Automotive Aftermarket Products Expo, making Las Vegas—which already has an anything-goes car culture—one seriously auto-obsessed city for a week. At the first SEMA Show, held in 1967 at Dodger Stadium in Los Angeles, just five cars were on display. This year, close to two thousand were. The convention is not open to the public—just exhibitors, buyers and the media—but it still attracted over a hundred thousand people. Within one million square feet of convention space, they wandered the aisles between the more than ten thousand booths. Some folks looked bedraggled, with eyes glazed over, while others oohed and aahed over cars and engines. Companies handed out swag (I waited in line to pick up a toy 1967 GTO at the Hot Wheels booth) and many booths featured the comely women, often with immodest clothing, who are trade-show and car-show staples and just one more reminder of the connection between cars and sex. The whole scene was further evidence that the fetishization of cars— especially powerful ones—won't end any time soon.

GIVEN THAT THIS YEAR'S theme was "Celebrating 40 years of American Muscle," SEMA was a place where the battle-weary Detroit automakers didn't need sex to feel good about themselves. Typically a mid-size, rear-wheel-drive machine with a big engine, the muscle car is back in favour as collectors eagerly snap up old ones and the Big Three scramble to release modern versions. Ford had already pumped up its Mustang, Dodge was planning to bring back its Challenger in 2008 and Chevrolet was promising to have its fifth-generation Camaro rolling off the line in 2009. The cars have particular appeal for baby boomers with the money to once again own the models they drove back when they were young, or who now finally have the money to afford what they couldn't afford in those days.

This may turn out to be a short-term strategy for the automakers given that the target market will soon be moving into retirement and forsaking expensive toys. "Chevy's new Camaro, like the new Dodge Challenger, is aimed directly at the balding and pot-bellied looking to extend their mid-life crises," wrote auto journalist David Booth in the *National Post*. "But, according to David Foot, he of *Boom, Bust and Echo* fame, the front end of the Boomer bulge is about to retire. Some time in the near future (he says 2011 or 2012), their free-spending ways will come to an end, just in time for Chevy to get a mere four good years out of Camaro sales. A shame, really, since it's a bitchin' ride."

No such discouraging words were on the lips of the speakers at the keynote luncheon the day before SEMA officially opened. Three cars—a Mustang and concept versions of the Challenger and Camaro—flanked a stage in a huge ballroom filled with round tables at the Las Vegas Hilton. Moderator Angus MacKenzie, the editor of *Motor Trend* magazine, defined American muscle as "more engine, less car" and "real performance on a working man's wage" and reckoned that the 1949 Oldsmobile Rocket 88 was the original. During the genre's glory years—from 1962 to 1972—they became icons of pop culture. Toward the end, the cars often displayed a real playfulness in colours, including bright oranges, lime greens and deep purples, and fun graphics based on cartoon characters (the Plymouth Road Runner, for example). But soon a perfect storm of outside influences—rising gas prices, insurance industry demands for safer cars, government regulations on emissions and competition from foreign manufacturers—brought an end to the era of affordable high performance. The situation grew especially dismal in the 1980s, when the

American carmakers really lost their way and the only vehicles that got people excited were trucks. "It does strike me that Detroit tried to build better Camrys and better Accords," said MacKenzie, "and forgot what its roots were and what the visceral American driving experience was."

The popularity of racing, particularly NASCAR, showed that no matter what Detroit did, Americans still carried a torch for fast cars. So, whether it's a genuine reawakening or an act of desperation from struggling companies, the muscle car is back. And as the automakers go retro, they're hoping to generate excitement among young people—just in case the whole boomer nostalgia trip really is the last gasp of an aging generation. The Camaro was the least retro of the three models on display: although it does pay homage to its stylish predecessors, it's a completely new design with a modern look because GM wanted to create a car that would strike a chord with young buyers as well as those familiar with the Camaro heritage.

Nostalgia being what it is, most people who dream of these rides have conveniently forgotten that the original muscle cars weren't exactly dream machines. Along with guzzling gas and spewing pollution, they handled poorly. As MacKenzie said, "Every road was an adventure if it had a turn in it." But the contemporary versions take advantage of advancements in design and technology to improve handling, increase fuel efficiency and reduce emissions.

An Australian with shoulder-length hair and dressed in a black suit, he shared the stage with six designers who sat in a row of director's chairs. One of them was former Chrysler engineer Tom Hoover, considered "the godfather of the Hemi" for his role in developing the 426 Hemi—an engine with a hemispherical-shaped combustion chamber; car lovers revere it for its power and, originally, its noise. Another panellist was Ralph Gilles, best known for his work on the Chrysler 300C. A four-door, rear-wheel-drive sedan with some echoes of the 300 series that Chrysler produced from the mid-1950s to the mid-1960s, it features a deep body and narrow windows, a Hemi V8 and a sticker price that's not outrageous. Some people didn't like it—inevitable given its bold design—but others loved it, including those who considered it a "baby Bentley" and those who were impressed that it appeared in hip-hop videos and was a favoured ride of rappers. Either way, the 300C won several awards, including being named the 2005 *Motor Trend* Car of the Year. And sales took off.

Although he's always insisted that designing a car is a team effort, Gilles got the credit—so much, in fact, that he became a celebrity. *Time* called him Chrysler's Bling King, *People* dubbed him the sexiest man in Detroit and *Black Enterprise* put him on its hot list. The son of Haitian immigrants who lived in New York when he was born in 1970, he grew up in Montreal crazy about cars. By the time he was eight, he'd started drawing concept vehicles and when he was fourteen, his aunt sent one of his sketches to Lee Iacocca. The response from the Chrysler chairman, which may have been a form letter, encouraged the teenager to keep at it and consider going to design school. Eventually, Gilles did go to Detroit's College for Creative Studies—one of the recommendations in the letter—and then landed at Chrysler in 1992. Later, he did an MBA at Michigan State, and now that he's vice-president of Jeep, Truck & Component Design for the company, he hopes to use his magic on the minivan with new versions of the Town and Country and the Caravan. Casually dressed in a black T-shirt and jeans, and with a shaved head, he looked like a rock star, but talked like a designer, pointing out that one of the advantages of industry globalization was that his company inherited Mercedes-Benz's stability control technology, which allows anyone to safely drive a large horsepower car, even in the snow.

Designer and car builder Dan Webb summed up the panel's attitude when he pointed to the models next to the stage and said, "I would much rather drive any one of these three cars across the country than a '68 anything." That prompted a big laugh from the people eating the rubber chicken, but few of them will be chuckling when they see the sticker prices on these new, improved vehicles. In 1964, the base Mustang sold for $2,368—or $15,506 in 2007 dollars. Today, the base model sells for about $20,000 and rises sharply with options. Ford's Pat Schiavone, the principal designer on the 1994 Mustang, was hopeful that more affordable models would appear—but then, he seemed to be optimistic about everything. "I don't want to be dipping into the oil reserves. I want something green; I don't want any emissions at all. And I think with the new technologies that are coming faster and faster, anything can happen," he said. "But what I do know is that people will still want to drive fast; they will still want muscle cars."

MacKenzie picked up on the cheerfulness in his closing remarks. "There's a new kind of horsepower war going on," he proclaimed unabashedly. "The cars themselves are more sophisticated, safer, faster, cleaner, but the core thing remains: more engine, less car, excitement when you get in and press that gas pedal, theatre and excitement when you bring it home and show your neighbours. I think it is 1966 all over again, and this time the glory years are going to last a whole lot longer."

DAN GRUNWALD AND HIS WIFE, Martha, sat at my table during the luncheon. When he was sixteen, his father gave him the broken-down family car, a 1959 Morris Minor. With some tinkering and three hundred dollars, he had his first automobile—and a lifelong passion. A few years later, his father told Martha that Grunwald would grow out of it, but that never happened. Today, along with a Jeep Wrangler, a Cadillac CTS and his wife's PT Cruiser, the jeweller from Geneva, Illinois, has a 1971 El Camino, a 1949 Chevy pickup, a 1967 Corvette and a 1966 Nova. "It's like a disease. It bites you, goes into remission for a little while, but always comes back and metastasizes itself into a different form somehow," said Grunwald, who has meaty hands and wore a red-checkered, button-down-collar shirt with a pen and reading glasses in the pocket. "Then we find ourselves re-living our glory days and buying and selling old cars."

A year ago, the Corvette club member sold a 1970 Vette as well as a 1964 Pontiac LeMans Convertible. Now, his current project is restoring the Nova and he spends eight to ten hours a week on it. "I work on jewellery all day, on little itty-bitty stuff under a microscope," he explained, "so if I can go home and take a big hammer and start pounding on things, it's great therapy for me." In addition, he moonlights as a freelance writer for *Sports Car Market* magazine and some local papers, a sideline he stumbled into several years ago after making a trip to the Barrett-Jackson Collector Car Auction in Scottsdale, Arizona.

For car guys, the January auction is one of the highlights of the year. A quarter of a million spectators show up in person and millions more watch on Speed Channel. The cars on the block are anything but old clunkers. In 2007, the thirty-sixth year, bidders paid nearly $112 million for 1,271 vehicles. Muscle cars that originally sold for a few thousand dollars went for a few hundred thousand dollars. One—an 800-horsepower 1966 Shelby Cobra 427 that was billed as "Carroll Shelby's Personal Supersnake"— sold for five million dollars, plus the 10 percent buyer's premium that Barrett-Jackson takes. Grunwald doesn't think the inflated prices will last and warns against buying one as an investment rather than a hobby. "Don't bet the college fund on it," he warned. "Eventually the market is going to falter and you don't want to be left without a seat when the music stops. The smart guys and the huge collectors are always out before then."

But that's a rarefied world. While the love affair is stronger than ever for collectors, restorers and other hobbyists, most people don't care about cars the way they used to, even if they're still prepared to go into debt for them. A fancy new muscle car may get the neighbours out for a gander, but most new wheels won't. "The telltale sign is that when the guy down the street gets a new car, nobody cares," Grunwald said, adding that it was different when he was a kid. "I don't care if you got a new Buick or an Oldsmobile or even a Ford Falcon, everybody on the block wanted to look at your car. Now everybody can afford to buy one and it's not very exciting."

THOSE NEIGHBOURS who aren't excited by new cars aren't the people who come to SEMA. The next day, I dropped by a Ford press conference in an area up a few stairs from the rest of the convention centre floor. A crush of people surrounded half a dozen 2007 Shelby GT500 Mustangs. Standing in the middle was the vehicle's namesake, the legend himself, eighty-three-year-old Carroll Shelby, dressed in a black shirt, black jacket and dignified broad-brimmed black hat. After accumulating many victories and setting plenty of records, he retired from racing in 1960. He turned to designing, creating the AC Cobra, a sports car that featured a Ford V8 engine in a lightweight British aluminum body, and then the Ford GT40 as well as the Mustang-based Shelby GT350 and Shelby GT500. The deal between Shelby and Ford ended in 1970; later, Iacocca, then at Chrysler, hired Shelby, who came up with the Dodge Viper.

A few years ago, Shelby and Ford patched up their differences and J Mays, the company's group vice-president of design and chief creative officer, introduced the Shelby GR-1 concept car at the 2005 North American International Auto Show in Detroit. Before joining Ford in 1997, Mays was instrumental in designing the successful new Beetle for Volkswagen, but he also relaunched the Thunderbird, which generated more publicity than sales, and Ford no longer makes it. The GR-1, a two-seat sports car, also created buzz: "A perfect body with smooth, shimmering aluminum skin," according to Mays, "the new Ford Shelby GR-1 concept is a rolling sculpture whose beautiful, flowing lines belie the raw, beastly V10 wedged under the hood." While there's no guarantee the Ford GR-1 will ever go into production, the new Shelby Mustang GT500 has been available since the summer of 2006.

"There's Carroll Shelby," someone squealed. Others pointed cameras and cell phones at their hero, and a man with a media pass around his neck snuck up to Shelby, introduced himself and asked for an autograph. A burly guy with a Ford badge seemed quite unhappy and moved in to protect the celebrity, who signed the autograph and let the man retreat before he was roughed up by the hired heavy. To be sure, part of Shelby's aura is his reputation as a racer, but his career ended long before that fan was born. Since then, Shelby has made an even bigger name for himself as a designer, even though it's hard to imagine anyone pushing through a crowd to get an autograph from many other Big Three designers.

With typically true aim, *The Simpsons* satirized American car design in a 1991 episode called "Oh Brother, Where Art Thou?" in which Homer discovers he has a half-brother named Herbert Powell who owns a successful auto company. Herb hires Homer as consultant, pays him two hundred thousand dollars a year and lets him design a car. The result, in an obvious reference to Ford's Edsel, is "The Homer," a completely over-the-top collection of features including a massive cup holder, tail fins, a bubble dome, shag carpeting, a horn that plays "La Cucaracha"—and a sticker price of eighty-two thousand dollars. The Simpson patriarch is thrilled with his design: "All my life, I have searched for a car that feels a certain way. Powerful like a gorilla, yet soft and yielding like a Nerf ball." Soon, a crane replaces the Powell Motors sign with one that reads "Kumatsu Motors."

In the real world, the trouble GM, Ford and Chrysler now find themselves in is due to years of uninspiring design, not one colossal error (even the Edsel didn't bankrupt Ford, which bounced back with hits such as the Falcon and Mustang). While the Big Three may have lost home field advantage and are still trying to sell some vehicles a lot of people don't like, they also create some appealing cars and trucks. The one piece of advice I heard again and again: take the power away from the bean counters and marketers and give it back to the car guys.

That may be too much to hope for, but back when I was in Detroit, at the beginning of my journey, Wayne Cherry, GM's retired vice-president, told me designers would decide the fate of the automakers and would be among the highest-paid people in the industry. "Design is becoming so important to companies, so much the differentiator, so much the emotional connection with the customer," he said, "that designers will have different pay scales." And with more movement between companies, as well as competition from the film, entertainment and other industries, designers will receive signing bonuses, just like athletes. No single person creates a car, but once lead designers are paid and fought over like athletes and movie stars, fame is sure to follow. And Gilles's celebrity status, though not quite in the Shelby strato-sphere, suggests that Cherry's notion is more than wishful thinking.

A NATIVE OF INDIANAPOLIS, Cherry made his first trip to Gasoline Alley at the Indy 500 as a nine-year-old. Later, he worked at Oldsmobile and Chevrolet dealerships, raced a 1955 Chevy, studied at the Art Center College of Design in Los Angeles and, in 1962, joined GM, where he was on the design teams behind the Oldsmobile Toronado and the Camaro. In 1965, he crossed the pond to work for GM subsidiaries, first at Vauxhall in England and then at Opel in Germany. He returned to the United States in 1991 and became design chief a year after that. Under his leadership, the company created a record number of concept cars—one hundred of them between 1999 and 2004—including the Cadillac 16, a stunner with a V16 engine that never went into production. Cherry, who was a leader in adopting computer-aided design technology, was also responsible for the

Hummer H2, the SUV with a look based on military Humvees; the Chevrolet SSR (Super Sport Roadster), a retro-looking pickup with a retractable hardtop; and the Pontiac Solstice, a two-door convertible roadster. He retired in 2004, but not before putting the booster cables to the Cadillac brand and proving that GM could still make a sexy, big car that sells.

Today, his own rides include a Silver Cloud Rolls-Royce and a Ferrari, but his daily driver is the first Chevrolet SSR to come off the line. When I met him at GM's Heritage Center in Sterling Heights, he was sixty-nine but looked and seemed younger. A tall guy with long legs, dark, thinning hair and grey sideburns, Cherry was full of enthusiasm; he talked with his hands and bounced around in his chair. My first question was: is it hard for designers to see their ideas actually make it to the road given that they have to deal with all sorts of outside forces, including marketing and finance people, government regulations and even environmentalists and safety advocates? He talked for seventeen minutes, touching on topics such as design in the 1950s and the importance of brands, before I pointed out that he hadn't really answered my question. "Oh, yeah, what was it?" he asked, laughing. Our one-hour meeting stretched to two.

Cherry, who now works with graduate students at the MIT Media Lab who are developing a city car of the future, was around when GM sold half of the cars in the country. He's seen the highs and he knows the lows, for both the company and design. "In the early days, design was king," he explained. "It was style over substance and science and everything else. Cinerama got bigger headlines than the polio vaccine. It was about visual things. It was about style." The designers may have gone too far with all the fins, chrome and flash, but they toned it down a bit in the 1960s, and produced a great variety of styles and sizes, which may be why many people consider it the most tasteful decade for automobiles. Back then, cars were American and nobody thought that would ever change.

While even people who weren't aficionados used to be able to tell an American car from a Japanese one in the blink of an eye, now I hear plenty of grumbling that all automobiles look the same. But Cherry pointed toward the exhibit hall of the Heritage Center and said that, in retrospect, cars from the 1930s and 1940s looked pretty much the same too. Later, though, he admitted that, "Years ago you could always tell a French car, a German car, an English car, an American car. I hope there's room for that today, but at the same time there will be cars that will be sold all over the world." Even if national styles are a thing of the past, the emphasis has to stay on design in the global market. Today, all automakers can turn out reliable, safe cars with lots of gadgetry and features, so what separates one car from another is the design and brand reputation: "The way to communicate the equity in a brand, the consistency in a brand and the value in a brand, is visually, through the design."

The front of a car—including the grille, the headlights, the shape of the hood and the look and placement of the emblem—is typically the most distinctive. And automakers who let their designers fiddle too much with that DNA do so at their peril. When he was a kid, Cherry played a game with himself that a lot of kids did—trying to see how soon he could identify a vehicle coming toward him. "That's brand identity," said Cherry, who talks a lot about brand and brand equity, terms normally associated with marketing, but then he believes good design is about art, engineering and business. So a designer has to be an innovator despite being stuck between the engineers and the marketing department—a job that is not always easy. In Europe, strong brand identity evolves slowly over many years. The Mercedes is a good example of this unhurried evolution; the old Volkswagen Beetle, which stayed basically the same for decades, may be an even better example. The look of North American cars, on the other hand, usually changes much more rapidly. "It is a different market here, and Americans are looking for something new and different," said Cherry, who noted that when asked to recommend a restaurant, Americans will suggest a place that just opened while a European will recommend one that's been around for ages. All that change makes it hard to maintain brand identity, though not all American auto executives cared about that. As a designer who worked for Chrysler in the 1950s told Chrysler Museum manager Barry Dressel: "Nobody ever told me, 'Make it look like a Chrysler.' They said, 'Make it look drop-dead gorgeous, so people want to buy it.'"

This constant search for the new means that designers must pull off a tricky balancing act. "The challenge for any brand of any kind of product is to keep it meaningful and relevant and not lose the brand's visual connection with the customer," he argued, while admitting that marketing departments and management are often only too happy to agree to radical change because they're tired of the same old thing. "The idea is you've go to do something different and keep the essence of the visual cues of that brand. When you can do both, that's when you've really accomplished something."

Cherry is particularly proud of rejuvenating the Cadillac brand with the introduction of the CTS in 2003. At the height of their popularity, Caddies were bold statements of luxury, but the definition of luxury had changed since the 1950s and the 1960s. Believing that people around the world respect America's technology, he wanted a design theme that would communicate the luxury of the advanced technology in the vehicle. As they concentrated on this goal, he and his team looked at a lot of pictures of different types of beauty. They compared a photo of a stealth fighter with one of a Learjet, for example, and a shot of a watch with a lot of dials with one of a timepiece that was an elegant piece of jewellery. He also wanted to recapture some of the brand's distinctive visual cues—such as the vertical lights—that had been lost over the years in the frenzy to come up with new looks. All Cadillac models now have vertical headlights and taillights and the characteristic Caddy grille. "I think we did a terrific job," he said almost matter-of-factly. "It was a significant move for Cadillac, but it still went back to the basic values and expressed the equity that was in the brand."

Cherry believes bold is the way to go when it comes to car design, even if it means that not everyone will like the result. "Things that appeal to too many people don't have as much impact," he said. And, after all, not everyone wants a Cadillac. (I have to admit that though I've always thought of Caddies as glorified land yachts, I test-drove a CTS and fell in love with it.) No matter what the product is, Cherry said, "If you have your brand identity and it's strong enough, and you're revitalizing it consistently, you don't have to follow design trends. Everybody else does. And so you're never out of date, because it's your look."

AN HOUR AFTER BEING IN—or near—the exalted presence of Carroll Shelby, I witnessed a very different scene at the Phoenix Motorcars event. Ed Begley, Jr., the tall, thin, blond actor who is one of Hollywood's most dedicated environmentalists, had come to SEMA to speak on behalf of the Ontario, California–based company. But the audio equipment hadn't arrived, and twenty-five or so media types were growing impatient. A woman who was with a TV crew went up to Begley, introduced herself and pointed out that the lining of his light grey suit jacket had ripped and was hanging below the hem. He thanked her and then asked another camera crew for some tape. Meanwhile, behind me, someone walked by, saw Begley and said, "Who is that guy? I recognize him."

Eventually, rather than watch the reporters move on to another press conference, the company asked everyone to move in closer and Begley spoke without the aid of a microphone. Pitching the Sport Utility Truck, a battery-electric fleet vehicle with a top speed of ninety-five miles an hour and a range of over one hundred miles per charge, Begley argued that we should all use the appropriate technology for our task. If he's driving around LA, he'll take his electric Toyota RAV4, but for longer distances, he'll ride in a hybrid Toyota Prius: "You don't need a sledgehammer to put in a carpet tack." Begley, who had a Mustang when he was eighteen, has been driving electric cars since 1970 (they've come a long way since then, he pointed out) and cited three reasons why the technology makes sense today: it cuts pollution, reduces America's dependence on oil from the Middle East and saves money. "It's not just about the environment, it's about the economy," he said. "I came here in a hybrid car that got a real-world fifty-one miles per gallon. It cost me twelve dollars to get from Studio City, California, to Las Vegas. So forget the environment—it's good for my pocketbook."

Green was a prominent theme at the show: Save the World Air, a North Hollywood, California–based company, held a well-attended press conference, though the passionate, articulate and attractive Erin Brockovich (the real one, not Julia Roberts who played her in the 2000 biopic) may have been a bigger draw than the technology, which remains unproven. Although the Environmental Protection Agency has already dismissed similar inventions, the company claimed that by using a magnetic field to reduce the viscosity of fuel, its EcoCharger products would reduce emissions, dramatically improve fuel economy and enhance engine performance. Whoever comes up with an effective and affordable way to make cars less environmentally damaging stands to receive untold riches. But the competition comes from around the globe. Despite the all-American theme of the show, it was impossible to overlook the increasing internationalization of the auto industry, which was evident at the booths and in the badges I saw on people—everywhere from Scandinavia to Israel to China.

Other trends at the show included donks, rat rods and drifting. Inspired by hip-hop, donks are custom vehicles featuring touches such as oversized rims, expensive, overpowering audio and home entertainment systems and colourful paint jobs—and even fur interiors and rhinestone exteriors. Rat rods represent the opposite approach to car culture: they are inexpensive do-it-yourself hot rods usually assembled from parts from different cars and finished with crude or incomplete paint jobs. "It's the creativity of the young person building the rat rod that gives the vehicle its character," said Cherry, who sees them as proof that the passion for cars is as strong as ever, even among young people. "There's no formula. They weld all sorts of pieces and bits of cars you've never even dreamed of to create these rat rods that are just phenomenal."

Finally, drifting might be best described as synchronized skid ballet. First popularized in Japan, it's the art of controlling a car while it slides sideways. I watched a demonstration outside at the *Motor Trend* Proving Ground. Three hot-dogging drivers in souped-up, late-model U.S. sports cars—a Viper, a Mustang and a Solstice—zoomed and pirouetted around the parking lot to much cheering, hooting and whistling from the large crowd. The cacophony of revving engines and squealing tires was accompanied by smoke and the smell of burning tires. Soon, my skin was covered in a fine spray of tire dust. Down at one end, a bunch of fans were doing the "we're not worthy" bow. Some American cars are as cool as ever.

A hankering for even more horsepower dominated the trade show, in spite of all the companies hawking green technology, and that made me worry that our fanatical relationship to the automobile will evolve into something healthier even more slowly than I had feared.

16 San Francisco Man versus the Internal Combustion Engine

MY NEARLY TWO WEEKS of travelling solo ended on Thursday night, when my agent David Johnston flew into town. He may not be the famed Samoan lawyer of Hunter S. Thompson's *Fear and Loathing in Las Vegas*, and I'm no gonzo journalist, but we finally left the blackjack table at 4:30 in the morning. A contractor from Red Deer, Alberta, named Garth sat beside me and acted as my consigliere, so I managed to make back all the money I'd thrown away at the roulette table and lost betting on my beloved Boston Bruins at the sports book. We weren't feeling exactly chipper the next day, and got a late start after a restorative breakfast. But I was happy to see Sin City, and all that car porn, in my rear-view mirror—and not just because we were driving into some dramatic scenery.

Although I'd read sensible advice to buy gas before entering Death Valley, I didn't heed it and ended up paying $2.95 a gallon for gas, the most I paid anywhere in the United States (the lowest was $1.99 a gallon in suburban St. Louis). Gas prices had settled back from the heights they'd hit during the summer of 2006 (in August, the average retail price of gas in the country was over $3 a gallon and I talked to people who'd paid as much as $5 in some places). Several folks I'd met along the way were convinced the lower prices were little more than a government plot in the run-up to the mid-term elections and that everyone would be paying more after November 7. And yet none of these cynics suggested they'd reduce their driving if the prices did start climbing again. This attitude reminded me of the old joke concerning Canadians and the weather: everybody complains about it, but nobody does anything about it.

Except that drivers *can* do something. And a few are—even if they aren't driving less, more and more people are buying hybrids such as the Toyota Prius. I hadn't seen too many on my trip until I'd reached Denver, but I knew the Prius was particularly popular in San Francisco, where David and I were headed.

Deserved or not, San Franciscans are saddled with a reputation not just for their wicked liberalism but also for their smugness. In a famous episode of *South Park* called "Smug Alert!" Stan writes a song called "Hey, People, You've Gotta Drive Hybrids Already" that convinces all the drivers in town to switch to the Toyonda Pious. They soon feel so virtuous about how much they're doing to save the planet that a menacing dark mass of toxic gas called "smug" forms over South Park. Soon the town's smug problem is second only to San Francisco's. Worse, as the two smug masses begin to merge, a "perfect storm of self-satisfaction" threatens to destroy both places. San Francisco completely disappears "up its own ass," but the people of South Park destroy their hybrids and switch back to their SUVs. They know a better solution would be to keep the hybrids and stop being so smug about it, but admit, "It's simply too much to ask."

Gas-electric hybrids such as the Prius may not represent the future of the automobile, but they prove there's a market for another approach. And despite *South Park*'s savage satire about environmental self-righteousness, at least California—led by Governor Arnold Schwarzenegger, who drives Hummers—is actually standing up to the car companies (something the politicians in Michigan or any of the other states that woo auto manufacturers with grants, tax holidays and infrastructure improvements would never have the guts to try). California plans to impose more stringent guidelines to reduce emissions of carbon dioxide and other greenhouse gases than the federal government's Corporate Average Fuel Efficiency (CAFE) standards, and to do it sooner. States have a right to set their own standards, but need to get a waiver from the Environmental Protection Agency. (Late in 2007, the EPA denied the waiver request, and the state is now suing.) The prospect of tougher rules has Detroit worried. It's not so much that automakers don't want to make cleaner cars, if that's what their customers want—GM even created a hydrogen Hummer prototype that Schwarzenegger uses—but they want to do it on their own timetable, not one set by California, which is the biggest auto market in the country and an influential trendsetter.

The search for alternative fuels to power our cars is far from just another left-coast fad. Automakers have trimmed tailpipe emissions that contribute to smog and now like to boast that burning a cord of wood in a fireplace produces more particulate than driving a new, properly tuned SUV around the world 3.7 times. But they haven't eliminated emissions altogether, and the only way to deal with the greenhouse gases that cause climate change is to stop burning fossil fuels. As human-generated global warming increasingly appears to be a real threat rather than a wild theory spread by ecological Chicken Littles, even some politicians agree that something must be done. In addition, while only a small portion of the country's oil comes from the Middle East, many Americans are tired of getting tangled in conflicts over there because of oil. And the prices—which are unlikely to drop below seventy dollars a barrel in the foreseeable future, and threaten to stay well above that level, especially with soaring demand from China and India—provide another incentive to kick the oil habit. But while possible alternatives abound, each of the technologies comes with its own trade-offs.

Most engines can handle up to 10 percent ethanol in gas, and some new cars can operate on E85, a blend of 85 percent ethanol and 15 percent gasoline. In the United States, ethanol is most often made from corn, which is great for American farmers and one reason politicians are so gung-ho about it. But growing corn sucks up both lavish government subsidies and so much oil that some critics argue that the amount of fossil fuels required to produce ethanol—to make the fertilizers and pesticides, harvest the corn, transport it and then distill it—actually exceeds the amount it replaces. Even a U.S. Department of Agriculture study showed that ethanol yields only 34 percent more energy than it takes to create, so it hardly seems worth the effort. Biodiesel, usually made from soybean oil, creates the same problems. So-called "second-generation" biofuels made from non-food crops may offer a better energy balance but are still probably not a viable long-term solution, especially because devoting arable land to fuel crops is already pushing up food prices. There has to be a better way.

BEFORE LEAVING LAS VEGAS, I visited the Center for Energy Research at the University of Nevada, Las Vegas. A yellow shack sat under solar energy equipment, and atop the building was a sign that proclaimed "Net Energy Produced" above a digital readout showing the rising total. I found Julian Gardner and Ron Fifield—who were developing a way to use hydrogen in existing vehicles—working on an ATV. In a fuel cell car, no combustion takes place, only a chemical reaction that produces power to run the electric motor and a small amount of heat and water. Gardner and Fifield's system uses hydrogen in the combustion process, and they hoped to reduce the drop-off in horsepower by injecting the hydrogen straight into the cylinder, so instead of the air and the fuel mixing during the intake stroke, it mixes after the intake valve is closed. They'd spent less than two hundred dollars on the parts needed to retrofit the ATV.

As they explained their project to me, their professor, Robert Boehm, rode up on his red bike. Tall and thin, he reminded me of Christopher Lloyd's character in *Back to the Future*, except that instead of a shock of wild tresses, the little hair on Boehm's head is close-cropped and he has a thin, white beard. And unlike the eccentric Doc Brown, who obsessed about the flux capacitor and the other components of the time machine he'd built out of a DeLorean, a sports car with gull-wing doors, Boehm is a mechanical engineer who specializes in solar energy.

We went inside the shack, found chairs amid the jumble of equipment and computers and sat down. He moved to UNLV from the University of Utah in 1990, reasoning that either Las Vegas or Phoenix would be the nation's solar capital. Both places were—and remain—fast-growing cities with soaring energy demands and plenty of sunshine. And yet, when he arrived, Boehm was shocked to see so little solar power: other than water heaters for swimming pools, there was nothing. In 1995, he created the Center for Energy Research to develop solar and other renewable energy projects, and today he's a bit more encouraged by ventures such as a sixty-four-megawatt solar thermal power plant going in near the Hoover Dam.

Despite his work in sustainable energy and his habit of commuting the three miles between his home and the university by bike, Boehm is a car guy. A long-time Corvair owner, he said, "I won't count how many I've had because they have not gone up tremendously in value, so it's fairly easy to get in and out of them. Easier to get into than get out of." Today he still keeps one Corvair. He and his wife also own a Prius, which they bought because they were impressed with the gas mileage and because "it's very big on the inside and not so big on the outside." When a local paper did a story on hybrids, most owners talked about buying the car for environmental reasons; none mentioned the improved torque that comes with an electric engine—except Boehm's wife, who told the reporter she loves her Prius because it gets off the line so fast. "She's serious about that, she just loves that part," admitted Boehm, "I said, 'If you'd ease up on that foot a little bit we'd probably get even better gas mileage than we do,' but electric cars really scream. It's really neat." His third set of wheels is a Pontiac Solstice, but he was a little ashamed to own up to that. "It's the most beautiful car I've ever seen, so that's why I got it," he said. "But I work in energy conservation and sustainability, and the Solstice isn't really built for sustainability. Gas mileage is the pits on it. But it's such a good-looking car, I gotta have that baby. I just love it." He'd have more cars if he had more room: "If I had garage space for 'n' cars—'n' could be any number—I'd have that many cars."

He'd also love to help solve the environmental problems posed by the automobile and thinks hydrogen is promising, but still a ways off. Some of his colleagues, though, argue vehemently that hydrogen is totally the wrong way to go, and tout electric vehicles that run on solar-generated electricity.

ELECTRIC CARS originally outsold gas-powered vehicles because they were clean, quiet and easy to operate. Unfortunately, the electrics were also slow, so cars with internal combustion engines invariably won the races (further evidence, as if any were needed, that speed is an essential attraction in driving). The electrics also developed more slowly, while Ford's Model T made gas-powered cars affordable, and Cadillac's introduction of the electric starter removed the hassle and danger of getting them going, which had been a major advantage of the electrics. In an era of cheap oil and few cares about the environment, the internal combustion engine was the winning technology. Fast, cheap and reliable was all American drivers ever really wanted.

That's too bad because even cars that ran on electricity generated by coal-fired plants would be cleaner than cars with internal combustion engines, to say nothing of the possibility of using electricity generated by renewable energy sources such as solar or wind. And since most of us would plug our wheels in at night, when power demand is lower, we might not need a huge increase in our electricity-generating capacity. But no one has yet overcome the battery's drawbacks, including making them affordable, finding ways to extend their life and, especially, increasing their range between rechargings. "The battery is always the Achilles heel," Boehm explained. "We're still using basically the same batteries as my grandfather used, so it's not like it's something that we haven't had time to think about." Despite years of research on traditional lead-acid batteries or the nickel metal hydrides used in the Toyota Prius, that technology is still not where it needs to be, and many people doubt it ever will be. Lithium-ion technology—common in consumer electronics such as laptop computers, cell phones and iPods—may be the solution, though for now it has the same problems.

The lithium-ion battery that General Motors expects to use in the Chevrolet Volt, the plug-in hybrid it's developing, will mean a range of only about forty miles. While it's true that most trips by most people are shorter than that, everyone wants the option of going farther. So for longer drives, the Volt will also have a small internal combustion engine that can recharge the battery. Unlike the Prius and other traditional hybrids, though, the Volt's gas engine won't power the car itself—it's really just a standby generator for the electric motor.

Smaller companies are hoping to take advantage of the industry giants who've been more leaden than lead-footed. Phoenix Motorcars has its electric pickup. And Tesla Motors, of San Carlos, California, claims its roadster, which uses lithium-ion technology, has a range of 245 miles per charge while the electric motor's torque means the car, which has a two-gear clutchless transmission, can go from zero to sixty in just four seconds in first gear and hit a top speed of 125 miles per hour in second gear. But as a sports car with a price tag of ninety-eight thousand dollars, the Tesla Roadster is not about to end up in every driveway.

GM hopes to start selling the Volt to a much broader market for about thirty thousand dollars as early as 2010. Some people dismissed the unveiling of the concept car in January of 2007 as a publicity stunt perpetrated by a company desperately in need of some good news; others argued that the battery technology wouldn't be ready by 2010. But a year later, the company said it was right on schedule, and the Volt has an influential champion in

Bob Lutz, now the vice-chairman of GM. A design guru with more than four decades in the industry, and known for fast and powerful cars such as the Dodge Viper, he's now pumped about the Volt. "This is now what I'm more excited about than I was about the Dodge Viper," he told *The New York Times*. "I think this can bring about the revolution and really make us independent of foreign oil and solve all the other problems."

Later, "Maximum Bob" Lutz dismissed global warming as "a crock of shit"—an embarrassing gaffe considering the fate of the EV1, an electric car created in the wake of California's short-lived Zero Emission Mandate, which dictated a growing percentage of vehicles sold in the state produce no emissions. Introduced in 1997, the EV1 was available only in California and Arizona and proved to be popular with Hollywood celebrities. GM can argue that demand for the EV1 was insufficient to make it a profitable product, and there were also battery problems, but the lackluster marketing and the fact the company forced lessees to return their cars, refused to sell them to willing buyers and then crushed the vehicles in 2003 is reminiscent of O.J. Simpson proclaiming his innocence after his jaunt in the white Bronco. Chris Paine's documentary *Who Killed the Electric Car?* argues that the auto and oil industries, aided and abetted by the Bush administration, overturned the Zero Emissions Mandate and stopped development of the EV1. I'm always skeptical of conspiracy theories, figuring that most bad decisions are due to incompetence or greed, but whatever the reason, GM's move to end the EV1 program meant sacrificing its lead in electric vehicle technology. Already, Toyota has also announced plans to have a plug-in hybrid powered by lithium-ion batteries on the road by 2010.

If GM had been prepared to swallow the EV1's short-term losses, the payoff—not just in long-term sales but also, more crucially, in technology development—would likely have been worth the investment. Instead of scrambling to create a practical and affordable Volt, the company might already have an even better and cheaper electric car on the road. But it's just that kind of thinking that has the Big Three in such trouble these days.

ELECTRIC CARS FACE technological, political and economic hurdles, but at least the power infrastructure is already in place. That's a huge advantage over the hydrogen fuel cell car. Hydrogen has the potential to be used where electricity can't—in planes and power-boats, for example—and might be the best solution for auto-mobiles. A hydrogen car is similar to a battery-electric one, except that instead of a battery—or a battery of batteries—it has a fuel cell and a hydrogen tank. Rather than plug it in, a driver fuels it up. The car has a regenerative braking system that saves energy when driving in cities, but can be switched off on highways to increase speed.

The only by-product from a hydrogen-power engine is water. (Converting an internal combustion engine to hydrogen provides a quick shortcut to the technology, though it will mean producing a small amount of nitrogen oxide.) But there's no infrastructure in place: we will need a distribution of hydrogen fuelling stations similar to—or even more widespread than—what we now have with gasoline, and that could be decades away.

The car isn't ready either, though not for lack of trying, as I discovered when I visited the California Fuel Cell Partnership (CaFCP). Backed by oil giants, technology companies, govern-mental agencies and eight major automakers, it operates out of suburban West Sacramento in a low-slung industrial building. The front atrium includes explanatory displays and a cutaway model of a fuel cell car; the automotive members use the service bays in the back, and the rear parking lot has a fuelling station. Juan Contreras handed me the keys to a small, light blue four-door car with a Mercedes-Benz logo on the front and "F-Cell" in big letters and "DaimlerChrysler" and "driving the future" in smaller type on the side.

I drove around the parking lot behind the building and was surprised at how unlike a traditional car it was: it wasn't just that it was so quiet and the acceleration was smooth and immediate, but the feel and sound were different. Instead of the engine revving up and the gears shifting, I heard just the whir of the compressors in the fuel cells, a sound that changed pitch when I stepped on the accelerator. After I'd tired of driving around a parking lot, Contreras took the wheel and we headed to the freeway. "It's fun to drive," said Contreras, who owns a Hyundai Sonata but takes his turn with the F-cell car. "It's exciting to get in a vehicle, press on the pedal and get this constant power flow." The range is around eighty miles and the top speed is about eighty miles per hour—a pace that's easy to hit unintentionally. "Sometimes you're driving and you're enjoying the constant flow and the smoothness so much that you forget your foot is putting way too much speed on the car," he admitted. "You look at the speedometer and you're going eighty and you have to ease off on the pedal."

The participating companies use the CaFCP primarily for demonstration and testing, as well as for servicing the 150 cars and 9 buses being used by organizations such as government agencies, local utilities and the University of California, Davis. But they do their primary research and development in their own facilities in other parts of the world—the partnership notwithstanding, it's a competitive business. As executive director, Catherine Dunwoody has to keep all the players working together, even though they all have their own priorities, have committed varying amounts of effort and money, have different ideas about what problems need to be addressed first and have individual timetables (the governmental members are a lot more impatient than the corporate ones). It's a job that must make her feel like a kindergarten teacher on some days, and she looks the part: tall and slim and conservatively dressed in a black-and-white top, grey pants and small hoop earrings. When Dunwoody arrived at the

CaFCP in 1998, one year before it officially launched, some people thought fuel cell cars would be available by 2003, the original end of the mandate. With the technology still far from perfected, a second phase kicked off to take the project to the end of 2007. In the fall of 2006, the partnership announced a third phase that will last through 2012. Dunwoody compared the first phase to a science experiment to determine if the technology worked, saw the second stage as a process of getting some cars on the road and expected the third step to be about building the foundations for a market. That's assuming that the technology continues to develop—by improving the durability of the fuel cells, bringing down the price and finding a way to store enough hydrogen to give vehicles a range of at least 300 or 350 miles—and fuelling stations proliferate. "So," she admitted, "it's by no means a slam dunk."

At least one partner grew tired of waiting. Late in 2007, Vancouver-based Ballard Power Systems sold its automotive fuel cell assets to Daimler and Ford so it could concentrate on adapting its technology to other markets where the costs weren't so high and the timeline not so long. Still, if the remaining companies can get everything sorted out, fleet sales could begin as early as 2010 and some models might start turning up in showrooms by 2015. Once the public accepts F-cell vehicles, which could take several years, replacing all the existing cars on the road could take another two decades. Even then, the technology won't be environmentally benign unless the hydrogen comes from a sustainable source. Currently, most hydrogen is generated using natural gas, a non-renewable fossil fuel. Electrolyzing water to split it into hydrogen and water is a possibility, but the process requires electricity and is, for now anyway, too expensive. In its favour, though, hydrogen can be generated locally—unlike oil, which often must be transported great distances—and by using whatever process makes the most sense: natural gas in one place, nuclear power in another and wind or solar technology in a third.

In the meantime, Dunwoody expects to see a mix of technologies on the road, including ethanol, natural gas, hybrid, as well as diesel and different kinds of renewable bio-fuels. The big danger for hydrogen is that it will take so long to get to market that competing technologies will improve or new ones will emerge, but Dunwoody, who spent fifteen years working on low-emission and zero-emission vehicle programs for the California Air Resources Board, isn't worried about battery electrics—which she allowed are fine for certain applications—overtaking hydrogen. "Fuel cell vehicles are electric vehicles," she said, "but they don't have the problems with batteries."

If hydrogen ends up as this era's winning technology, it may be the middle of the century before everyone is driving an F-cell car—and that may be too late for the planet. "One of the biggest misconceptions out there today is that there is a quick-fix solution," said Dunwoody, who drives a Honda CR-V but takes a hydrogen car one week a month. "There really isn't, other than to buy smaller cars and drive less. That's the quick-fix solution."

EVEN FACING higher gas prices, too many drivers remain reluctant to switch to hybrids or smaller cars. Nor are they keen to use their cars less. Long before making that move, they cut back on their maintenance (keeping their tires, for example, six or twelve months longer than they should). I wasn't taking any chances with my old car, especially with such a long trip ahead of me. Before I left Toronto, I took it to my mechanic, Gord Donley, for a pre-launch checkup. "Well," he told me, "there's no reason why it shouldn't make it."

That wasn't the most reassuring assurance, and so when it finally happened, I wasn't really surprised. David and I woke up on a cold morning in Bridgeport, California, loaded up the car and hopped in to begin our drive to San Francisco. Click. Click. Nothing. The car wouldn't start; it wouldn't even turn over. But I took some silent satisfaction in the fact that this happened when I was with my agent. Originally, I'd planned to rent different iconic and innovative cars—a Cadillac, a Hummer, a Prius—as I drove across the country, but that would have been too expensive and too impractical, so I settled for my Maxima. When I'd told David about the change in plan, he'd said cheerfully, "Well, your old car should provide its own adventures." I was secretly glad he was with me for this one.

Capricious cars have always been a huge frustration for their owners. When I asked Mike Shanahan, the Newmarket Ford dealer, what features buyers are looking for, his answer was simple: "First and foremost, quality and reliability." Although American automakers have upped the quality of their cars over the past few years, they're still trying to shake a reputation for selling unreliable ones. David MacDonald of Environics and his wife both had cars that were built in 1991. His was a Dodge Spirit; hers was a Toyota Tercel. "In about six years, I easily spent ten times more than she did on repairs. I could have bought the car again," he said. "All she ever did was change the oil and the brakes. But my car—the goddamn transmission went, there was a distributor arm problem, suspension problems. Every year it was six or seven hundred dollars. She said, 'I will never, ever buy domestic again.'"

Being in the industry, MacDonald reads the data and knows that some domestics are high quality while others aren't. But most people aren't knowledgeable enough to know which are which, so that inconsistency has created the negative perceptions that are the big challenge for the Big Three. "There are a lot of people who won't be won over, or it will be a long time before they're brought back."

People who see the automobile as an appliance will be the toughest to bring back, but people with an emotional attachment to their cars are more easily wooed by style and design and brand meaning than by brand reputation. "They're like Volkswagen people," said MacDonald, pointing out that for some people there's just something about owning a German ride. "Talk to

Volkswagen owners: they love their cars, but they have some of the worst repair problems. Our accountant had a lot of trouble with his Jetta. What'd the guy do? Traded it in, and got another Jetta."

Even the best-made and best-maintained cars may occasionally require time at the shop. "Anything that's emotional or passionate goes both ways," said Shanahan. "The love side of the automobile is what it is. The hate side is that it's not perfect, so it breaks or something goes wrong with it." He explained that dealers have two different relationships with customers—one on the sales floor and one at the service desk. And though a successful dealer has to master both of them, it's a lot easier to keep the buyer happy than the owner whose car needs to be fixed. A service department customer wants a friendly person dressed like a doctor to pull out a screwdriver to make a quick adjustment, right away, at no charge. Instead, a service technician with greasy hands and dressed in dirty coveralls must hook up the car to expensive equipment to diagnose what's wrong. Then, before he can fix the defect, he usually has to order the part. "It becomes an unpleasant experience because, right off the bat, what they want they can't have," admitted Shanahan. "So we're managing a relationship of disappointment."

Sitting in Bridgeport, I felt more helpless than disappointed. Rather than asking if anyone had booster cables, I foolishly assumed the worst. But the only mechanic in the tiny town was a Jehovah's Witness and would not be working on a Sunday. So I called AAA, and a mountain of a man in a big yellow truck eventually showed up. He wore wraparound shades, a blue AAA ball cap and a big plaid shirt over his overalls. The handles of his moustache hung down four or five inches. He immediately assumed it was the battery and had us driving away in no time.

We kept the engine running all the way to San Francisco, except when we had to refuel near Sacramento. The car restarted and we drove into surprisingly heavy Sunday afternoon traffic as people returned from weekend excursions. (On Monday, my car wouldn't start again and I had to get to Sacramento. I quickly hailed a taxi—easy to do in Frisco—and took it to a car rental outlet where I picked up a Toyota Corolla. I found it lighter and tinnier than my Maxima, and since it didn't have an iPod jack and I hadn't brought any CDs, it mostly reminded me why I hate commercial radio.)

As we'd crawled along Interstate 80 late Sunday afternoon, driving into the sinking sun, David and I had grown increasingly excited just seeing our destination. It was the first really impressive skyline I'd seen in weeks. San Francisco is one of America's greatest cities: beautiful, vibrant and livable. With almost 750,000 people living on a chunk of land that's just seven by seven miles, the place has a population density of close to 16,000 people per square mile. Even if it's an accident of geography—being perched on the tip of a peninsula means there's no room to sprawl—San Francisco stands out as an ideal advertisement for the joys and benefits of density. Traffic can certainly be thick, especially on the highways leading in and out of the city, but people have so many other options, including regional commuter rail, a light rail and subway system, streetcars, trolley and diesel buses, ferries and the famous cable cars. Biking is also popular here: forty thousand people cycle to work and the city has forty miles of bike lanes, twenty-three miles of bike paths and ambitious expansion plans. And even with the steep hills, it's an inviting walking city.

Nothing illustrates this success better than the reclaimed waterfront. The Embarcadero Freeway was a wide double-decker elevated expressway originally destined to connect the Bay Bridge with the Golden Gate Bridge. After the first part, from the Bay Bridge to Broadway, opened in 1959, a citizen's revolt against inner-city freeways put an end to any further construction. But what remained of the expressway was ugly, noisy and sooty and cut the city off from San Francisco Bay, and for years some citizens wanted to raze the depressing concrete eyesore. Others, predictably, argued that drivers needed to get around in their cars and, in 1987, they defeated a proposal to tear it down. But two years later, in fifteen seconds of seismic violence, the Loma Prieta earthquake revived the issue. Although plenty of people wanted to rebuild the damaged monstrosity, common sense and the vision of Mayor Art Agnos triumphed, and the city now has a street-level boulevard called The Embarcadero. Each direction offers three car lanes, a bike lane and a parking lane, and the old Ferry Building— once stranded and unwelcoming, but now refurbished—is full of upscale shops and restaurants. With improvements to the piers, the waterfront is a place where San Franciscans and tourists go not only to catch a ferry, or even just to shop or eat, but to stroll, jog and cycle. On Saturday mornings, the farmers' market is packed. The waterfront is a triumph and people want to live and work near it, fuelling further development of both commercial and condominium buildings.

The major downside to San Francisco's high density is the lofty cost of housing, but that's just the free market finding the true value of residing in such a livable city.

DAVID AND I STAYED at the Royal Pacific Motor Inn on the edge of the Chinatown and North Beach neighbourhoods. The old motel, which surrounds a courtyard parking lot, is around the corner from the City Lights bookstore. Co-founded in 1953 by poet Lawrence Ferlinghetti, the shop soon became holy ground for the Beat Generation, many of whom spent a lot of time a few steps away—just across what is now Kerouac Alley—at Vesuvio. We watched the election results at the old bar, and all the customers and staff seemed delighted to see the Republicans spanked so hard.

The next day, I walked downtown to visit the offices of the Sierra Club. The group, which has been around since 1892, bills itself as "America's oldest, largest and most influential grassroots environmental organization" and claims to have 1.3 million members and supporters. Its battles include fighting to increase CAFE standards and promoting the development and adoption of alternative fuels, but it also advocates in favour of smart growth as a way to reduce sprawl.

One of the leaders on this issue is John Holtzclaw. A tall, thin man whose hair and moustache are going from grey to white, he is a mostly retired consultant who does research for environmental groups. He also serves as the chair of the Sierra Club's Transportation Committee. Though he grew up in the car culture of suburban Tulsa, he now lives in North Beach and hasn't owned a car since 1978, a not uncommon boast in his neighbourhood. He moved there in 1971 after completing grad school at UCLA, but after seven years of rarely using his car he decided to see if he could get along without it. "It was," he assured me, "pretty easy."

He talked excitedly, was quick to laugh and occasionally pounded his desk when making a point. Though he abhors sprawl, he never says there's an ideal density and, in fact, argues for a variety of densities. "We're not saying, 'You've got to move into a high-density area.' And we're not saying we're going to tear down all the suburbs. They're built, let them exist," he said, adding that what he wants to see is new housing going up in the centres of existing cities and towns, particularly around the transit lines. "Give people those kinds of alternatives they don't have now, except at extremely expensive rents and house prices." For Holtzclaw, the high cost of real estate in central neighbourhoods is proof that Americans don't want to live in sprawl and will pay to be able to walk and take transit. "People want to live in convenience rather than density," he said, "but you need density to get that convenience."

Developers who once constructed little but sprawling subdivisions—and defended it by saying, "I have to build this because people don't want to live in density"—are increasingly turning to denser projects, such as condominiums. But they often run afoul of politicians and bureaucrats who obsess about parking, which is a subsidy for the car, wastes space and increases building costs. Several years ago, a developer wanted to put up a mid-rise residential building west of the Transbay Terminal and proposed including half the usual amount of parking. When the planning department, which was less enlightened than it is now, said that wasn't enough, the developer counter-offered with the idea of unbundling the cost of parking from the cost of housing—he'd put in only a half a space per unit and then charge for the parking rather than offering it for free. If enough people were willing to pay, he promised, he would hire a service to park the cars more densely. "The planning department agreed," said Holtzclaw, "and he's never had to hire that service."

To learn more about the new attitude among developers, I took a trip out to Berkeley to meet Tim Frank, a land use consultant and chair of the Sierra Club's Challenge to Sprawl Campaign Committee. Berkeley sits on the eastern shore of San Francisco Bay and is home to a little over one hundred thousand residents at a density of nearly ten thousand people per square mile, but maintains a smalltown feel. The city, perhaps best known for its long history of activist politics, is well served by public transit, and both cycling and walking are popular. Frank walks most places around Berkeley, but drives his Subaru Outback when he needs to go to Sacramento or somewhere else out of town. To get into San Francisco, he walks a mile and a half to the BART station. "When we think about transit-oriented development, we really aren't usually talking about development that's a mile and a half away, because a lot of people won't walk quite that far," he admitted. But he likes the idea of getting a brisk walk in and finds it doesn't really take much longer than driving because of the time it takes to find parking. "So I get to BART and I've had a little bit of exercise and when I get to the other end, I'm a happier person."

Frank lives in a small, bluish-grey bungalow filled with old furniture, including a grandfather clock. Wearing a fleece vest, blue jeans, white socks and white penny loafers with no pennies in them, he sat in a blue chair and happily reported, "Developers actually want to do this good, old-style development again. People may react to the word 'density' but you show them pictures of really good density and they like it." Some examples would make anyone cringe, but others prompt even people who think they don't like density to say, "Wow. Boy, would I love to live there."

Holtzclaw takes people to San Francisco neighbourhoods and asks them how dense they think it is. "He gets estimates that are so wildly inaccurate," said Frank. "It's just amazing." I wondered how I would do. I associate bungalows with sprawl, but I was sitting in one just off a main street in an old streetcar suburb built in the 1920s. The homes sit on small lots at a rate of about eight units per acre—not exactly sprawl, but not high density either. What I hadn't noticed until my host pointed it out was the nearby four-storey apartment building. By mixing homes and apartments, the neighbourhood had a density of about fifteen units per acre.

When he joined the Sierra Club in 1988 to work on land use issues, one of his jobs was to negotiate with developers to preserve wilderness areas, win trail easements and extract similar concessions. Now, he often supports developers asking for higher densities or hoping to build fewer parking spaces. Sometimes the builders seek out the Sierra Club; sometimes it's the other way around. For developers, the economic benefits of putting more units on less land are obvious, but Frank can marshal several different arguments in favour of density—everything from social justice (the benefits of encouraging a range of incomes in a neighbourhood) to fiscal conservatism (more compact development means government can be smaller, leaner and more efficient because providing police, fire and other public services is cheaper).

Even good projects face opposition from NIMBYs, but Frank can make the case that increasing density improves quality of life in three ways. First, sprawl spawns traffic congestion, which is annoying, stressful and robs people of valuable free time. Second, it increases pollution, which is not only unhealthy but unpleasant. And, third, it eliminates open space, which should be enjoyed rather than gobbled up. When Frank testifies at planning and community meetings, he has credibility because the Sierra Club has no financial stake. In one case, he spoke on behalf of a mixed-use project with residential units above retail space proposed for the main street in Windsor, a town on the Highway 101 corridor in Sonoma County. "Beautiful project, great architecture, something I'd be proud to make a neighbour of mine," thought Frank. But some residents complained, "No, we don't want it. It's different." And it was different—it wasn't the traditional collection of detached single-family homes on large lots separated from commercial strips. "That format," he noted, "forces you to use lots of land and forces people to drive for every trip."

With the developers already onside, politicians are coming around. "It's a myth that somehow sprawl is a function of the natural course of the free market," he insisted. "Public policy is part of what got us in this pickle in the first place." Indeed, governments at all levels have been making bad decisions for decades. The federal government's redlining practices, which lasted from the 1930s to the 1970s, made it harder for people to get mortgages in denser, more racially diverse downtown neighbourhoods. And local governments outlawed mixed-use development, even though the traditional main street, with residential above retail, had always worked well. But Frank sees that changing. "Even in places like Arizona," he said, adding that he was convinced Phoenix would find opportunities for in-fill development and take on more urban characteristics. "Citizens are going to demand it because the present course of just falling all over the place is going to have such a tremendous impact on the quality of life that people are going to revolt against it." In Tampa, residential high-rises, which haven't gone up for decades, are returning. And all across the country, old, failed malls offer big parcels of land—anywhere from ten to forty acres—ripe for redevelopment into mixed-use neighbourhoods with a variety of housing choices close to shopping.

Local residents who don't see the connection between density and the presence of shopping and entertainment choices as well as the viability of public transit aren't likely to completely fade away; but both Frank and Holtzclaw admitted that even within the Sierra Club, not everyone understands how sprawl exacerbates climate change. Although global warming and energy use are the number one issue for the organization, some environmentalists are so focused on their own issues and projects that they don't see the larger picture. "It's not just building more hybrid cars but building more cities so people don't have to drive as much," Holtzclaw said, adding that people who live in multi-family housing share walls and a roof, so they use less energy for heating and cooling and tend to have smaller appliances. "There are lots of ways that the global warming effort benefits from building more compact cities."

He is also excited about the social benefits of living in a diverse community. The night before we met, Holtzclaw watched the mid-term election results at the office with his colleagues, and perhaps inevitably our conversation sometimes touched on politics. He argued that when people have to drive everywhere, that hurts the social environment. "You know your neighbour-hood from the windshield. You don't know your neighbourhood from walking around and meeting your neighbours, chatting in the coffee shop or meeting them casually in the supermarket," he said. "You don't build up both the sense of community and the sense that people who look different really aren't that different. And so you are gullible to the Bush-type fear appeals." Decrying "our country's arrogance" toward people of different religions and races, he suggested, "that attitude doesn't carry too well in the city, where you're meeting all these people" and if more people lived in cities, the spirit of this country could change "from one of fear and hate for people who are different." Intolerance would become inclusiveness.

Maybe San Francisco wasn't liberal because of its history of beatniks and hippies but because of its density. Indeed, if Holtzclaw was right, no one should be surprised that two of the country's densest big cities—New York and San Francisco—are its most liberal. People who live closer together and are less dependent on the automobile develop a different attitude toward citizenship and activism. As he pointed out, "People take responsibility for their community if they feel a sense of community."

SOMEDAY WE MAY all live in tolerant and diverse communities, but we'll still want cars—if only so we can visit other tolerant and diverse cities. So, one way or another, we need to find a technological solution for a problem technology created in the first place. It's like that sage show-ending toast in *The Simpsons* episode called "Homer vs. The Eighteenth Amendment," in which Prohibition returns to Springfield, and Homer, who becomes a bootlegger known as the Beer Baron, declares, "Here's to alcohol: the source of, and answer to, all of life's problems."

Someday we may be able to say the same thing about technology and be just as right, but so far no one has come up with any easy answers or even a surefire path to the future. Ethanol, biodiesel and hybrids are, let's hope, transitional technologies. Plug-in hybrids, when they become available, will be an improvement, but our goal must be cars that don't use fossil fuels or internal combustion engines.

Either battery-electric power or hydrogen offers carmakers the opportunity to completely rethink the design and manufacturing of vehicles. But even if the ideal technology suddenly emerges and everybody says, "Oh, boy, the next car I buy is going to be one of those kinds of cars," it will take years to replace all the gas hogs. After all, I was driving across the continent in a fifteen-year-old set of wheels. Boehm had stated the obvious: "There's no way you're going to snap your fingers and wake up tomorrow morning and it's going to be a hydrogen world or an electric vehicle world or whatever."

We need to step up the research and development, and cross our fingers. But, at the same time, let's not forget that we wouldn't be so desperate for a technological fix if we didn't drive so much— if more cities were like San Francisco and more people walked to work, to shop and to play.

17 The Pacific Coast Highway
Conflicted

I PARKED MY MAXIMA at the airport in San Francisco and rented a silver convertible Mustang for the drive to Los Angeles and back. My sidekick for the trip south was Mike Harper, who owns two Porsches and races one of them, and admits to being a devout car worshipper. But since he was going through a crisis of faith, it turned out that I was to be his confessor over the next few days.

As a preteen growing up in Kitchener, Ontario, Mike fell for his dad's exotic automobiles, including a BMW Bavaria, a couple of Jaguars and an old Morgan. "I couldn't drive them but I certainly enjoyed driving in them," he told me. "And I got to wash them. So from an early age I literally had hands-on experience with cars. I got close to them and noticed the curves and the artfulness of special cars and started looking forward to the day when I could start driving them." When he was a teenager, his family had six sets of wheels and only three drivers, so Mike did much of his driving in a Fiat Spyder. At twenty-one, he bought his first car, which he is embarrassed to admit was a two-tone Pinto wagon. He then bought his own Fiat Spyder, nicknamed "Fix it Again, Tony"—and his mechanic really was named Tony. He sold it after the hassle and expense of keeping it on the road became too much for him.

In 1994, he bought a Porsche 911 and started racing, reasoning that it would be a shame to have a car like that and not take it on the track and really learn how to drive it. He joined the local Porsche club, started out at the lapping days and then progressed up the various levels. "Half of it is the racing," he explained, "and the other half is the race culture and the people."

Though he owns three other vehicles—a 2000 Porsche Boxster S, a Saab and a pickup truck he uses at his place in the country— he has a special attachment to his 911, which has been through many iterations, from street car to track car, back to street car and finally to a full race car. Someday, he'll probably convert it to a street car again. "I've never had a car that I had a deeper relation- ship with," he said. "It's doubtful that I will ever sell that car." But he was having second thoughts about his Boxster, which he liked but considered a bit of a poser car—the kind of car driven by men who aren't car guys but have lots of dough. This wasn't the first time Mike had let peer pressure sway his opinion of a car. He liked his Mazda Miata, except that it was the source of too much ridicule from his friends, who considered it a "chick car." Finally, after one guy asked him if he had pink racing gloves to go with it, he decided to sell.

Since he lives in central Toronto, close to the subway, and enjoys riding his bike, he doesn't need to get behind a wheel every day, but still racks up twenty thousand kilometres a year on his four vehicles. "I wish we could have cars that we could live with and enjoy," he said. "Cars have made life so much better for so many people, but they've now put the world into a tough position so we have to change our attitudes about them. We have to change our behaviour because doing more of the same is going to end in disaster."

He's so conflicted that, lately, he wonders if his cars will be the last he'll ever own. "Most days I torture myself thinking about what my next car is going to be, but then sanity creeps in," Mike confided, adding that the ones he already owned had as many kilometres left in them as he was likely to drive the rest of his life. "One part of me says, live with what you've got and be happy with what you've got," he said. "So instead of thinking of what my next car will be, I start thinking, will I ever have another car? Should I ever have another car?"

Before we hit the Pacific Coast Highway, we were going to San Jose to stay with people I didn't know. Bruce Spencer and I are both on an internet mailing list devoted to our favourite hockey team, the Boston Bruins. We'd never met or even really emailed each other privately, but when he heard about my road trip, he insisted I visit him.

San Jose was a small farming city with fewer than 100,000 people in 1950, and the area was known as the Valley of Heart's Delight. Today, the city is the booming high-tech centre of Silicon Valley with a population of more than 950,000, which makes it bigger than San Francisco. Early growth policies that encouraged sprawl through the annexation of surrounding land gave way to ones that promoted intensification and managed growth. That's meant that the density of the city itself has improved, but the sprawl has continued outside San Jose's borders and, as Spencer warned me, the road and transit infrastructure hasn't kept pace, exacerbating the traffic congestion in the area, something Mike and I experienced first-hand when we arrived in town late Friday afternoon.

Because it was the end of the week and we were out-of-town guests, Spencer invited his in-laws over for a barbecue. As Al Correa, the oldest in the clan, told me more than once, when the family gets together, they're a party all by themselves. And all of the men are car guys. Originally from Massachusetts, Spencer moved west in the mid-1980s and was soon struck by the richness of California's car culture and how people take greater pride in their vehicles than Easterners. The CPA, who owns a tax preparation company, has owned more than two dozen cars (and half a dozen motorcycles) over the years. He bought his first set of wheels, a late 1960s model Toyota FJ40, when he was fifteen and then counted down the days until he turned sixteen and could drive it. His next ride was a 1973 Pinto. Though the Pinto sold well, the Ford subcompact gained considerable notoriety after several fuel tanks exploded in rear-end collisions. Undeterred by that reputation, Spencer moved on to a 1979 Pinto wagon, complete with faux-wood exterior. That was good for hauling his music gear around, but by his senior year of high school he needed something with a bit more style. So he bought a silver 1976 Pontiac Firebird, the first car he really fell in love with. It was also the first car he learned to work on, partly out of necessity, partly out of desire. "I spent weekends pulling that thing apart for no reason, other than to jam it back together late Sunday so I could drive it to school," he remembered. "You know that commercial where the guy pulls his car apart to clean a piston with a tooth-brush? Well, that was me. And you know how later on that week he reaches in his pocket and pulls out an extra piece of the car that didn't make it back in? Yep, that was me, too. I'm proud of the maintenance I was able to do, but I also screwed up a few things pretty bad."

He traded in that one for an orange 1974 Firebird Limited and regretted it almost immediately, so he replaced it with another 1976 Firebird, but it just wasn't the same as his first. Since then, he's owned a string of Monte Carlos, Ford and Chevy trucks and SUVs and the odd Maverick. He can count on one hand the ones that weren't American: the FJ40, an Isuzu Trooper, two Porsche 911s and his current ride, a Nissan Xterra, which he is delighted with. His wife, Diana, drives a Chrysler Town and Country minivan—a tough thing for a Porsche lover to accept, he admitted. "It killed me to get a minivan."

Another car enthusiast who married into the Correa family is Mike Murray, a thin, heavily tattooed UPS driver with a shaved head. Although it soon became clear that he really wanted to show us his car, he didn't want to come out and say so; instead he waited until his brother-in-law forced the issue. Murray took us out front to see his white 1964 Buick Riviera, which he'd lovingly restored and customized, including redoing the interior in red leather, installing both air and helium tanks for the hydraulic suspension and shaving the door handles, a modification that involves removing the factory handles and then using a remote door popper to get in (though Murray admitted the cheap remote he'd bought no longer worked and he had to stick his hand in through the car's triangular side window). As he demonstrated the various heights and configurations possible with the suspension system, opened the hood to show off the V8 engine and let everyone hear its loud primitive rumble, his eyes lit up with childlike pride. Correa, who once owned the car, looked on wistfully. He probably regretted his decision to sell it given the way Murray had restored it, but he entertained us with the story of how, many years ago, he'd driven the car into a telephone pole, giving it a large, perfectly semicircular dent in the dead centre of the front.

Though it gets just seven miles per gallon, Murray uses the Riviera as his daily driver. "It's the only car I want," he told me. His wife, on the other hand, drives a Honda Civic. "I love my country and I'd love to buy American," he said a little sadly, "but I had to buy the best car for my wife."

By now, this was a familiar refrain. The Big Three can wrap themselves in the flag, but for all the patriotism across the land these days, more and more people are buying their cars with their heads instead of their hearts. And given how expensive cars are, one bad experience can really stick in a car owner's head. Other countries' carmakers also issue recalls and produce the odd lemon, but when Americans have problems with an American car, they take it personally, as I really started to understand Saturday morning as Spencer, dressed in jeans, a green golf shirt and a green ball cap, cooked up a breakfast of eggs and sausages.

"My ideal car for a long, long time was a Jeep Grand Cherokee," he told me. In fact, he sold his 1984 Porsche Carrera so he could afford a fully loaded metallic-blue 2001 Jeep Grand Cherokee. "It was the car I wanted for so long and I spent a lot of money on it thinking one of the kids would take it to college. But it didn't treat me right back," he said, sounding like nothing so much as a spurned lover. "That car was in the shop every six months." Three or four years later, he finally cried uncle. His breaking point came one day when he was playing softball with his brothers-in-law: his wife called to say one of the windows wouldn't go up and it was starting to rain. "I couldn't go out for a beer with the guys because I had to go home and deal with that. Here we had this American car, desired and loved for so long, and we had nothing but problems." Even more proof, as if any were needed, that nothing should ever come between a man and a beer with his buddies. Not even a car.

MIKE HOGGED THE WHEEL all the way to Los Angeles. The way he figured it, I'd have plenty of time with the Mustang after he flew home. Spencer's brothers-in-law had spent a good deal of effort trying to convince us to skip LA because of the traffic, and go all the way to San Diego. That sounded like fun, but I actually wanted to experience LA's traffic.

We left San Jose and headed for State Route 1, commonly known as Highway 1 or just the Pacific Coast Highway. After stopping in Monterrey for a bowl of clam chowder, we travelled leisurely along Seventeen-Mile Drive, the famous scenic route along the coastline through Pacific Grove and Pebble Beach. Well worth the nine-dollar entry fee. And then we were really off. Just south of Carmel, we passed a yellow road sign promising, "Hills and Curves Next 63 Miles."

Mike turned to me and said, "That's the sign every driver wants to see."

While my driver manoeuvred the Mustang along the winding road, I soaked up the stunning scenery: cliffs down to the rocky shore to my right, cliffs up to the blue sky on my left. By the time we got to Morro Bay, it was well past dark. The tourist town is sometimes known as the Gibraltar of the Pacific because Morro Rock, the last of the Nine Sisters, a series of volcanic plugs running up the coast from San Luis Obispo, sits in the middle of the harbour. Once a valuable navigational aid for mariners, the

576-foot-high rock is now a sanctuary for peregrine falcons and other birds. When we were there, most of the tourists seemed to be couples, so after dinner we walked inland a few blocks and found a bar filled with locals and Cal Poly students, an entertaining band and a shuffleboard table. We stayed late.

The next morning, not too early, we kept going south until we reached Santa Barbara. We gaped at the money, the attractive people and the expensive cars and then stopped for lunch. When Mike asked our exotically gorgeous young waitress why people came to Santa Barbara, she seemed surprised by the question and said, "Because it's so beautiful."

As we returned to the Pacific Coast Highway and headed south to Los Angeles, Mike admitted that thinking about cars takes up an embarrassing amount of his time. "I love what they do. I love how some of them sound. How they look. The freedom that goes with them," he explained, adding that he's rarely more relaxed than when he's driving. "I'm happy sitting here in a convertible, which is the ultimate driving experience in terms of the open air, the sun in your face." He doesn't need or want to listen to the radio, preferring to find deliverance in the sound of an old car's exhaust as he revels in the power and the handling. "I enjoy the feeling of being in control of something and going where I want to go. I just hope we will always have two-lane highways because that's where the fun is."

Watching Murray start his Riviera the night before had taken Mike back to when he was a kid and getting a car going wasn't a certainty and often took some finesse. The introduction of fuel injection solved the problem, but Mike missed the drama of the carburetor era. What he didn't miss were the emissions. As Murray brought the car to life, Mike stood behind it to enjoy the deep bass of the classic big block engine, but also to see the two exhaust pipes. Sure enough, smoke shot out of them.

A few months after our road trip, he sold the Boxster and bought his dream car: a Porsche 993. By the end of 2007, he'd also sold the 911—he would never be able to tell his fellow racers this, but he just couldn't justify the environmental cost of racing it. That didn't make it any easier to sell a car he thought he'd never give up, though, and Mike confessed: "I moped about it for weeks."

18 Los Angeles
Suburbs in Search of a City

I'D HEARD A LOT about the car culture in Los Angeles long before I arrived. "You are your car," was a typical warning. "In LA, you're centred in your car," Montreal art curator Peter White told me. "You live in your car and you get out here and there. Your car is where you are and other places have a secondary role. There's this inversion that takes place."

It didn't take me long to see how that could happen. I was staying in the Hollywood Hills with Amy Spach, a friend since we went to McGill University together. She showed up in a Camaro for second year, even though downtown Montreal is not a place anyone, especially a student, needs a car. But it wasn't like that where she grew up—car-conquered suburban New Jersey. (In third year, she took me home for American Thanksgiving: I'd never seen a drive-in bank before, and found the thought of one completely preposterous.) Amy obtained her driver's licence on her seventeenth birthday, the first day she was eligible to do so. All her friends drove; in fact, I was the first person she ever knew who didn't. But later, while living in Manhattan and London, she went nine years without wheels. "I fantasize about that time," she admitted. That's because she moved to LA in 1989.

Today, she must drive ten to twelve minutes down a steep and winding canyon road just to get to the nearest store. She can't get a pizza delivered. And she has to drop her son off at the car pool because none of the other parents wants to drive up to get him. Much to her son's embarrassment, she gets around in a 2002 Nissan Altima. While functional, the car is far from glamorous in a city where everyone else seems to be driving Porsche Cayenne

SUVs, Jaguars and other luxury cars. It's also old: most people she knows rarely keep a car longer than two years. "I am in the minority in LA because I don't love my car," she said, adding that she resists the peer pressure to take her ride to the car wash every few days. Though she works from home, she spends at least an hour a day in her car and it's far from uncommon for her to be behind the wheel for four hours. "Initially, the car was my liberation," declared the one-time Jersey girl, "but now it feels like my entrapment."

If LA's car-obsessed excess were a vehicle, it would be a Hummer. The in-your-face monster appeals to some people but, as the numerous anti-Hummer websites attest, is despised by others. And few sights are as ridiculous as an extremely thin woman driving one of these massive machines.

My non-driving wife, Carmen Merrifield, is a Hummer-hater; in fact, she believes that it's the duty of every right-thinking citizen who sees one to give the driver the finger. So I accepted General Motors's offer to let me test-drive one for a couple of days with wry amusement. As it turned out, Carmen was flying into LA to meet me on the same day I was to pick it up. My mischievous plan was to pick up the beast, then surprise her with it at the airport. But it wasn't going to be ready in time. So we went together to pick it up in Torrance and then headed to the coast. Luxurious and fully loaded—with leather seats, XM satellite radio, built-in GPS—the H3 is smaller than its predecessors, but it didn't take long to get a reaction from someone other than my wife. At Redondo Beach, while we waited at a stoplight, a driver in a Toyota Prius sneered at me and my Hummer as he made a left turn in front of us. That scene said it all: a hybrid built by a Japanese company versus a behemoth built by Detroit. Both have their fans, of course, but one seems like the future and the other reeks of the past.

LOS ANGELES ONCE APPEARED to be the future of the American city. From 1920 to 1940, with the movie business and the aviation industry booming, two million people moved here, tripling the area's population. Since many of people arrived by car, it was no surprise that they wanted to stay in their vehicles. The endless summers also helped make Southern California a perfect incubator for a lifestyle built around the automobile.

Because most Eastern cities started with a dense core and then expanded in a radial pattern, especially after the arrival of the automobile, most people blame the suburbs on the car. But there were railway and streetcar suburbs long before the car arrived. "The automobile didn't create suburbs," argued the Chrysler Museum's Barry Dressel. "Suburbs were a preoccupation all during the nineteenth century. But what the automobile did was allow people to gratify that urge by dispersing the population farther out." Even if it's true that the suburbs helped create the car rather than the other way around, the old streetcar suburbs had the benefit of being denser than the new ones. And once the car led to housing developments farther and farther away, the easiest way to move people around was to build highways.

In the East, that meant destroying downtowns, but most of LA's significant growth came after the car, so it developed differently. If Henry Ford wasn't thinking about LA when he said, "We shall solve the city problem by leaving the city," he should have been. Certainly writer and renowned wag Dorothy Parker was when she quipped, "Los Angeles is seventy-two suburbs in search of a city."

All those suburbs have given LA an unenviable reputation for sprawl, and the smog that inevitably goes with it. And yet, the Los Angeles–Long Beach–Santa Ana urban area, which has a population of close to twelve million, has a density of more than seven thousand people per square mile—denser, in other words, than the New York area. "Turns out LA is not really the paradigm of sprawl," said the Sierra Club's Tim Frank. "You have to go to someplace like Atlanta to find that." There, developers are still building plenty of houses on one- and two-acre lots out on the periphery of the city. LA doesn't have that option because it has mountains and the Pacific Ocean constraining it, which has tended to mean smaller lots and more in-fill development.

And yet LA doesn't always benefit from its density. "LA is a conundrum," mused James van Hemert of the Rocky Mountain Land Use Institute. "People say they don't want to be like LA because it's sprawled, but in fact the average population density in the LA metro area is almost twice Denver's. But it's still very auto-dependent, so you have high density with cars." That's because cramming people into an area won't make a difference to the amount they drive unless there are workplaces as well as shops, restaurants and other places worth walking to nearby. The ideal urban form isn't just dense; it encourages a mix of homes, retail outlets and offices.

IF LOW-DENSITY SPRAWL begets congestion, auto-dependent high density begets even more congestion. No one likes being stuck in traffic, but the thing about people who complain about it is that they are the traffic. Except for a couple of days in the H3, I was driving a convertible and I was there for only a week anyway, so I didn't complain too much, but I was shocked by how few miles I travelled for all the time I spent in the car. One evening, it took me ninety minutes to drive from Santa Monica to the Hollywood Hills—a distance of just twelve miles. There I was stuck on Santa Monica Boulevard, late enough in the day that I could no longer bask in the mid-November sun, and unable to move even though the light was green. We were in gridlock.

The irony is that when we choose the "freedom" of driving, we are captive to the actions of the many—more captive, in fact, than the people who take public transit. Perhaps because their freedom is so often compromised, Angelinos tend not to be the most courteous drivers. When we first arrived in LA, Mike was amazed at how no one would let him in after he found himself in the wrong lane. For the rest of my week there, I tried to let other cars in whenever possible—it was my small act of subversion.

While LA is famous for its traffic jams, congestion is a problem in cities all over North America. And it's not just frustrating and time-consuming; it's expensive and bad for the environment. Between the 4.2 billion lost hours and 2.9 billion gallons of wasted fuel, traffic costs the U.S. economy $78 billion a year. On an individual basis, each year the average peak-period driver spends an additional 38 hours in the car and burns another 26 gallons of fuel, most of it greenhouse gas–producing fossil fuels. Not surprisingly, the situation is worst for Angelinos—at a cost of an extra 72 hours and 52 gallons every year.

Before I left on my road trip, I paid a couple of visits to the University of Toronto, where Baher Abdulhai and Eric Miller are engineering professors who have offices next to one another—but very different perspectives on traffic. To get to work, Abdulhai drives his Mercedes E320 into the city from the suburbs; Miller walks about forty minutes and feels guilty when, after walking home, he hops into his Toyota Sienna minivan to drive his sons, through rush-hour traffic, to a hockey arena out in the suburbs.

When I asked each of them about the Spadina Expressway, which Jane Jacobs and other citizens stopped, I heard two opposing opinions. Miller thinks it was "absolutely" the right decision. If Toronto has a reputation around the world as an interesting place, he pointed out, it's not because of what's going on in the suburbs; it's the older downtown neighbourhoods, which would have been wiped out, that impress people. "We didn't need it. People don't need freeways to get downtown, and I think that's one thing we've proven," he argued. "Toronto has boomed because we put transit in and we've encouraged people to live and work downtown."

His colleague disagreed. Though Abdulhai grew up in Egypt and didn't arrive in Toronto until nearly three decades after the battle over Spadina, he thinks killing it was a mistake. "Freeways are arteries, so you can't say, 'I don't want to depend on my artery going to the heart, I'm going to clog it and rely on the tiny little vessels to feed the heart.' No, it doesn't work that way," he said, adding that a city's arteries are essential for moving people and goods. "Extremes are bad in either direction: no highways whatsoever, you're going to choke the city; highways everywhere, it's expensive, you'll hurt the environment and they create overconsumption. So balance is the key." Because he believes in balance, he sat on the board of GO Transit, the region's commuter rail and bus system, and is a big proponent of investing not just in roads but also in public transit.

Abdulhai is also the founder and director of the University of Toronto's Intelligent Transportation Systems Centre and Testbed. ITS takes advantage of information and communications technology to manage traffic in order to ease congestion, increase safety and reduce pollution. By monitoring traffic using cameras, global positioning systems and detection devices built into roads and then feeding the information into computers, it's possible to detect collisions and anticipate congestion, forecast how long the tie-ups will last and disseminate information to drivers or use it to decide to control access to roads, change traffic lights or even adjust speed limits. "All of these things are simply algorithms that are sitting in a computer sniffing the numbers and deciding how to play with them," he explained as we sat in a conference room with a glass wall that gave us a view of the lab, which consisted of rows of computers and a wall of television screens showing different roads and highways.

I hoped Abdulhai would be able to answer a question I'd long had about traffic. I'd heard that even hours after the police have cleared away a crash, traffic continues to slow down in that spot. So, I wondered, does traffic have a memory?

"Yes," he said, "we teach this to undergrads."

Since a little traffic flow theory is necessary to understand the concept, he explained that the three main variables for describing traffic are speed (the rate the cars travel on the road), volume (the number of cars that use the road) and density (the number of cars on the road at a given time). In the wee hours of the morning, a highway is likely to have little volume and low density, but as rush hour approaches, both the density and the volume increase until the road reaches capacity. At that point, because the cars are so close together, drivers will start to slow down, resulting in a drop in volume but an increase in density. Eventually, so many cars squeeze onto the road that the traffic reaches critical density, breaks down and results in a traffic jam. As more cars arrive, the boundary of the congestion moves farther and farther up the road like a shock wave. Once traffic starts moving again, there's another shock wave as the cars at the front of the congestion start speeding up. But it takes five to ten times longer than the original disruption for the second shock wave to catch up with the first one and the congestion to completely dissipate, meaning that if two cars collide and it takes the drivers six minutes to get their cars to the side of the road, it can take up to an hour before all traffic is moving again. It also means that if I come along forty-five minutes after the collision, I will hit the congestion much sooner than I would have had I travelled on that stretch of road half an hour earlier. "The whole highway is like an accordion," he explained. "Whenever you pass through congestion, you don't need to see a burning car at that location—it could be another location another time and that congestion is spreading."

He sketched a diagram on a piece of paper as he talked, but then went to get his laptop so he could demonstrate the theory on a computer simulator and show me how traffic engineers can ease congestion by controlling signal lights at the entrances to highways. Often called "ramp metering," it's common in many American cities, especially in California. First, he let me see typical nighttime flow. "Everything is hunky dory," he said. "It's fast, and when a few people join in from the on-ramp, life is rosy and nice." He then increased the main flow to capacity so that the little black cars on the screen slowed down but continued moving, though he kept the ramp closed so no cars could join the main flow. Even so, he explained, demand was high enough that something as simple as a jittery driver jumping on his brakes could create congestion. Then he opened the ramp, overloading the road and bringing the little cars to a halt.

But if cars flow onto the highway at a controlled rate, they don't create congestion. While he acknowledged that ramp metering is not popular with drivers, Abdulhai assured me that it is effective and pointed out that when highways are clogged, drivers can't enter them anyway. "So these guys," he said, pointing to the cars on the simulator's ramp, "are better off if those guys move."

But humans are funny creatures, and that means they're often the weak link in ITS. Many cities use signs to alert drivers about clogged routes—some even send the information to cell phones or directly to cars—but there will always be those who try to outsmart everyone else. If the sign on Toronto's Highway 401 indicates that the express lanes are moving slowly and the collector lanes are moving well, some drivers will inevitably conclude: "Hmm, everybody's going to the collectors now, so I'm going to take the express lanes." One way to reduce this problem is to offer more explicit information such as specific travel time estimates for each route.

Another ITS technique, currently being tested in Europe, is dynamic speed control, or adaptive speed limits, which promises to reduce congestion by using signs that can change the speed limit on a road so cars won't simply roar up to a traffic jam at full speed. Drivers approaching a jam at one hundred kilometres per hour will only add to the congestion and be stuck longer. But if they reduce their speed to sixty kilometres, the slowdown may have a chance to dissipate before they reach it. This would be safer and reduce both gas consumption and driver aggravation.

As costs drop and more technology starts showing up in cars, ITS will become even more powerful. A traffic department could, for example, use beacons to communicate to vehicles about a hazard or collision ahead. "The ITS guys have been doing all kinds of wonderful things in isolation, and we've been doing things in isolation," GM's Tom Odell noted. "Someday, very soon, we're going to start to talk and this magic will start to happen."

WHAT FRUSTRATES DRIVERS the most is the unpredictability of their travel time, according to Shashi Nambisan and Walter Vodrazka, both transportation engineers at the University of Nevada, Las Vegas. They live in a city where the traffic is bad and getting worse: Vodrazka commutes a little over four miles, each way, in his Ford Taurus and sometimes it takes him six or seven minutes. Sometimes it takes as long as half an hour. So to avoid being late—and to spare himself a lot of aggravation—he tries to leave home no later than 7:45 to ensure he'll get to campus in plenty of time for his 8:30 class, even if many of his students are tardy.

When it comes to easing congestion, there are two opposing approaches. One view says we need to tame traffic, making do with the roads we already have; the other says we have to add capacity to serve the demand. Nambisan would prefer to avoid either extreme but knows that will require some behaviour modification, including changing when we travel and the routes we take. Employers must also play a role by allowing more flextime and letting people work from home more often. (Just think: if everyone who now drives to his or her job could work from home one day a week, it would mean a 20 percent drop in commuter traffic.)

For their part, transportation experts can introduce car-pool lanes, ramp metering and adaptive speed limits, but they are in a tough spot because they're trying to reduce congestion even as they know that they could do much more if the problem grew much worse. London introduced a congestion toll only after traffic slowed so much that people were willing to accept such a drastic measure. "But is that our role in society, as transportation professionals?" asked Nambisan. "To get the system to a breaking point before we can get it better?"

Of course not, but we are hurtling toward that point nonetheless. Abdulhai favours using a variety of weapons—including ITS, the expansion and better management of transit, and road expansion. But for economic and environmental reasons, new roads are likely to be increasingly rare. Besides, adding more roads just attracts more cars. "You don't have to provide more capacity for cars; they'll go away, they'll find something else to do," said Miller, citing Jane Jacobs. "You expand the road, you attract more cars; you shrink the road or keep it the same, you don't get more cars. People will adjust."

Once again, Abdulhai didn't agree. Because of latent demand, new roads or lanes will attract more drivers and become more congested. So the expanded highway will be worse than the day it opened but better than the day before it opened, and the additional capacity means that more people can use the road.

When it comes to transit, he divides people into three groups. At one end of the spectrum are transit loyalists, who either love riding buses, streetcars and subways or can't afford to get around any other way. At the other end are people who are dependent on the car for a number of reasons—"some of them are good reasons, some of them are bad reasons"—and it's completely unrealistic to expect them all to start taking the bus everywhere. But in between is a segment of the population that will take whatever is most convenient, and there are two ways to sway these people: one is to make travelling on freeways a miserable experience, something that's gradually happening; the other, better approach, is to improve transit so people will take it because they want to, not because they have to. "If you increase highway capacity only and you ignore transit completely, then you're going in the wrong direction," Abdulhai argued. "You're telling people their better option is the car and that is not what I'm promoting. I'm saying expand transit to accommodate transit users, expand highways to accommodate the must-use highway users and make transit more attractive to the in-betweeners."

But adding transportation infrastructure to our cities, while essential, is really just treating the symptoms rather than attacking the disease of bad urban planning. "Transportation begins with the way you build the city, and if there's a villain, it's not the car, it's the way we've built our city with single-use suburbs," Miller said. "We put all the people here and we scatter office buildings and stores hither, thither and yon and we don't think about the transportation. We assume everybody can get there by car, but we don't think about the congestion that's created."

Sprawl isn't the only cause of traffic, but high-density mixed-use development—which means residents have the option of taking public transit, riding a bike or walking—is part of the solution. "People just drive a lot more in low-density areas," insisted the Sierra Club's John Holtzclaw, and that's why a growing number of cities are trying to change their development patterns. "We sometimes say—I don't know if you can quote me on this but—traffic congestion is our friend. Traffic congestion lets people know how bad things are."

"Why do you say you're not sure I can quote you?" I asked.

"Because the right—the pro-sprawl people—will say, 'Hey, they want this! They want you to have to live in traffic congestion.' No. We want them to move into some place that's more convenient so they don't have to live in traffic congestion."

HISTORY AND GEOGRAPHY would probably have been enough to guarantee that LA ended up dominated by the car, but just to be sure, a consortium led by GM bought one of the city's two streetcar systems in the 1930s and replaced the comfortable and convenient trolleys with buses. But today, Angelinos have the option of using a mass transit system that includes commuter rail, buses and an expanding network of above-ground light rail and underground subways. So one thing I wanted to do was talk to someone who lived happily without a car.

And James Kushner couldn't be happier. He lives in a loft in a converted building in Old Town Pasadena and takes transit to Southwestern Law School in Wilshire, just blocks from the towers of downtown LA, which he can see from his office window. A bald, stocky man dressed in a colourful short-sleeved shirt, he has owned Corvettes and driven the Pacific Coast Highway with the top down, so he knows what fun cars can be. "But I've never been happier to be done with the car," he told me. "I'd rather walk three or four miles than have the 'convenience' of a car." He not only finds the car-free lifestyle healthier, less stressful and less time-consuming, it also helps him get out of doing things he'd rather not do. "If somebody wants me to go somewhere and give a speech or come to a party, I just say, 'I don't drive. I can't go.'"

LA isn't normally on the list of desirable cities for non-drivers, but that doesn't faze Kushner. He thinks the combination of weather and transit means he's actually in one of the best places in the country. He spends a lot of time in other cities and figures he could also live in San Francisco; Seattle; Washington, D.C.; Manhattan; and possibly Boston and Chicago, though it starts to get a little cold up there. Since he also teaches at Utrecht University in the Netherlands, he travels throughout Europe and admires the compact cities there. He's also a fan of Vancouver. "When you ride a bus in LA, you know you're riding with the bottom 10 or 15 percent of the income group of the city, but you don't have that feeling in Vancouver. So, the transit is comfortable and I think even some of the suburban communities are really quite walkable," he said. "They were planned in quite a nice way so that you can walk to services, you can walk to shopping. You don't have to get in a car. They're not like American suburbs where you can't get anywhere unless you're in a car."

Kushner's interest in living without an automobile isn't strictly personal. Raised in Philadelphia, he joined the Peace Corps and went to Venezuela, where he studied municipal management. After returning to the United States, he worked for Volunteers in Service to America, in Canton, Ohio, representing residents of urban renewal neighbourhoods. Then he joined a legal services program in Kansas City, where most of his cases had to do with highway projects or urban renewal plans or other housing issues. Then it was off to the National Housing and Economic Development Law Project, a think tank in Berkeley, before landing in LA in 1975. At Southwestern, he teaches courses in land use, community development and constitutional law, while his many books include *The Post-Automobile City: Legal Mechanisms to Establish the Pedestrian-Friendly City* and, most recently, *Healthy Cities: The Intersection of Urban Planning, Law and Health*, which is about what legal mechanisms could be used to redesign cities to improve individual health and reduce the burden the car puts on the health care system. He's worried not just about the trauma from collisions but also the high costs of the sedentary lifestyle that comes from driving everywhere, including obesity, diabetes and heart disease, and the asthma caused or aggravated by pollution. "You can create communities that are walkable, that are attractive," he said. "And you could reduce dramatically the cost of health care, which I think is rapidly becoming an impossible situation for Western countries and even Eastern ones."

We've hit the point where moving farther out no longer makes sense because the cost of commuting is greater than the benefits of the less expensive house in the boonies. When U of T's Miller studied suburban living, he found that, as expected, the money people devoted to transportation rose dramatically as they moved away from downtown. What surprised him was that housing costs also went up. He acknowledged that in the overheated Toronto market, downtown homes were more expensive to buy, tended to be smaller and often had higher repair bills because they're likely to be older; but using data that included the taxes, utility bills and mortgage costs, he concluded that suburban residents may not have found the bargain they think they have. "You're getting more house, but it probably costs you more," he said. "People talk about affordable housing and cheap land, but there really is no such thing as cheap land—you pay for it one way or the other. You pay for it in transportation and congestion, and it's not just you who pays for it—society pays for it." And the study didn't even take into account the cost of people's time, the cost of the pollution or any of the social, personal or psychological costs of long commutes.

Meanwhile, the design and location of the options in denser neighbourhoods are increasingly attractive. Changing demographics are also helping as the population ages and the families with kids—many of whom will still want the big suburban yard—become a smaller percentage of the mix. "As I go around the country and look at what cities are doing, I am optimistic that great changes are occurring under our eyes. My friends have no idea," Kushner said, "because if you don't ride the light rail you can't tell what's happening at the stations, and if you don't ride the subway, you don't see the increasing crowds."

As someone who moved from a four-bedroom house in the suburbs to a one-room loft and now says, "I don't need any more room," he thinks more people realize they've been over-buying and don't really need so much space, which just means more to keep clean anyway. "Empty nesters are the shock troops of urban redevelopment," he argued, noting that as soon as they move in, Starbucks coffee shops, Whole Foods Markets, bookstores, art house movie theatres and other businesses are sure to follow.

In the last decade, Kushner has seen a dramatic shift in attitude away from the single-family home in the suburbs, which 80 or 90 percent of Americans sought, toward urban living, which 30 to 40 percent now want. As developers see the soaring demand, their attitudes are also changing. "These guys looked at density as insane," said Kushner. A builder once told him, "Nobody wants to live over a restaurant. That's the craziest thing I've ever heard."

Now, high-density apartments and condominiums are profitable projects. "The developers of the single-family home in America right now are dying. The industry's dead," he said." Ten, fifteen years from now, in cities like Atlanta and LA, I think people are going to say, 'Wow, I had no idea.' It's that kind of a thing that creeps up on you. Until you see an article in *The Wall Street Journal* or *The New York Times,* you don't know the changes are underway."

Along with the homebuyers and the developers, the politicians are starting to come around. But while they are increasingly open to higher-density development, they're slow to stop subsidizing the car. In Manhattan, parking is expensive and usually inconvenient because drivers often have to keep their cars blocks away from their apartments. So most people don't bother to own a car. If politicians do away with subsidies—"the thumb on the scales," according to Kushner—the market will go in the direction of high-density, compact communities. "I'm not about being fascist and saying nobody's going to have a car if I'm in charge," he said. "I don't think that's where we're likely to go. But I do think the costs have to be understood by people and they have to make informed decisions."

TWENTY YEARS AGO, Old Town Pasadena was a sketchy part of town with little housing and lots of dive bars and struggling businesses. Now it's a thriving mixed-use neighbourhood with offices for people to work in and shops, restaurants and nightclubs that attract people from all over Los Angeles. "It's such a cool, hip, inviting place to go, and when you've got that, people want to live there too," Frank told me before I left San Francisco, adding that developers quickly started building new condos and converting old buildings. "It feeds on itself."

The day after meeting Kushner, I had lunch with Amy in Old Town Pasadena. Afterwards, we walked around, and as she checked out the shops, I took in the historic buildings that had been restored to their former architectural glory and noted all the people walking around. Many were shoppers or tourists, but plenty appeared to be office workers taking a break. (This was in marked contrast to Melrose, where people looked like they just drove there to shop.) But I could see what Kushner had meant when he'd warned me about the commercial gentrification. Big-name chains have moved in, pushing up rents and squeezing out many of the independent stores. When that happens—and it happens in cities all around the world now—it wipes out much of a shopping district's unique charm and results in fewer shops that cater to the everyday needs of the people who live in the neighbourhood. But Pasadena is still a model for others. "Developers want to replicate it," said Frank, who remembers the area as skid row when he was growing up in LA. "And then cities also want to replicate it because Pasadena shows them how economic activity has helped make the city fiscally healthier."

Santa Monica is another model, as I learned when I met Denny Zane, the Prius-driving former mayor. Now a political consultant whose cell phone rings frequently, he wore a white T-shirt, jeans and running shoes. The issue that initially drew him into local politics was rent control, and he sat on council for twelve years, two as mayor, before leaving in 1992. He remains chair of Santa Monicans for Renters' Rights, an activist group he co-founded. After rent control, he's best known for the revitalization of the Third Street Promenade, formerly called the Santa Monica Mall. The transformation started at about the same time as the one in Old Town Pasadena, but while the private sector drove most of the changes in Pasadena, the Promenade, which was the centrepiece of the revival of downtown Santa Monica, was the product of city council's policy decisions.

The Promenade had been a pedestrian mall since the early 1960s, but it was a commercial failure. Some people thought the solution was to build a large shopping centre at the south end, and the three-storey Frank Gehry–designed Santa Monica Place opened in 1980. But all that did was suck out what was left of the street's retail life. A few years later, Zane and his fellow councillors set their minds to the problem but couldn't find anywhere in America that had done what they wanted to do: revitalize downtown without tearing it down. They considered attracting movie theatres as an anchor for the area, but quickly learned that they didn't have a hope because nearby Westwood had such a large concentration of cinemas. So Zane suggested that outdoor dining could be the street's salvation: instead of having one big anchor such as a shopping centre, they'd aim for a lot of mini-anchors that would create something distinctive. Despite its ideal weather, LA had no outdoor dining district at the time. Zane blamed car culture for that. "We had no sidewalks. That is, not no sidewalks—we had utterly inadequate sidewalks that were just too narrow," he explained, adding that the city had widened its streets and narrowed its sidewalks to accommodate more traffic. "People were presumed to get from place to place by driving and not by walking. But here we were looking at this space that, for twenty-five years, had had no cars on it. So the sidewalks were ours to create."

Not surprisingly, most of the local merchants thought a much better idea was to close the pedestrian mall and let cars back on the street. A bitter debate ensued until a designer came up with a compromise that included wide sidewalks, two-car lanes and bollards that could be raised or lowered to either prevent or allow traffic on the street. It was a brilliantly simple solution to a vexing little problem and everybody went, "Bingo!" Santa Monica didn't compromise its outdoor dining for the car; instead, it forced the car to accommodate the outdoor dining and the pedestrians.

Just as construction was underway, the city received several proposals for movie theatres, but none of them were for the Promenade—just other parts of town where the neighbours didn't want more traffic or parking problems. Before prohibiting movie houses everywhere except on the Promenade, Zane took the cinema executives on a walking tour to show them they'd be better off there anyway. Afterwards, they all said, "You're right. This makes sense." When council unanimously passed the ordinance, it also limited the number of cinemas to three, which left some companies disappointed, but city council didn't want the theatres to overwhelm the outdoor dining, which was to be the street's real competitive advantage.

Almost immediately, the Promenade was a success as people eagerly filled the theatres and the first half-dozen restaurants with patios. But the residents were growing antsy about heavy traffic because several office projects were going up. "They're fortresses that people drive to, stay in, and then leave," noted Zane. "And they're lousy tax generators. They're just traffic generators." The community backlash led to a push for slow-growth policies, with some groups touting draconian measures that might have hurt the downtown's ability to get back on its feet. Because there wasn't much housing stock in the area, and what did exist was dilapidated, council rezoned the streets around the Promenade to de-emphasize office space and promote housing above the ground level. Developers could go higher with residential buildings than with commercial ones because housing not only generates less traffic, it provides customers for local businesses, making them less dependent on tourists.

Wider sidewalks and mixed-use development are right out of Jane Jacobs's playbook, but Zane confessed he hadn't read much more than fifty pages of her writing. "This was not applied theory. This was just practice, addressing local issues and local dilemmas about traffic."

Two decades later, the pedestrian mall is busier than ever. Carmen and I ate lunch there after we picked up the Hummer, and even on a Wednesday afternoon, the place thrummed with people. The project exceeded expectations, in part because so many Angelinos who don't have their own local options drive to it. Some residents lament the hordes of tourists, and it's true that on Saturday nights, especially in the summer, the crowds can be overwhelming. But Zane's satisfied with the demographic mix.

"Weekend nights are younger than other times, but there are enough middle-aged people," he said. "We're like the control rods in a nuclear reactor. The young adults are more like the fuel rods—they've got all the heat and energy and razzmatazz. They're kicking about, having a good time and stuff. But us middle-aged guys keep everything cool and under control."

Commercial gentrification is also a concern here. Success attracts corporate retailers who wave money around and drive up rents. We just happened to be sitting on the patio of an independent café called the 18th Street Coffee House, where Zane was eating a piece of cheesecake and drinking a mocha.

"So you get a Starbucks instead of something like this?" I asked.

"*A* Starbucks?" he said incredulously. "I think there are four Starbucks on the Promenade. What the hell is that about? There used to be a wonderful café like this—very cool—but they couldn't pay the rent."

The lefty independent bookstore is also gone, replaced by both a Borders and a Barnes & Noble, and the usual suspects—including Gap, Pottery Barn and Apple—now dominate the mall. But the farmer's market is popular, and it even offers free valet parking for bicycles on Sundays.

The most gratifying sight is people walking their dogs because Zane knows no one drives to Santa Monica to do that. The best thing that could happen is for other communities to develop similar projects, so people wouldn't have to cram onto the Third Street Promenade. In fact, Zane told me—only half joking, I think—that his original motivation for wanting to revive downtown was that Old Mahoney's, his favourite bar, closed and he didn't want to have to travel to Hollywood to enjoy a drink. "You shouldn't have to drive halfway across LA to find a restaurant or a movie or whatever," he said. "But of course we hadn't figured that all those other people out there didn't have something either."

Soon, representatives from other cities started showing up to see how Santa Monica had done it. "In some ways it became the template for what we later learned was smart growth," he said. "But we were just being smart about our own problems, both political and planning." Unfortunately, many places bastardized the template. A common mistake is to opt for a theme. "If you want a short life," he insisted, "that's what you do." A theme might prove popular for a couple of years, but the fickleness of the marketplace will make sure it doesn't last long. "People come to the Promenade because it's real life, not because it's theme life. People live here. It's real life happening, warts and all."

In Southern California, sprawl has always been possible because of the ready availability of cheap land, but developers are running out of buildable land that doesn't have some nearby political resistance, so communities and developers must look for other options. "This is the convergence of necessity and good judgment," he said. "The smart thing to do now turns out to be the only thing to do."

My fear is that even if the urban planners, designers, developers and politicians all get together and create the perfect urban form—and that's a hell of a big if—it doesn't mean that drivers will get out of their cars. As Kushner had told me a day earlier, "The hardest part will be for people to just get past the love of the automobile. There's a culture in this country where you grow up looking at cars, looking at the cars you can't afford, remembering the car that you lost your virginity in. It's part of the American myth." We've taken that myth and added convenience and comfort and a sense of control to induce a hardcore addiction.

But Zane argued that we don't need everyone to leave the car behind because incremental improvements can make a huge difference. He argued that if as few as 2 or 3 percent of drivers started taking transit, it would help. "The air pollution would be much better, the congestion would be much better. In a way, you don't have to give up the car culture; you just have to add to it. The car gets to do what it does well and the transit system does what it does well, and they can happily do very well together."

Of course, this can only work if politicians start taking public transit more seriously—and throw some serious money at it. While LA is adding to its network of light rail lines and subways, it's still not enough for such a car-oriented city. Kushner admitted that he gets frustrated at the slow pace of transit development. "If we went full-bore with that, I think we'd have something amazing pretty fast."

But at least attitudes are changing. Just fifteen years ago, when he talked to his students about transit-oriented development and similar ideas, he'd get nothing but puzzled looks and fierce arguments. Now, even the conservatives agree with him. The environmentalists, the Christian movement, the real estate developers, the corporate community, the Democrats and the Republicans may finally have something they can all agree on. "In this country, we've had split politics for as long as anybody can remember, and now we're finally seeing a consensus beginning around these issues of urban growth and design, and that's why I'm probably most optimistic about the future," he said, "I can't give you an exact timetable, but as I see new developments, as I go around the country and look at what cities are doing, I am optimistic that great changes are occurring under our eyes."

Although Kushner praises the transformation of Portland as the most successful rejuvenation of a downtown in the United States, he doesn't think the answer is simply for everyone to move downtown again. For one thing, not everyone wants to do that; for another, it can just create a new set of problems, including what to do with brownfields, with the homeless, with concentrations of poverty and, in some places, with still-simmering racial tensions. Instead, he'd like to see the development of attractive and walkable high-density mixed-use nodes connected by public transit: "I see the future as being this kind of concentrated suburbanism that offers an urban lifestyle in suburban nodes."

If Kushner is right, then all those suburbs that make up Los Angeles may finally find their city—and provide a sustainable model for the rest of the world.

19 The Road Home
Avoiding Carmageddon

FOR SEVEN WEEKS, I had enjoyed near-flawless weather. A morning of heavy rain in Detroit, a torrential all-day downpour in Oklahoma and a blizzard in Denver—but other than that, I'd been travelling under clear skies for longer than I deserved. But that all changed the morning I left San Francisco for the second time. Carmen and I had driven back up the Pacific Coast Highway and then she flew home. I planned to join her there in two weeks and headed north on the Redwood Highway. The rain didn't stop me from enjoying downtown Portland or Thanksgiving weekend in Seattle, but I arrived in Vancouver just in time for the first few flakes of what would turn out to be the largest snowfall in twenty years. My wife and mother wanted me to sell my car in Vancouver and fly home to avoid driving across the continent in the winter. But I wasn't about to cut and run.

Besides, all those hours in the car were going to give me time to digest what I'd seen and heard on my road trip. I'd witnessed a hard-core addiction to the automobile—even when people who knew their habit was bad for them, they felt helpless. "I live here, my job is there and a car is the only feasible way to get between the two," they reason. "And what's one more car on the road?" But every car on the road contributes to sprawl, environmental damage, traffic congestion, health problems and the decline of civic involvement.

And it's getting worse, not better. Decades ago, when the husband worked and the wife stayed home with the kids, a man could live near his job, though usually he didn't, especially after the flight to the suburbs. But today, with the two-career family so common, living near two different jobs is not even a possibility for many couples, especially in polycentric cities. In 2005, 74 percent of Canadian adults made all their trips by car, up from 70 percent in 1998 and 68 percent in 1992. The lower the density of the city, the higher the automobile use: 77 percent of Edmontonians rely exclusively on the car, while only 65 percent of Montrealers do. The density of the neighbourhood and the distance from downtown also make a difference: 74 percent of people who live fifteen kilometres or more from the city core are car dependent, compared to only 43 percent of residents within five kilometres.

Most people my age started driving in their teens, but before that they walked to school and to visit friends. So they know how to walk, even if they rarely do it now. Worse, they drive their kids everywhere. Part of it is fear; no parent today would do what mine did: send me to school on public transit from the age of ten. James van Hemert of the Rocky Mountain Land Use Institute told me that he and his wife made their kids walk or bike to school—to a lot of disapproving incredulity. "The implication was we were cruel, uncaring parents," he said. "We're not. And now I have kids who walk for miles." Just because we now live in an overprotective society doesn't mean we have to drive our kids everywhere—and we should be as vigilant about childhood obesity and the other health risks associated with car culture as we are about pedophiles. (A walking bus—a group of children accompanied by two adults, one in the lead, one bringing up the rear—is one way to deal with the fear factor while letting children walk to school.) As soon as they're old enough, we buy them cars even though the crash rate for teenagers is horrifying. We are training a generation of kids to never be pedestrians or transit users.

North America isn't the only place on a bad automobile jag. I'd seen it in Argentina, and a few months after my road trip, I flew to London to get a sense of the car culture there. As every tourist knows, it is a great walking city; the famous black cabs, while not cheap, are easy to flag down; and there's an extensive public transit system consisting of buses and the Underground, better known as "the tube" (though it is old and, in the summer, can be unbearably hot). And yet Londoners, like all Britons, are car crazy.

I stayed with my sister and brother-in-law and niece in a mews house near Sloane Square. This has always been a posh area, but the amount of money here, and in surrounding neighbourhoods, is staggering. Even before I heard about the real estate prices or paid for a meal in a local pub (a typical example: US$100 for a Sunday pub lunch for two), I could see it in the cars. Normally, the sight of a Rolls-Royce, a Bentley or a Lamborghini is a rare treat; not here—the place is lousy with them. And since most people park on the street, many of these fancy cars are always on display rather than hidden away in garages. Mercedes-Benzes, Porsches, Jaguars and BMWs are standard rides. Anyone who drives a Lexus, a Volkswagen or one of the many Minis is not really keeping up with the Joneses. Smaller cars predominate here—which makes sense given the narrow roads, tight parking spaces and high gas prices—and I saw a lot of Smart cars and plenty of Priuses. Even away from this rarefied neck of the woods, American cars aren't plentiful and I didn't see one pickup all week. But SUVs, which Londoners call "Chelsea tractors," are surprisingly common. Mostly, though, the people here prefer the stylish and luxurious to the simply big and brutish.

While in London, I watched two very different television shows. The first was *Top Gear*, a hugely popular BBC series hosted by car lover Jeremy Clarkson. The second was the first episode of a four-part BBC documentary called *Are We There Yet?*, in which journalist John Ware described the car culture in his country this way: "It's mad, it's bonkers, it's a sort of mad carmageddon, it's ugly, it's smelly, it's grim, it's Britain."

But as much as Europe, like South America, struggles to cope with the automobile, if there really is going to be carmageddon, it's likely to be in India or China. Shashi Nambisan, the University of Nevada, Las Vegas, transportation engineer, emigrated from

India two decades ago. When he returns to his native country, he finds driving in the overwhelming congestion a white-knuckle experience and is convinced that the American love affair with the automobile is contagious. "It's spreading across the world," he said. "I see far more problems coming up in China and India and Indonesia than we will ever experience here because cars are becoming more affordable to a larger section of the populace." The recent release of the Nano, a $2,500 model from the giant Tata Motors, will mean a lot more drivers in India.

The automobile obsession in England was scary because that country has far less sprawl than North America does, so it has alternatives, including an excellent train system. In addition, a quarter of all the trips people take are shorter than two miles, making them ideal for walking, biking or taking transit. That just fed my fear that even if planners could come up with the ideal urban form—comfortably dense with wide, inviting sidewalks, plenty of safe bike lanes and an extensive and efficient public transit system—too many people still wouldn't get out of their cars. The only solution may be to make people pay for their decision to drive.

A FEW MONTHS BEFORE I left on my trip, I visited the Toronto Traffic Management Centre. At 7:30 a.m., the room—which had fifty-seven television monitors—was quiet; in fact, only one employee was at his post. Les Kelman, Toronto's director of transportation systems, assured me that the place was not like that when there were problems on the roads, but it was the morning before the Canada Day holiday, so traffic was much lighter than usual. With so little going on in the command centre, we moved to his office, where he kept an orange safety vest on the back of the door. Short and bearded, Kelman is an impish man with a wry sense of humour, a Scottish burr and a great love of soccer. "One day," he predicted, "road space is going to be more valuable than gold."

No doubt he was exaggerating for effect, especially since most cities aren't as choked with traffic as all the complaining from drivers would suggest, but the situation is deteriorating around the world. A few places have been smart enough to invest heavily in transit: in the last decade, Madrid has more than doubled the size of its subway system, which is now the third largest in the world with over three hundred kilometres of track. But most cities haven't shown the same gumption and simply expect transportation engineers to struggle with little more than new technology to ease gridlock.

Since it's obviously going to take more than that, politicians will have to get serious. Two weeks before Toronto's municipal elections in 2003, mayoral candidate David Miller mused that if the senior levels of government didn't pony up their share for transit funding, perhaps drivers who took the main highways into the city would have to pay a toll of $2.25 for the privilege, the same as the cost of hopping on a subway, streetcar or bus at the time. Commuters were outraged, and John Tory, a frontrunner for the job, seized the opportunity to paint Miller—who in the previous weeks had made an impressive charge from behind to become a serious contender—as a typical tax-and-spend politician. Miller might have blown his chance, but he quickly backtracked and said Toronto would never have tolls as long as he was mayor. The about-face was certainly crucial to his eventual electoral success and now, as mayor, he will only talk about tolls as a regional solution.

For all his progressive talk, Miller is just one more politician without the guts to take tough decisions against cars and drivers—unlike Ken Livingstone. At the C40 Large Cities Climate Summit, a New York City conference in May 2007 that put municipal leaders and corporate executives together in an effort to tackle climate change, the mayor of London admitted that he faced a lot of opposition when he introduced a congestion levy in his city. "There was this drip, drip, drip of negativity and it took a toll on my poll ratings," he said. "But within a week of the congestion charge starting, my opinion poll rating had gone up 12 percent."

Livingstone congratulated New York mayor Michael Bloomberg's "courageous" plan to introduce an eight-dollar congestion toll for Manhattan. If it goes through, the charge will generate an estimated five hundred million dollars a year, revenue that will be spent on tunnels, commuter railroads, subways and buses. The famously left-wing Londoner also gave the billionaire Republican some advice: "There may be one or two people who predict doom and gloom. Ignore them. We can't solve the problem of global warming without getting a better balance between mass transit and the motor car."

In 2003, London started charging five pounds for vehicles entering, leaving, driving or parking on a public road in the central zone between 7 a.m. and 6:30 p.m. (since cut back to 6 p.m.) on weekdays. Taxis, hybrids and electric cars are exempt. The fee increased to eight pounds in 2005, and just a couple of weeks before I arrived in March 2007, the city expanded the zone westward. (Initially designed to reduce congestion, the charge is increasingly also an environmental measure. The next step, if Livingstone has his way, will be to raise the cost for Chelsea tractors and other vehicles that emit more than 225 grams of carbon dioxide per kilometre to twenty-five pounds.)

The proceeds don't go into the city's general budget and must be spent on improving public transit. In the first year, the toll led to an 18 percent decrease in the number of cars and trucks entering the zone and an increase of between 14 and 21 percent in the speed they travelled. Congestion has increased since then, but traffic would have increased without the charge and at least now it's growing from a lower base. As a tourist, I definitely noticed a difference from the last time I'd been there five years earlier. During the week, at least; on Saturday, when the charge doesn't apply, the traffic thickened and slowed to what I remembered.

Not everyone is as impressed as I was. I heard plenty of moaning, and Chris Prior, who sees the toll as "a blunt instrument" and "an example of everything that's wrong with government," was upset enough that he decided to run for mayor against Livingstone. As the leader of the Stop Congestion Charging Party, he will, if elected in May 2008, abolish the toll on his first day in office. His arguments against it include that too much of the charge—about two-thirds, in fact—goes to collecting it rather than improving public transit, it's regressive because it takes more of a nurse's salary than a banker's and it just forces the congestion outside the zone. Instead, he'd improve public transit and marry communications technology with new, more flexible forms of transportation such as shared taxis and smaller, electric buses.

Prior drives a Prius—and not just because hybrids are exempt from the toll—but dressed in a dark blue suit, crisp white shirt and sober tie, he appeared to be the stereotypical Conservative and, in fact, he told me, "I believe very much that government should be about cutting taxes and improving the quality of public administration." By contrast, Livingstone may best be known by his "Red Ken" moniker. The irony is that congestion tolls—now derided as tax grabs, restrictions on freedom and a plot hatched by lefties and tree huggers—were first touted, decades ago, by the likes of Alan Walters, who went on to be chief economic advisor to Margaret Thatcher, and Milton Friedman, the economist who was so influential in the rise of neo-conservatism in the 1980s. To thinkers of this ilk, drivers only consider their own costs when they take a congested road; they don't take into account the cost they impose on others by slowing everyone down. When drivers must pay to use a road, they face the true cost of their decision, which reduces demand and creates a more efficient use of the capacity.

Although all drivers can figure out what they pay for gas, insurance and other car-related expenses, and some can even put a value on their time, few ever think about what economists call an "externality"—the public cost of congestion. Since Georgina Santos, a lecturer at the University of Oxford's Transport Studies Unit, has looked into this and co-authored a paper titled, "Road Pricing: Lessons from London," I took the train to Oxford. Best known for its university, the city is also the home of a BMW plant that has produced over one million Minis, but I was impressed by the sea of bikes locked up at the train station, and at lunchtime I saw far more bikes than cars on the road, and the sidewalks were crammed with people.

Inside her tidy office, Santos, who is originally from Argentina, explained that external costs vary with the type of vehicle and amount of congestion. Theoretically, if a government charges more than the true cost, it will reduce traffic too much, stunting economic activity; but if it doesn't charge enough, the roads will remain clogged with traffic. In practice, politics determines the price: Livingstone initially decided to make both cars and trucks pay five pounds—an easy-to-remember round number—even if that meant the plan overcharged cars and undercharged trucks. "I'm not a politician, I'm an academic," admitted Santos, a slim woman who wore several bracelets that jangled on her wrist as she talked. "Any academic economist would say, 'You are crazy, you cannot charge the same toll to cars and to trucks. That is against economic theory, completely against.' And yet, he got traffic congestion down and the benefits in time-savings have been considerable."

She recommended that cities thinking of copying London's example do three things. First, ensure the tolled zone is well served by public transit; otherwise, people have no option but to pay the charge. Second, consult the public, and tweak the plan based on that input, but don't hold a referendum, because people won't vote for it. Third, keep it simple. London initially chose a small area with clear limits and a flat toll that was easy to understand— even if it didn't exactly hold to economic theory.

Despite the success of the original plan, the westward expansion was controversial. Even supporters questioned the decision to give residents a massive discount (though that did mean the wealthy denizens of Kensington and Chelsea suddenly switched from being the biggest grumblers to placated beneficiaries). That concession worries Stephen Glaister. A professor of transport and infrastructure at London's Imperial College, he is an economist who needs a congestion charge for his office: the large room was overflowing with papers, files, reports and books on shelves, on the floor and in file boxes. I sat down in a chair behind a pile of papers on the long table attached to his desk. It was late afternoon, and the tail of his rumpled white shirt was no longer tucked in at the back and his red-and-blue tie hung a couple of inches below his undone top button. As we talked, he rose several times to grab a book or a report and I was impressed at how quickly he located them, though at one point several file boxes tumbled to the floor.

A member of the Transport for London Board, which is the executive agency for the mayor, Glaister supports the congestion charge, but while he understands why the city gave people in the original zone the discount—the charge was new and the residents were few—he fears that maintaining the special status for those in the new area will jeopardize future expansions. "There's absolutely no point in even thinking about introducing a congestion-charging scheme if you give discounts to residents," he said. "Once you do that, you've given it away because most traffic is local."

That precedent is particularly unfortunate since he's really more interested in road pricing for London as a whole and for other parts of England. "Congestion actually is much more serious in outer London than it is in the centre," said Glaister, who owns a Prius but cycles to work. "That's where the grief is. This is because it's much like the rest of the country: public transport isn't an alternative out there." The solution is to invest money to improve transit in outer London and then introduce the congestion charge to pay for it. But that will require not just dinging all residents but also replacing the daily fee with one based on how far a driver travels and when, which would require more advanced technology.

Glaister also had advice for other cities. "Number one, look at the facts. Don't listen to taxi drivers and the general public," he said. The second step is to take a lot of care in the design of the plan, not just how, where and when drivers will be charged—and which ones will get exemptions or discounts—but what the money collected will be spent on. Some jurisdictions may want to reduce gas taxes to make the toll revenue neutral; others will dedicate it to public transit. "Then be very careful to present the complete picture to the public before you give them half a chance to go off on the wrong foot."

TOLLS MAY BE AN IDEA that some people and some cities are finally willing to debate, but free parking remains the blind spot in urban and transportation planning. During my trip, I'd heard various estimates (four, eight, thirteen) for the number of parking spots per car in North America and I have to admit that, initially, I was shocked. After all, like most people, when I'm driving around hunting for a legal space—all the while burning fossil fuels, spewing emissions and adding to the traffic congestion—it never occurs to me that North American cities devote so much space to parking. But the typical driver has a parking spot at home and one at work (usually bigger than the cubicle he or she spends all day in) as well as shared spots at malls, stores, restaurants and even churches. We're so accustomed to abundant free parking that we resist paying for it, hate looking for it and, most of all, dread getting tickets. As Donald Shoup, America's parking guru, told me, "Everybody thinks parking is a personal problem, not a policy problem." But everybody is wrong.

Born in California in 1938, Shoup was living in Honolulu when the Japanese attacked Pearl Harbor in 1941. Now a professor at UCLA's urban planning department and the author of *The High*

Cost of Free Parking, he has a growing band of followers who call themselves Shoupistas even though the market-oriented policies he advocates could best be summed up by the battle cry, "Charge whatever the traffic will bear." He'd offered to arrange "free (or rather fully subsidized) parking" for me, but I wanted to take the bus in order to experience public transit in Los Angeles. I made it to UCLA forty-five minutes early and spent the time checking out the campus and then went up to his office and found a bald man with a grey beard sitting at a desk with a radio in the shape of a parking meter on it.

Shoup isn't sure what the ratio of parking spots to cars is—he suspects it's at least three or four to one, probably more—but he knows it's too high. He's also convinced that free parking not only encourages people to drive—it's actually expensive because subsidizing it costs the economy more than the government devotes to Medicare. Turning to his computer, he showed me aerial photos of several cities to demonstrate how much land we waste just to give drivers a place to leave their wheels. "Parking is the single-biggest land use in almost any city and almost everybody has ignored it," he told me. "It's like dark matter in the universe: we know there's something there, and it seems to weigh a lot, but we don't know what it is. If only we could get our hands on it."

While he was at his computer, he also gave me a virtual tour of Old Town Pasadena, with before and after photos that showed how it had gone from skid row to upscale destination. One of his ideas was instrumental in that transformation. The city faced a common problem: parking was free, but the few merchants who were still in business complained that it was inadequate. The people who worked in the stores took most of the spots, leaving customers to drive around searching for one—or just staying away. Meanwhile, the city had a vision of a revitalized downtown but no money to repair sidewalks, plant trees, increase security or take any of the other steps necessary to attract people. Shoup recommended charging enough for parking to maintain an

85 percent occupancy rate and using the money shoppers dropped in the meters to improve the neighbourhood. The revenue couldn't go into the city's general coffers; it had to be spent on the streets. Once that happened, the business community started to invest too—even sandblasting and renovating derelict buildings—and soon the shop owners, who had initially opposed meters, wanted to charge for parking until midnight. They wanted the money for the improvements, but they also discovered that their fears about scaring away customers were unfounded—anyone who really wanted to shop or eat in the area was willing to invest a few quarters. As the area became more popular, the meters raised more money for more improvements, which increased the popularity. And so on. The city now collects one million dollars a year to pay for upkeep that includes sweeping the sidewalks nightly and steam-cleaning them twice a month.

In Calvin Trillin's *Tepper Isn't Going Out*, a slight but charming novel about a man who becomes a New York folk hero because of his parking acumen, once Murray Tepper finds a parking spot he just sits there and enjoys it. But when Shoup and I talked about the book, he pointed out that Tepper wouldn't have stayed put so long if Manhattan charged the right price for street parking. The right price is the one that means there are always one or two open spots per block. Since the cost encourages turnover, time limits are unnecessary; in fact, any place that needs to impose time limits is not charging enough. A city should adjust the rate every quarter to ensure the 15 percent vacancy rate, always letting the market decide the price. "Nobody can tell you what the right price of gold is, or the right price of wheat or apples," he argued. "It just happens."

Free off-street parking isn't something that just happens, though, because planning departments always insist that developers include a minimum number of parking spots. Shoup doesn't have much respect for the ability of urban planners to determine how many spots are necessary. Since planners don't learn anything about parking in school, they learn it on the job, but because parking is so political—NIMBY neighbours constantly squawk at the thought of anyone parking on their street—what they really learn is the politics of parking. "Planning will be looked back on as worse than phrenology, because phrenology didn't do any harm," he said, referring to the nineteenth-century pseudoscience that claimed to be able to determine character and other traits from the size and shape of a cranium. The harm abundant free parking does feeds on itself: all that land dedicated to parking, which often sits empty for much of the day, increases sprawl, and that sprawl makes alternatives such as public transit and walking less feasible, which forces more people into cars, which increases the need for more parking.

Again, Shoup argued that the market should decide: freed from the arbitrary and capricious demands of the planners, developers will put in the right amount of parking—enough to meet their customers' needs, but not so much that they waste valuable space or money. When the Westfield San Francisco Centre reopened in September 2006 after a major renovation, it was triple the size, featured high-profile tenants such as Bloomingdale's and expected twenty-five million visitors a year—all without adding any new parking. A lot of people shook their heads at that, but the mall is close to thirty-two transit lines and sits across the street from a large parking garage that was rarely anywhere close to full.

In 1992, the state of California adopted another Shoupism: under the parking cash-out law, companies that pay for employees' parking must offer the equivalent in cash to non-parkers. So someone who works for a firm that pays $150 a month for each spot in an underground lot can opt to forgo the spot and pocket the cash. After the law came in, 13 percent of employees took the money—most switching to car pools or taking public transit, though a few started riding a bike or walking to work.

Although his ideas seem like so much common sense, Shoup still feels they're underappreciated. Many places want to thrive the way Old Town Pasadena has, but few realize how crucial the meter money was to that success. Still, he knows some planners are curious because he receives more invitations to speak than he can accept. Cities pay him large lecture fees, fly him first class and then wine him and dine him, but they don't all do what he suggests because parking is so political. "All I can do is go and say, 'You're doing everything wrong,'" said Shoup, who rides a bike 2 miles to campus, puts just 3,500 miles a year on his Infiniti and admitted that he's often mistaken as an enemy of the car. He insists he's not; it's just that people would live differently—read: drive less—if they had to pay for parking. The good news is that all that parking space is an accidental land reserve for housing that can bring in tax revenue even as it helps ease traffic congestion, air pollution and energy dependence. "The nice thing is that when cities adopt what I'm saying,"—he snapped his fingers—"like that, it works."

DRIVERS WON'T BE KEEN on shelling out more for parking, congestion tolls and gas or carbon taxes, but such measures are probably inevitable and they make sense as long as the revenues are strictly dedicated to public transit, local improvement projects and, in the case of gas levies, the development of cleaner fuels. Either that, or these charges should be revenue neutral: a carbon tax, for example, can mean a reduction in income taxes. North American governments should also be investing some of this money in high-speed trains in well-travelled corridors. France's TGV and similar rail services in other countries offer a fast, efficient and comfortable— and environmentally sensible—way to visit other places. Ultimately, though, individuals need to make the choice to drive less.

For some people who live in cities, an alternative to owning a second vehicle—or even any at all—may be to join a car-sharing service. Kevin McLaughlin is the president of Toronto-based AutoShare, which allows members to pay an hourly rate to drive its vehicles, which are parked at over one hundred locations around the city. Gas and insurance are included in the cost, so the service is ideal for people who need a car for the occasional chore. The average member drives about ten hours a month. I met with McLaughlin in the spring of 2006, several weeks after Massachusetts-based Zipcar arrived in Toronto. Initially worried about such a well-financed competitor, he soon realized his new rival would not only help to build the market, it would also validate that market, making it easier for him to get the financing he needs to expand. Convinced that there's the potential for his company to sign up as many as 10 percent of Torontonians and to have a fleet of several thousand, he said his biggest constraint, aside from raising capital, is finding and paying for places to park the company's cars.

McLaughlin grew up with posters of race driver Gilles Villeneuve on his bedroom wall, his uncle raced cars and his father still owns a 1938 Cord and a 1929 McLaughlin-Buick (in fact, his family is distantly related to Sam McLaughlin, the Canadian automaker who sold his company to General Motors). And he has been able to combine his youthful love of cars with his adult concern for the environment. McLaughlin, who worked as an environmentalist in Vancouver, admitted that the reaction from people in the movement has been mixed. Many have applauded his attempt to reduce the number of cars on the road, but some don't like that cars are involved at all. "This isn't the solution, but there really isn't *a* solution," he said. "It is part of the solution."

MY ROAD TRIP ALSO HELPED me to better understand why many people love cars so much. And my own affection for the automobile grew as I started to see the car—even my old car—less as an appliance and more as something fun. It certainly wouldn't be the first thing I've enjoyed that was bad for me. As always, I gather, moderation is necessary. The members of the Classic Car Club, in London, may have found the right balance. James Evans, the club's co-owner and managing director, was unshaven and dressed in jeans. We sat in old leather chairs and he explained that his members are car lovers who are "money rich and time poor." In the last few years, he has seen an attitude adjustment, especially after the congestion charge came in. "They just can't be bothered owning a car in London," he admitted. "It's just become such a hassle, such a chore. And it's become very expensive to own a car."

Evans grew up just outside of Glasgow, the son of a Jaguar-loving mother and an auto-hating father. "He would always have a rubbish car, like a Vauxhall Viva, which is dreadful, and he would drive a car until it physically stopped," he remembered. "And the number of times I was in the car and it would break down—I'd have friends with me, and be like, 'Oh God, this is so embar-rassing'—so one day I decided the one thing I would always have would be a nice car." In 1997, he was saving up to buy a Ferrari 308 when he heard about the Classic Car Club, which had started two years earlier with eight vehicles. He joined, then started working there, then bought it in 1999.

Located in an old garage on the edge of The City, London's financial district, the club doesn't look at all fancy from the outside. Even the office is far from elegant, though it does feature a foosball table and a jukebox dominated by 1970s and 1980s music—from The Stranglers' "No More Heroes" to Dexy's Midnight Runners' "Come On Eileen"—as well as an Esso gas tank bubble gum machine, a half-height Michelin Man, and steering wheels and a Jaguar grille on the walls. There's also an old dentist's chair, and when I asked Evans about it, he joked, "Oh, that's to make people join."

Seems to work: the London site has 450 members and the club now operates in Edinburgh, Glasgow, Copenhagen and New York, with plans for further expansion in other U.S. cities. For an annual fee, members can book a car by redeeming points based on the type of car, time of year and day of the week they want to drive it. A Saturday in the summer, for example, is worth more than a Wednesday in winter. The club has three mechanics and two valets to fix and clean the sixty-vehicle collection, which is worth more than one million pounds and includes forty or so classics and sports cars, from Rolls-Royces to Porsches to E-type Jaguars. The rest range from a Mini and a VW Beetle to several high-end SUVs (since some members have given up their own cars, opting instead to take transit or walk to work, the club now offers cars suitable for family trips).

Evans and I stepped out of the office and into a large space crammed with cars, and he proudly showed off some of the gems, including a 1965 Buick Riviera, a 1985 Ferrari Mondial and a 2006 BMW Z4M Coupe. One of the most popular cars with the members is the 1967 Citroën DS Pallas; Evans opened the door and insisted I sit in it. I sank into the leather seat and marvelled at how comfortable it was.

"Man, it's so luxurious, I could sleep in here," I exclaimed.

"They don't make them like they used to, as they say," he boasted. "You could go all the way across the States in that, couldn't you?"

If I had, I'm sure I would have stayed on the road a lot longer.

I HAD NO COMPLAINTS about my Maxima, though. I spent a few snowy days in Vancouver with my friend Grahame Arnould, who is a cartoonist. He then joined me on the drive through the mountains to Calgary. Grahame wanted to hook up with a red-headed Pilates instructor in Nelson, B.C., and that wasn't too much of a detour so I said sure. But the morning we were to leave, we awoke to a travel advisory for the main highway, so we took an alternative route to Hope, crawled along an icy road for the first part of the day and lost so much time that we never made it to Nelson. Instead, we spent the night chatting with Norm the ex-con bartender at the Hot L Saloon in the tiny border town of Midway. The next day, it was getting dark by the time we reached Fernie; hearing reports of blowing snow in the Crowsnest Pass, we decided to spend the night. In the morning, we cleared several inches of snow off the car and left town despite a travel advisory.

In Calgary, I did a night on the town with Blake O'Brien, a friend who runs his old Mercedes station wagon on cooking fat, and predictably enough, my start the next morning was later than I'd planned. For the rest of the trip I was on my own, trying to get back to Toronto safely but quickly.

The snow seemed to blow constantly on the Trans-Canada Highway. Sometimes it wisped across in straight lines; sometimes it swirled across in a ghostly dance. The white road ahead was disconcerting, but it was bare underneath. After dark, though, the blowing snow made the visibility poor, so I tried to limit my driving to daylight hours and stayed a night in Swift Current. After I crossed from Saskatchewan into Manitoba, the sky cleared and I saw a rainbow, but it was soon snowing again. And it had been bitterly cold for days.

From Winnipeg, I headed south to North Dakota, past Fargo, through Minnesota to Eau Claire, Wisconsin. I woke up to more snow on the car and drove through flurries and blowing snow for about an hour before it cleared up. I started to make good time. Driving past Chicago was a hassle, but I was beginning to think I'd make it home late that night. Once I reached Michigan, though, the skies filled with dark clouds, and soon I faced more flurries and then heavy snow. I drove past several collisions, including an SUV upside down in the ditch, and by 5 p.m. reluctantly conceded that I'd be spending one more night in a hotel.

The next day, nine and a half weeks after I started, I arrived home. My car had made it. In fact, the dead battery in Bridgeport, California, was the only mechanical problem I'd encountered during the 14,992 kilometres through seventeen states and five provinces. A few weeks later, though, my mechanic Gord Donley suggested I start saving up for my next car because the fuel and break lines were rusting badly. He figured I might get another winter or two out of it, but six months, almost to the day, after I returned from my road trip, he pronounced my wheels dead. Well, he didn't so much say the car was dead as recommend euthanasia.

It was early in June when I dropped it off, but when I checked my messages later in the day, it wasn't his usual, "Your car is ready." Instead, I heard, "Please give me a call." Donley said the brake line was leaking and he wouldn't even let me drive it home. Fixing it would cost two thousand dollars and the car wasn't worth that much; although it had only 176,255 kilometres on the odometer, it also had oil and coolant leaks and busted air conditioning.

I was bummed, naturally. I had no wheels. But there was more to it than that: it had been my first ride, and though I'd never given it a name and or lost my virginity in the back seat, I'd had some good times in it. I'd done a road trip to the Maritimes, travelled to Maine and back and enjoyed my great adventure to California in it. As the day wore on and the news sunk in, my melancholy grew.

Somehow I'd driven across the continent and back and my love–hate relationship with the automobile had only deepened. I knew that on both a personal level (my finances) and a global one (the environment), I should just join AutoShare, but possessing my own car now seemed even more crucial. I wasn't going to kid myself that a car would bless me with status, power or freedom, but I still wanted one. Sure enough, at the end of summer, I bought a Sunlight Silver Mazda3 with manual transmission, cup holders and an iPod jack. I rationalize my decision by saying my ride isn't too bad on gas, and since it's small and new, I've at least reduced my emissions.

That doesn't mean I don't feel guilty. I do. I've seen and heard more than enough to understand how the car is hurting our planet, our communities and ourselves. I also realize that whatever other lofty meaning we imbue our automobiles with, they really are just appliances. The problem isn't that we own cars but that we subsidize them, design cities for them and build our lives around them. We drive too much. So while my sporty sedan is great fun and I can't wait to go on another good long road trip, I won't be putting many miles on it. I am still a committed pedestrian.

Appendix
Car Song Playlist

NO MATTER WHAT the audio system is, music rarely sounds better than when it's cranked up during a road trip with friends. And automobiles never seem more full of promise—more essential—than in the lyrics of a good song about a beloved set of wheels, driving or the road. And there are a lot of them.

I aimed to craft a killer playlist of car tunes, but that's no easy task, especially since I wanted them all to fit on an eighty-minute CD, a limit that turned out to be quite painful. I ended up cutting a lot of tracks I didn't want to lose. That caveat aside, here is an annotated version of my completely idiosyncratic playlist of the most indispensable car songs:

"Rocket 88"
JACKIE BRENSTON & HIS DELTA CATS (1951)
This may be the first rock 'n' roll song. Even if it isn't, it's a classic about cars, boozing and cruising. (Ike Turner's Kings of Rhythm actually made the recording, but since Brenston, normally the group's saxophone player, did the singing, the band used the Delta Cats moniker.)

"No Particular Place to Go"
CHUCK BERRY (1964)
Although Berry, who worked on an auto-body assembly line, recorded several noteworthy car songs, including "Maybelline," "No Money Down" and "You Can't Catch Me," I've chosen this rocker about a guy and a girl "cruising and playing the radio." They park but the girl has a "safety belt that wouldn't budge."

"Little Red Corvette"

PRINCE, *1999* (1983)

Sure, using a car as a metaphor for a woman is nothing new, but this funky pop song is Prince at his best.

"Low Rider"

WAR, *WHY CAN'T WE BE FRIENDS?* (1975)

This Latin-rock take on lowrider culture is hard to resist.

"Little Deuce Coupe"

THE BEACH BOYS, *SURFER GIRL* (1963)

No car-song playlist would be complete without the Beach Boys. Although the great American pop band has plenty of automobile-related material to choose from—"Fun, Fun, Fun" and "409" would also have been fine selections—I've chosen this hot rod ode because of the stunning vocal arrangement.

"Driving Sideways"

AIMEE MANN, *BACHELOR NO. 2* (2000)

A lovely song about travelling with a woman who won't navigate because she's afraid she'll be wrong. A metaphor for a doomed relationship.

"Brand New Cadillac"

THE CLASH, *LONDON CALLING* (1979)

Although Vince Taylor wrote this song, the Clash recorded the definitive version. A great tune from what may be the greatest rock 'n' roll album of all time, so of course it's going to make this list.

"Roadrunner"

THE MODERN LOVERS, *THE MODERN LOVERS* (1976)

This infectious garage rock anthem is about avoiding loneliness by listening to the radio and driving fast in Massachusetts. "Radio on!"

"The Passenger"

IGGY POP, *LUST FOR LIFE* (1977)

My playlist includes more songs from the 1970s than any other decade. Perhaps that's because I was a teenager back then and not because the era was the high-water mark for car music. Still, this popular proto-punk song about cruising around at night, when the city is asleep and the stars are out and "everything looks good," is an obvious choice.

"Autobahn"

KRAFTWERK, *AUTOBAHN* (1974)

An improbable hit on both sides of the Atlantic, this hypnotic bit of electronic pop—complete with cars zooming by, squealing tires and other road sounds—captures the exhilarating monotony of long-distance highway driving. The fact that most English-speaking listeners misheard the song's oft-repeated line *"Fahren fahren fahren auf der Autobahn"* as "Fun, fun, fun on the autobahn" only makes it better. (*Fahren* means driving in German.) There are various versions available, ranging from three minutes to nearly twenty-three minutes in length—I've chosen the nine-and-a-half-minute one so this playlist will be burnable on a CD.

"Radar Love"

GOLDEN EARRING, *MOONTAN* (1973)

Widely considered the best driving song of all time—just try sticking to the speed limit while this song blasts from the car stereo. Just try.

"Crosstown Traffic"

JIMI HENDRIX, *ELECTRIC LADYLAND* (1968)

Cars as sexual metaphor again—this time from one of rock's most revered guitarists. The narrator, who will only drive ninety miles an hour, compares a "hard to get through to" woman to heavy traffic because she is slowing him down.

"Old Blue Car"

PETER CASE, *PETER CASE* (1986)

Although it earned a Grammy Award nomination, this song from Case's solo debut is perhaps the least known on this playlist. But everyone can relate to what it's about: he and his friends pile into an old car that will take them anywhere they want to go.

"Long May You Run"

THE STILLS-YOUNG BAND, *THE STILLS-YOUNG BAND* (1976)

Today, Neil Young is a devoted car collector. But back in 1965 (not in 1962 as the song suggests) he had to abandon his beloved first car—an old hearse nicknamed Mort—after it broke down near Blind River, a small town in Northern Ontario. This is his elegy to Mort.

"Passenger Side"
WILCO, *A.M.* (1995)
A whimsical alt-country ballad about a driver who has lost his licence and must rely on his friends to drive him around. The wasted passenger doesn't like riding shotgun—or that his equally wasted designated driver is swerving all over the road.

"Windfall"
SON VOLT, *TRACE* (1995)
The narrator of this alt-country anthem sure loves the road trip he's on. I'm particularly fond of the part where he finds an all-night AM radio station from Louisiana that reminds him of 1963 and "sounds like heaven."

"This Year"
THE MOUNTAIN GOATS, *THE SUNSET TREE* (2005)
This song is not about cars; it's about a seventeen-year-old kid determined to survive one more year with his abusive stepfather. But I've included it here because songwriter John Darnielle does such a masterful job of using the car as a narrative vehicle. On Saturday morning, he finds freedom by getting in the car and driving away, fast. He gets drunk, plays video games and then meets his girlfriend (they are, he sings, "twin high maintenance machines"). The car, stuck in second gear, screams as he turns into the driveway when he arrives home at dusk to face another inevitable ugly confrontation with his stepfather.

"(Looking for) The Heart of Saturday Night"
TOM WAITS, *THE HEART OF SATURDAY NIGHT* (1974)
I'm tempted to pick "Ol' 55," from Waits's *Closing Time* album, but I'm going with this tender, melancholic ballad about cruising around on a Saturday night in an Oldsmobile.

"Racing in the Streets"
BRUCE SPRINGSTEEN, *DARKNESS ON THE EDGE OF TOWN* (1978)
Given that The Boss grew up in New Jersey, it's no surprise that cars make appearances in many of his songs, but this one from the last of his

four great albums is my pick as the best of the genre. Springsteen often masks dark lyrics with rousing music, but this is no rocker; it's a slow, seven-minute masterpiece and an unabashedly poignant portrayal of adult despair and what a car can really mean to someone. Springsteen's working-class characters rarely see cars as simply freedom or adolescent salvation despite all their talk about promised lands: the man wooing the porch-bound Mary in "Thunder Road" knows any redemption from their loneliness that he and his car can offer will be only temporary and the cruising kids in "Born to Run" have nowhere to hide on the broken hero–jammed highways. But the narrator in "Racing in the Streets" is past even that; for him, the car represents survival. Unlike other men his age—most of whom have given up and started slowly dying—when he's finished working at his dreary job he goes out and races his souped-up 1969 Chevy for money. His aging girlfriend wallows in her shattered dreams and even when he says he'll drive her to the sea to wash away their sins, it's hard to sense any optimism about it. His car and his ability to beat other drivers are all he has left.

Acknowledgments

MY ROAD TRIP wouldn't have been nearly as much fun without my fellow travellers: Chris Goldie (who also read the first draft), Scott Tomenson, David Johnston (my great agent), Mike Harper (who was beyond generous with his car knowledge), Carmen Merrifield (see below) and Grahame Arnould.

Several people invited me into their homes just when I began to dread hotels: Margot Hartford and Pieter Leezenberg in San Francisco, Bruce and Diana Spencer in San Jose, Amy and James Spach in Los Angeles, Terry and Beth Drayton in Seattle, Grahame Arnould in Vancouver and Blake O'Brien in Calgary. Later, Nicky Falconer and Steve Baker hosted me in London.

I'm indebted to a number of people who helped me write this book. Thanks to my ever-patient editor Helen Reeves, who also had the idea, and to Diane Turbide, for suggesting I could pull it off. Ian Pearson and Matthew Church read the first draft, and their advice proved invaluable. Brian Banks assigned a magazine piece about my road trip, which meant a little money and made sure I didn't wait until I arrived home to start writing. Researchers Wendy Glauser in Toronto, Dawn Makinson in Buenos Aires and James Fontanella in London made my life so much easier. Wendy also transcribed for me, as did Heather Stonehouse and Gabriela D'Angelo, who also translated. Copy editor Tara Tovell challenged my ideas and the way I expressed them. And production editor Sandra Tooze made sure it all got done on time. Any errors are, of course, mine alone.

Special thanks to my mom and my four sisters and to all my friends who, against all odds, continue to put up with me.

Finally, thanks to the astonishing Carmen Merrifield for twenty-five years of love and indulgence.

Tim Falconer
Toronto
January 2008

Trademark Notices

AC Cobra is a registered trademark of AC Cars.

"We Try Harder" is a registered trademark of Avis.

The following are registered trademarks of BMW: 320, Bavaria, Mini Cooper and Z4M Coupe.

The following are registered trademarks of Chrysler: 300 (Chrylser), 300C (Chrylser), Aires (Dodge), Airflow CU Sedan (Chrysler), Caliber (Dodge), Caravan (Dodge), Challenger (Dodge), Charger, Charger Daytona, Charger R/T 440 Magnum (Dodge), Cherokee (Jeep), CJ (Jeep), Cordoba (Chrysler), Dart, Golden Eagle (Jeep), Grand Cherokee (Jeep), Gremlin (AMC), LeBaron (Chrysler), Pacifica (Chrysler), PT Cruiser, PT Cruiser Limited Edition, Ram 350, Reliant (Plymouth), Road Runner (Plymouth), Spirit (Dodge), Stratus (Dodge), Six (Plymouth), Town and Country, Town and Country Minivan (Chrysler), Viper (Dodge), Voyager (Plymouth), Wagoneer (Jeep), Willys Jeepster (1949), Wrangler (Jeep), YJ (Jeep), "Look at all three!" (Chrysler, 1932) and "If you can find a better car—buy it" (Chrysler).

The following are registered trademarks of Daimler: E320 (Mercedes) and Smart Car.

De Tomaso Pantera is a registered trademark of De Tomaso.

308 and Mondial are registered trademarks of Ferrari.

The following are registered trademarks of Fiat: Sorpasso 1300 Series and Spyder.

The following are registered trademarks of Ford: 150 XLT (Ford), 500 (Ford), Bronco (Ford), Brougham (Ford), "Bubble Top" (Lincoln), Continental (Lincoln), Crown Victoria (Ford), Edsel (Ford), Expedition (Ford), Explorer (Ford), F-150 King Ranch (Ford), F-350 (Ford), Fairlane, Falcon (Ford), Falcon Futura, Falcon Sprint, Fiesta (Ford),

Focus (Ford), Galaxie 500, GT40 (Ford), Grand Marquis LS, High Country Special, Lincoln Continental, Mach 1 Mustang, Maverick (Ford), Mustang (Ford), Mustang GT, Mustang GT-390 Fastback (Ford), Mystichrome Covertible Cobra, Shelby Cobra 427, Shelby GR-1 (concept car), Shelby GT350, Shelby GT500 Mustang, Model A (Ford), Model T, Pinto (Ford), Police Interceptor (Ford), Ranch Wagon (Ford), Ranger, Taurus (Ford), Thunderbird, Torino (Ford), "Only Mustang makes it happen" (Ford), "Quality is Job One" (Ford) and"Help move America forward" (Ford).

The following are registered trademarks of GM: 454 (Chevrolet), Avalanche (GM), Aveo (Chevrolet), Bel Air (Buick), Blazer (Chevrolet), Brickyard (Camaro), Cadillac 16 (concept car), Camaro (Chevrolet), Camaro Rally Sport SS, Camaro SS-427, Camaro Z28, Camaro Z28 SS 30th Anniversary Edition, Camaro ZL1, Celebrity (Chevrolet), Chevette (Chevrolet), Chevy II Nova (Chevrolet), Club Coupe (Cadillac), Corvair (Chevrolet), Corvair Monza Coupe (Chevrolet), Corvette C6.R, Corvette Stingray, Cutlass Supreme (Buick), DeVille (Cadillac), CTS (Cadillac), El Camino, Eldorado (Cadillac), Equinox (Chevrolet), Escalade (Cadillac), Firebird (Pontiac), Firebird Limited (Pontiac), GTO, Hummer H2, Hummer H3, Impala (Chevrolet), LeMans Convertible (Pontiac), LS7 (Corvette), Lucerne (Buick), Malibu (Chevrolet), McLaughlin-Buick, Montana, Monte Carlo, Z28 (Camaro), Northstar (Cadillac), Nova (Chevrolet), Riviera (Buick), Roadmaster (Buick), Rocket 88 (Oldsmobile), Safari, Silverado (Chevrolet), SRX (Cadillac), SSR (Super Sport Roadster) (Chevrolet), Suburban (Chevrolet), Tahoe (Chevrolet), Toronado (Oldsmobile), V8 (Cadillac, 1948), Vega (Chevrolet), Viva (Vauxhall), Volt (Chevrolet), "The standard of the world" (Cadillac), "See the U.S.A. in your Chevrolet, America is asking you to call,""Drive your Chevrolet through the U.S.A.," "America's the greatest land of all" (Chevrolet), "Baseball, hot dogs, apple pie and Chevrolet," "The Heartbeat of America" (GM), "Keep America Rolling" (GM), "An American Revolution" (GM), "This is our country. This is our truck" (GM) and "Escape Greatly" (Hummer).

The following are registered trademarks of Honda: Accord (Honda), Civic (Honda), CR-V (Honda), CSX (Acura), Element (Honda), Fit (Honda), Odyssey and Prelude (Honda).

Accent and Sonata are registered trademarks of Hyundai.

Trooper is a registered trademark of Isuzu.

TRADEMARK NOTICES | 329

The following are registered trademarks of Land Rover (now owned by Ford): Defender 90, Discovery and Range Rover.

The following are registered trademarks of Mazda: 626 LX, Mazda 3, Miata (Mazda), Millennia and "Zoom Zoom."

Minor (Morris, 1959) is a registered trademark of Morris Motor Company.

The following are registered trademarks of Nissan: 300ZX, Altima, Infiniti, Maxima and Tiida.

DS Pallas (Citroën) and Peugeot 404 are registered trademarks of Peugeot Citroën.

The following are registered trademarks of Porsche: 550 Spyder, 911, 911 Cabriolet, 928, 993, Boxter S, Carrera and Cayenne.

Megan (Renault) and Torino 380 (made by Industrias Kaiser Argentina, which was bought by Renault in 1975) are registered trademarks of Renault.

Silver Cloud is a registered trademark of Rolls-Royce.

Outback is a registered trademark of Subaru.

Nano is a registered trademark of Tata.

Roadster is a registered trademark of Telsa.

The following are registered trademarks of Toyota: Camry (Toyota), Celica, Corolla (Toyota), Crown (Toyota), FJ40 (Toyota), Highlander (Toyota), Prius, RAV4 (Toyota), RX (Lexus), Sienna (Toyota), T-100 (Toyota), Tacoma (Toyota), Tercel (Toyota) and Yaris (Toyota).

The following are registered trademarks of Volkswagen: Beetle, Golf, Jetta, Polo, Rabbit, "Think small," "Lemon," "It's ugly, but it gets you there," "If you want to show you've gotten somewhere, get a beautiful chariot. But if you simply want to get somewhere, bet a Bug" and "Polo. Small but tough."

S40 is a registered trademark of Volvo.

Yugo is a registered trademark of Zastava.

Index

Abdulhai, Baher, 282–86
accidents. *See* automobile safety; traffic safety
Adams, Michael, 13
advertising, 18, 60–74
  annual spending on, 61
  history, 62–67, 73
  and the internet, 72, 73
  jingoism in, 70, 71
  safety/practicality used in, 69, 70, 159
  sex in, 65, 66, 70
  and social status, 63–65
  and SUVs, 73, 179
  and unsafe driving, 60, 61, 179
  Volkswagen strategy in, 65–66, 68
  women in, 62, 63, 65, 66, 70
air pollution, 9–10, 107, 290. *See also* environmental protection standards
Albuquerque, New Mexico, 156, 157–58, 217
Alejandro, Adrian, 201–2
alternative fuel vehicles, 247–58
  biofuels, 249–50
  electric, 244–45, 251, 252–55
  fuel cell, 250, 255–58
  hybrids, 248
American Graffiti (film), 2, 123
American Motors, 40, 195

American vs. Canadian values, 11–13, 15–16, 28–29
Americans for Fuel Efficient Cars, 48
Animal House (film), 82
Argentina, 68–69, 90, 164, 198–203, 205–9
Arnould, Grahame, 315
Atlanta, Georgia, 280
automobile clubs. *See* car clubs
automobile design
  and brand identity, 242–44
  and the "Forward Look," 22
  and national styles, 242
  and the status of designers, 239–41
  and tail fins, 22, 132
automobile industry. *See also* specific auto companies
  economic importance of, 13, 35, 142, 147
  and foreign competition, 34, 45, 51–54, 147–48, 259, 274
  history, 16–17, 19, 21–22, 37–40, 44, 252
  internationalization of, 245
  and introduction of consumer credit, 17
  quality issue in, 51–54, 259–60, 274–75
  and snobbery against American cars, 156–57